A   B   C

CAMBRIDGESHIRE   SUFFOLK

HERTFORDSHIRE

MIDDLESEX

LONDON

KENT

1

Hadstock
Gt Chesterford
Bartlow End
Sturmer
Ovington
Ashdon
Helion Bumpstead
Birdbrook
Ashen
Lt Chesterford
Steeple Bumpstead
Ridgewell
Tilbury
juxta Clare
Elmdon
Strethall
Littlebury
St Aylotts
Moyns Park
Stambourne
Lt Yeldham
Chrishall
Saffron Walden
Hempstead
Gt Yeldham
Audley
Tiptofts
End
Wendens Ambo
Wimbish
Radwinter
Cornish Hall
Toppesfield
Langley
Arkesden
End
Sible
Castle

2

Newport
Broadoaks
Gt Sampford
Hedingham
Hedingham
Wicken
Bonhunt
Debden
Lt Sampford
Spains Hall
Clavering
Finchingfield
Rickling
Widdington
Lt Bardfield
Wethersfield
Quendon
Thaxted
Berden
Henham
Gt Bardfield
Shalford
Gosfield
Manuden
Ugley
Chickney
Lindsell
Bardfield Saling
Farnham
Broxted
Gt Easton
Panfield
Elsenham
Tilty
Stisted
Stansted
Lt Easton
Gt Saling
Bocking
Mountfitchet
Stebbing
Birchanger
Gt Dunmow
Lt Dunmow
Rayne
Braintree
Takeley
Lt Canfield
Barnston
Felsted
Black Notley
Cressing

3

Gt Hallingbury
GtCanfield
High Roding
North End
White Notley
Lt Hallingbury
Ford End
Lt Leighs
Faulkbourne
Hatfield
Aythorpe Roding
Pleshey
Leez Priory
Broadoak
Fairsted
Sheering
Leaden Roding
Gt Waltham
Gt Leighs
Terling
White Roding
Good Easter
Lt Waltham
Hatfield
Matching
Margaret Roding
Mashbury
Broomfield
Peverel
Roydon
Latton
Harlow Abbess Roding
Berners Roding
Chignal
Boreham
Lt Laver
Beauchamp Roding
Shellow Roxwell
Springfield
Ulting
Gt Parndon
Netteswell
High Laver
Bowells
Lt Baddow
Magdalen Laver
Moreton
The Willingales
Writtle
Nazeing
Northweald Bassett
Bobbingworth
Fyfield
Widford
Chelmsford
Epping Upland
Shelley
Norton Mandeville
Gt Baddow
Danbury
Epping
Greensted
High Ongar
Sandon
juxta Ongar
Chipping Ongar
Galleywood
Warlies Park
Coopersale
Stanford Rivers
Blackmore
Common
Bicknacre Priory
Waltham Holy Cross
Theydon
Stondon Massey
Margaretting
E Hanningfield
Upshire
Garnon
Theydon Mount
Fryerning
Woodham
Theydon Bois
Stapleford
Kelvedon
Ingatestone
Stock
W Hanningfield
Ferrers
High Beech
Abridge
Tawney
Hatch
Doddinghurst
Buttsbury
S Hanningfield
Loughton
Navestock
Mountnessing
Rettendon
Lambourne
Stapleford Abbots
Shenfield
Hutton
Downham

4

Chingford
Havering
Noak Hill
Billericay
Runwell
Chigwell
Chigwell
atte Bower
S Weald
Brentwood
Ramsden
Woodford
Row
Gt Burstead
Bellhouse
Rawreth
Thorndon Hall
Ingrave
Ramsden
Barkingside
Harold Hill
Lt Warley
Lt Burstead
Crays
Nevendon
Walthamstow
Wanstead
Romford
Gt Warley
Laindon
Rayleigh
Leytonstone
Hornchurch
E Horndon
Dunton
N Benfleet
Thundersley
Leyton
Ilford
Bulphan
Pitsea
Bowers Gifford
Hadleigh
Upminster
Langdon Hills
Vange
S Benfleet

5

Stratford
N Ockendon
Horndon on
Fobbing
Plaistow
Barking
Dagenham
the Hill
Corringham
Canvey
W Ham
S Ockendon
Stanford
Island
Canning Town
Rainham
Belhus
Orsett
le Hope
E Ham
Mucking
Wennington
Aveley
Stifford
R Thames
Silvertown
W Thurrock
Chadwell St Mary
Purfleet
Lt Thurrock
E Tilbury
Grays Thurrock
W Tilbury
Tilbury Dock

A   B   C

A Select Guide to
Essex Churches and Chapels

Great Canfield, St Mary. Limited-edition print by Richard Bawden, reproduced by kind permission of the artist.

A
SELECT GUIDE
TO
ESSEX CHURCHES
AND
CHAPELS

by Members of
The Friends of Essex Churches
edited by
John Fitch

PAUL WATKINS
STAMFORD
1996

.

© 1996 Friends of Essex Churches

Typeset and designed by the publishers

Published by

PAUL WATKINS
18 Adelaide Street
Stamford
Lincolnshire, PE9 2EN

ISBN

1 900289 07 5

Published in association with
The Friends of Essex Churches
Box FEC,
Guy Harlings
53, New Street,
Chelmsford, CM1 1AT

Printed and bound by Woolnoughs of Irthlingborough

CONTENTS

FOREWORD

by Col. Hugh Hunter Jones, President of the Friends of Essex Churches

The Association of the Friends of Essex Churches was founded in 1951 in order to collect money and make grants to churches and chapels of all Christian denominations that faced heavy repair costs to their fabrics. After its amalgamation in 1984 with the Essex Churches Support Trust it was also able to give advice and assistance to parishes as how best to raise funds themselves.

The constitution of the new 'Friends' includes the aim to 'take part in stimulating interest in the history of such churches'. The publication of this Guide is designed to help fulfil that purpose.

However, the project could never have been undertaken without a most generous gift from Lord Sainsbury, of Toppesfield, which has covered all the expenses for the research and compilation of this volume. We express our very deep gratitude to Lord Sainsbury by dedicating this Guide to him.

We are also greatly indebted to all those who have given freely of their time and skill in contributing towards the production of this book. Though too numerous to name all individually each deserves our most sincere thanks.

We acknowledge most gratefully the invaluable work of our four sub-editors and co-ordinators – Nancy Briggs, Judith Cligman, David Andrews and James Boutwood – who have so kindly given us the benefit of their wide experience in shaping this Guide.

To Robin Soames also we are particularly in debt for his drive and dedication that have kept up the momentum of the enterprise firmly on course throughout its lengthy germination and gestation.

Finally, we pay a most special tribute to our editor, Canon John Fitch, whose energy, scholarship and deep knowledge of the subject have so unreservedly been placed at our disposal with such an impressive result.

I hope our Guide will bring as much pleasure and enlightenment to its readers as it has to its creators.

ACKNOWLEDGEMENTS

The editor acknowledges with most grateful thanks the help of all who have assisted in any way in the compilation of this book. Special thanks are due to Lord Sainsbury, of Toppesfield, for his generous financial support which made its publication possible, and to the four sub-editors or co-ordinators, Nancy Briggs, Judith Cligman, David Andrews and James Boutwood, to the 'volunteers' who visited and reported on many of the churches, and to Robin Soames who provided valuable transport and encouragement.

To them must be added Christopher Stell, F.S.A. of the Royal Commission on Historical Monuments and the Chapels Society, for valued assistance with Essex Chapels; Dr Norman Scarfe, F.S.A., author of *The Shell Guide To Essex*, for permission to quote freely from his works, and his readiness to answer questions; to the clergy and churchwardens who welcomed us to their churches; and to Penguin Books for permission to quote freely from the late Sir Nikolaus Pevsner's great book on Essex in the Buildings of England series.

With regard to the illustrations, we are particularly indebted to Richard Bawden for his fine etching of Great Canfield which forms the frontispiece; to Mark Arman for the lovely wood engraving reproduced overleaf; to the Essex Record Office for making various old prints available; to Olive Cook for permission to use the photographs of Stebbing and Tilty interiors by her late husband, Edwin Smith; to the Bishop of Brentwood for kindly allowing us to use the colour photograph of his Cathedral which was also used in the Pitkin guide; and to Peter Rogers of Essex County Council for his colour photograph of Lambourne interior. The remaining photographs, both in colour and in black and white, are by members of the Friends, including myself, and we are only too glad to make this contribution.

I must here record my massive debt to the printed sources listed in the bibliography and to innumerable guide books to individual churches, as well as to clergy, ministers and others for giving us access, making us welcome and giving us much useful information.

Last but not least, may I say what a pleasure it has been to work with our publisher, Shaun Tyas, and his assistant Marion Cutforth (who typed the original text), and thank them for their patience and forebearance.

John Fitch

7

The parish church of St John the Baptist, Our Lady and St Laurence, Thaxted. Wood engraving by Mark Arman, originally printed at The Workshop Press, Hanna's, Bolford Street, Thaxted.

AN APPRECIATION OF ESSEX
CHURCHES AND CHAPELS

'What's so special about Essex churches to warrant a new book on the subject?', I hear you ask. 'Read this book and use it on your travels round the county and you will see' is the equally inevitable rejoinder.

In one sense, *all* churches (and chapels) are 'special' – however *apparently* uninteresting or unattractive. For a Christian church, cathedral, chapel or meeting house, whether old or new, large or small, Romanesque, Gothic, Classical or Modern, is primarily functional. It was planned, designed, built, furnished, consecrated (or dedicated) and set apart, for the worship of God by His people, the *living* church – that is for common prayer, the preaching and hearing of the Word (His Word), and the administration of His Sacraments. Such a building can only be properly understood and appreciated, whether by Christians or others, bearing that in mind. Churches are not museums.

But, of course, most of them are *more* than simply functional. Medieval people, and others, however mixed their motives, built to 'the glory of God'. Everything in the churches they built had, by its beauty, by the excellence of its art and craftsmanship, to express and reflect, however dimly, the surpassing excellence that is divine.

That said, no two churches are identical. Their character and contents, plan and design, vary enormously according to history, fashion, and particular local circumstance, from place to place, village to village, and in England, from county to county.

Every historic English county has its own marked individuality, differentiating it from all others. Essex is no exception; and these characteristics, deriving from its geological, historical and sociological make-up, are inevitably reflected in its churches, chapels and meeting houses, especially the older ones.

This book is compiled by the Friends of Essex Churches, which exists not only to raise funds to help keep these churches in good repair, but also to arouse, stimulate and inform a practical concern for, and pride in, this vital sector of our county heritage. Hence this book.

WHY WE HAD TO SELECT

The large Anglican diocese of Chelmsford, created by Act of Parliament in 1914, is coterminous with the *original* county of Essex. Stretching from Harwich in the north east and Saffron Walden in the north west to Barking,

Walthamstow, West Ham and Stratford on the very threshold of the City of London, it contains within its boundaries over six hundred Anglican parish and district churches. Of these 410 represent ancient (i.e. medieval) parishes. The rest are modern (i.e. nineteenth and twentieth centuries). On top of that, the number of places of worship of all Christian denominations put together could well bring the grand total to something not far short of a thousand, perhaps even more. From St Cedd's lonely little missionary 'cathedral' built *c.*654 on the wall of the Roman fort at Bradwell right through to churches of the early 1990s, such as Emmanuel, Billericay and the new Roman Catholic Cathedral at Brentwood, the range and variety in age, size, shape, style and building materials, to say nothing of liturgical use, is enormous. That is what makes this study so fascinating.

But it will also be obvious from what has already been written that in compiling this book we have had, regretfully but inevitably, to be selective. To have attempted to include all the churches and chapels would have made it impossibly unwieldy and defeated our purpose. We have taken great pains over this business of selection and honestly tried to include as many churches of especial interest or beauty from all periods, all areas and all denominations, and to make the gazetteer as widely representative as possible.

If, as will sometimes have happened, your favourite church has been left out, please forgive us and accept that the omission was not malicious! There are many difficult borderline cases. One category generally omitted was many ancient Essex churches extensively 'restored' by the Victorians. Conversely we made a point of *including* those with 'atmospheric' interiors which somehow escaped 'restoration' (e.g. Bardfield Saling, Belchamp Otten, Bradwell by Coggeshall). But we have included several notable churches *built* in the nineteenth century (e.g. St Edward's, Romford, St Thomas's, Brentwood and Stansted Mountfitchet St John) as well as (we hope) a fair sample of the equally large number built this century. At the same time, we felt it right to give most prominence to earlier churches, especially medieval. Selection has been most stringent, regrettably, in 'London over the Border'.

So much by way of clearing the ground.

OUR CHURCHES: BUILDING MATERIALS

Let us begin our study of Essex churches by looking at the extraordinary variety of materials with which they were built – in contrast to the churches say, of the limestone belt, from Lincolnshire to Somerset, or of flint in Norfolk and Suffolk.

First, *timber*. In the great church building period of the middle ages, much of Essex, especially in the west was still largely forest – Hatfield, Waltham, Epping. So good timber, especially oak, was always plentiful. It is no accident that Essex can lay claim to the oldest wooden church in the world, Greensted by Ongar, built of vertical split logs. Or that in mid-Essex we find so many of those wonderful pagoda-like timber belfries uniquely characteristic of this county. Blackmore, Navestock, Margaretting, Stock and West Hanningfield are simply the best examples.

Although Essex cannot rival Suffolk and Norfolk in the sheer virtuosity of their church roofs, it can boast not only fine double hammer beams at Great Bromley, Gestingthorpe, Castle Hedingham and Sturmer, but also point to three of its finest fifteenth-century churches, Thaxted, Saffron Walden and Clavering, which retain all their original, low pitched roofs. They can stand comparison with any. All of these, significantly, are near the Suffolk border, but down south, Shenfield, Theydon Garnon and Navestock all have something *not* paralleled in East Anglia – good *timber* arcades. We have, too, many fine timber porches (e.g. South Benfleet).

Finally, doors: how often do we stop to look at them? Hadstock's Saxon church still has its original door, which must be one of the oldest in England; and Castle Hedingham's great Norman church has no fewer than three original doors. Others abound.

Next, *stone*: Essex has no good building stone, no quarries. With the sole exception of Greensted, all our surviving ancient churches, even Thaxted, were built mainly of what came to hand locally, and that means chiefly pebble and flint rubble from the fields, dressed as and if their builders could afford it, with limestone from quarries as far away as Lincolnshire and Rutland. Wealthy parishes like Saffron Walden imported ashlar (dressed, squared stone) on a large scale but it must have been terribly expensive.

Having said this, it immediately needs qualifying. For there was stone of a kind, or to be precise, of four kinds, available near at hand. On the north west Essex-Cambridgeshire border there was *clunch*, which can be described as a hard chalk or soft limestone. It was sometimes used in church interiors to build arcades, as for example, at Steeple Bumpstead and Sible Hedingham, and because it was soft enough to take incisions easily, it was ideal for graffiti, in which both these churches, and others like them are rich. (They are described and illustrated in detail in V. Pritchard, *English Medieval Graffiti* (Cambridge, 1967)).

Next there was *Kentish Rag*, quarried in the North Downs near Maidstone and imported across the river into South Essex on a large scale for church building. It is familiar to us in the handsome towers of Canewdon, Prittlewell and Rettendon: in the first of these it has been effectively combined with knapped flint on the parapets of tower and porch. Whole churches were built of it, from St Margaret's Barking to as far from Kent as Tolleshunt D'Arcy, and it is used in the new R.C. Cathedral at Brentwood.

11

Clunch and rag both had to be obtained from across the county boundary. *Septaria* and *puddingstone* were to hand locally. 'Septaria' writes Norman Scarfe (*Shell Guide* p. 22) 'crops up in the London claybed, mainly in the north-east corner of the county. It takes the form of lumps of clayey limestone, ironstone or the like ...' It 'looks like petrified clay and varies in colour from ginger to saffron yellow'. The Romans used it to build the town walls of Colchester, and the Normans, the castle keep. It is found in church walls and towers from the Stour as far south as the Blackwater. In Lawford tower, it is combined with *puddingstone* and *flint*, and three shades of brick, to give what Scarfe describes as 'the richest patchwork of building materials in Essex' (*op. cit.*, p. 128).

Puddingstone is what geologists call a conglomerate. It 'largely consists of flinty pebbles and small lumps of sandstone, united into a very inedible-looking dark brown "pudding" by a natural cement of iron oxide or some siliceous material' (Alec Clifton-Taylor, *Patterns Of English Building*, 1962). It was widely used in churches in much the same area as septaria. At Boxted, overlooking the Stour valley, the Normans used it to build the church tower; with the upper stages in sixteenth-century brick, Pevsner thought 'the whole in its variety of textures happens to look extremely lovely' (*Essex*, p. 84).

Before we leave these various Essex stones we must return briefly to *flint*. Across the border Suffolk is famous for its superb use of knapped and squared flints and for its flushwork (a combination of knapped flint with freestone to form patterns or inscriptions). But, while the most spectacular Essex flushwork is in the gateways of the abbeys of St Osyth, and St John, Colchester, we have the dazzling porch of Chelmsford Cathedral and those of Fingringhoe, Great Bromley and Ardleigh, and the lovely tower parapet of Earls Colne, with its de Vere mullet and coat of arms – to say nothing of the noble flint towers of Brightlingsea and Dedham – to boast about.

We also have a variety of flushwork *not* paralleled, so far as I know, in Suffolk, and that is the three striped towers of West Thurrock (horizontal stripes of black flint and Reigate stone), Purleigh and Fingringhoe (both with horizontal bands of flint and stone).

At last we come to *brick*. In an earlier draft of this essay I wrote that Essex is pre-eminently a county of brick. I was rightly taken to task for overstatement. Nevertheless Essex has every reason to be proud of its brick churches and church brickwork; they are a rich and distinctive ingredient in our county heritage.

The Romans made wide use of bricks and tiles and it seems strange that after their departure the technique of brick making was lost for so long. In at least a hundred of our Saxon and Norman churches Roman brick and tile have been re-used, in the absence of stone, in a variety of ways. They are prominent in the Saxon tower of Holy Trinity, Colchester, in the west

INTRODUCTION

Reused Roman bricks in the west doorway of the tower of Holy Trinity, Colchester

facade of St Botolph's Priory Church, and were used to form the (Saxon?) chancel arch at White Notley.

The first signs of a native revival of brick making may be found at Little Coggeshall in the gate chapel of the Abbey, dedicated to St Nicholas and built *c*.1225. In this little building we find extensive use of brick dressing and, says Pevsner, the 'brick is definitely not Roman. It is supposed to be the earliest medieval brickwork in England' (*Essex*, p. 251).

By the end of the fifteenth century production was so widespread and sophisticated that to it, and to the skill of Essex bricklayers, we owe our noblest early Tudor red brick towers and porches: Ingatestone, Gestingthorpe, Rochford, Castle Hedingham, Rayne, Thorpe le Soken, Sandon, Fryerning, Tolleshunt Major, Theydon Garnon and Wickham St Paul, and the distinguished porch and south nave wall of Feering. To this seemingly endless list we must add three complete churches, East Horndon, Layer Marney and Chignal Smealy. Almost all of these buildings exhibit diapering in vitrified blue brick. There are brick clerestories at Great Baddow, High Easter and Wethersfield. At St Osyth and Blackmore there are brick arcades and at Chignal Smealy there is even a brick font.

The tradition persisted after the Reformation – whole churches at Woodham Walter (1564), Theydon Mount (1614), and the mildly Baroque Ingrave (1735) – all red brick – with brick towers at Toppesfield (1699), Bradwell Juxta Mare (1706) and Terling (1732). Not parish churches only but seventeenth-century Quaker meeting houses (Stebbing and Earls Colne, both 1674) and an Independent Chapel (Little Baddow *c*.1700) are all in red brick. By the early nineteenth century the fashion had changed to white bricks. The elegant Wesleyan Methodist Chapel at Manningtree (1807), Eld Lane Baptist Chapel Colchester (1834), Harwich Parish Church (1821), neo-Norman St Botolph's Colchester and octagonal East Donyland / Rowhedge (both 1838) are all in white brick. A recent example of honey

13

coloured brick blending well with concrete is St Paul's, Harlow New Town (1959).

Turning to roofing materials, probably most of our humbler village churches were originally thatched, in reed or straw, as a number still are in Suffolk and Norfolk. The only two Essex thatched churches known to this writer (neither of them parish churches) are Duddenhoe End, Elmdon (a sixteenth-century barn made into a church for the hamlet in 1857) and Silver End, Rivenhall. How good they both look. Otherwise locally made clay tiles for pitched roofs, and lead for flat ones, were the rule until slate began to be imported in the nineteenth century. For spires, shingles (wooden tiles) were often used in Essex.

OUR CHURCHES: DEVELOPING STYLES

Now for a rapid, necessarily sketchy, survey of the historical development of Essex church building over thirteen centuries.

The Gospel was first proclaimed, and the Church established, in Essex, the kingdom of the East Saxons, by the Celtic missionary/monk/bishop Cedd. Inspired and trained by the pioneer St Aidan at Lindisfarne in Northumbria, he sailed down the east coast and after founding a monastery at Tilbury on the Thames estuary, made his headquarters at Bradwell on the Dengie peninsula just south of the mouth of the Blackwater, where there were the remains of a Roman fort. There, near the site 1300 years later of the nuclear power station, he built St Peter's (on the Roman wall) to serve as the spiritual power station for Essex. One of the oldest Christian churches in England, it is a pilgrim shrine for Essex Christians, comparable to Lindisfarne and its parent Iona. It was rare in those days for a church to be built of anything but timber, but as plentiful Roman materials were at hand they were duly re-used to build this church c.654.

Soon after St Cedd's death in 664 the missionary and diocesan headquarters was moved to London. Essex remained in that diocese until 1845. Wooden churches were built by local magnates in the years that followed; one of them, Greensted, still stands. Others have been found by excavation. Churches with Saxon dedications (Saints Osyth, Botolph, Edmund, Edward, Ethelbert) probably indicate Saxon progenitors. There are some twelve Essex churches with recognisable Saxon features, but all except Bradwell and Greensted are believed to be of the century before the Norman Conquest. Most impressive are Hadstock, nave and transepts, possibly belonging to a minster church founded by St Botolph, another missionary monk, to whom it is dedicated; Strethall chancel arch; and the tower of Holy Trinity, Colchester.

In the Norman period, 1066-*c*.1200, England was brought fully into line with the Romanesque art and architecture of Western Europe. As has already been said, a great many Essex churches have retained some Norman features overlaid by later developments, a doorway here, an arch or window there, or a tower, but very few are complete (a notable exception is Rainham) and few (it has to be said) outstanding. To see Essex Norman/Romanesque on the monumental scale you must go to Waltham Abbey; only a fragment of the once great abbey church survives, the nave, but *what* a fragment! Compare it with the impressive ruins of St Botolph's Priory, Colchester. To get the feel of a Norman *parish* church you must go, with plenty of time to spare, to Copford, with its evidence of former tunnel vaulting and its famous wall paintings, albeit over 'restored' (i.e. repainted) most, not all, of them by the Victorians. There are massive, generally unbuttressed, Norman towers, square, like Corringham, Felsted, Finchingfield, Heybridge, Stambourne, Boreham, Great Tey (the last two crossing towers) and round, Great Leighs, Broomfield and Lamarsh. There are apses at Copford, East Ham, Hadleigh, Pentlow, Great Maplestead, Little Braxted and Little Tey. Finally, visit Castle Hedingham, a noble church built by the de Veres up at the castle towards the end of the Norman period (*c*.1180), there to note signs of the gradual transition to a new and revolutionary style with the round Norman arches giving away at the east end of the nave to the much stronger pointed arch – Gothic. The most beautiful transitional arcading in Essex is at Little Dunmow.

The Gothic style was invented at St Denis near Paris with the building of the abbey church choir there, completed in 1144. Its main features were the pointed arch, the flying buttress and the rib vault. Gothic did not really arrive in England for another half century. Known as Early English in this country, where it is exemplified at Salisbury and Lincoln Cathedrals, it came to fruition in the thirteenth century. Of this period there is a fair scattering in Essex of arcades (e.g. Wethersfield) and lancet windows (Tilty nave, Easthorpe, Berden and Fairstead, chancels) but apart from Little Coggeshall (not a parish church), no complete church to which we can point. Horndon on the Hill comes very near.

The elegant simplicity of Early English soon gave way to the increasingly fanciful, elaborate, almost frivolous complexities of (so called) Decorated in the fourteenth century, nationally exemplified at Exeter Cathedral and the Ely Octagon and Lady Chapel. It is best seen in Essex in the wonderful chancels at Tilty and Lawford, both dazzling examples of showmanship; in the richly embellished south aisle of All Saints', Maldon and also in the (heavily restored) rotunda at Little Maplestead; and in the entire churches of Stebbing, with its elaborate stone screen, and Shalford.

After the Black Death (1348/9) brought all building to a temporary halt, a new and plainer style took over, exemplified in the naves of Canterbury and Winchester Cathedrals, and in King's College chapel, Cambridge, and appropriately called Perpendicular from its emphasis on vertical, straight lines as opposed to the sinuous curves of Decorated. It reached its apogee in the fifteenth and early sixteenth centuries and is the quintessentially English style. Essex has its perfect expression at Saffron Walden (with its affinity to King's). Dedham, Bocking, Clavering, Rayleigh, Brightlingsea and Great Coggeshall and also the Tudor brick towers and churches enumerated earlier are all Perpendicular. (Thaxted, perhaps the most glorious of all Essex's larger churches, is predominantly Perpendicular, but its lovely nave arcades are a little earlier, c.1340.)

The vast cumulative achievement of medieval church builders over more than five centuries was brought to an abrupt end by the Reformation. In the tumultuous quarter century between 1534, when Henry VIII declared himself Supreme Head under God of the Church in England, and 1559, when his daughter Elizabeth I began her reign by reversing her half-sister Mary's Catholic reaction, the transformation brought about in our churches and in the centuries-old forms of worship that went on in them, was nothing less than cataclysmic.

In 1534 the walls and windows of *all* churches and indeed most of their furnishings (rood screens especially) glowed with bright colours and vivid imagery. In days when literacy was rare, these wall paintings were the Poor Man's Bible, effectively telling, with some legendary embroidery, the gospel story of our Redemption, focused in the majestic awesome central figure of the crucified but victorious Redeemer; and they confronted worshippers (who in those days comprised the entire community), in the Doom (Last Judgement) so often painted on the wall over the chancel arch above the Rood (Christ crucified), with the stark and terrifying alternatives of Heaven and Hell. Churches, too, were then the focal point of *all* parish life, the naves used for miracle and mystery plays, church ales, etc. with only the thinnest of veils dividing sacred from secular.

By 1559 most, if not quite all, the old colour and imagery had gone, the murals whitewashed over and replaced with edifying or admonitory texts; the Rood, and all other 'Popish, idolatrous' images taken down, smashed or burnt, soon to be replaced with the Royal Arms; the stone altars replaced with one moveable oak communion table; the accumulation of altar plate, linen and elaborate vestments sold and replaced by a plain surplice and communion cup and cover/paten; the old Latin service books put on the bonfire, to be replaced by Coverdale's Great Bible (1539) and the Elizabethan compromise revision of the Book of Common Prayer in Cranmer's sonorous English, its use enforced by the Act of Uniformity. For the time being some stained glass remained although most of it was later smashed by seventeenth-century Puritan iconoclasts. Churches became much lighter, less cluttered. There was gain too, as well as loss, especially

16

in the simplification of the Liturgy and the haunting beauty of its English, 'the vulgar tongue'.

There was surprisingly little church building in Essex in the two and a half centuries that followed the Reformation – fewer than ten new Anglican churches altogether. Of these only four survive in use – Woodham Walter (1564), Theydon Mount (1612), Ingrave (1735) and Wanstead (1790 – a fine example of late Palladian classicism), all described in this book, along with four older churches – Messing, where the chancel is a rare survival of the Laudian High Churchmanship of the 1630s, and Lambourn, Debden and Helions Bumpstead, medieval churches delightfully transformed in Georgian times. The nave and tower of Dagenham St Peter and St Paul deserves special mention as an essay in late Strawberry Hill Gothick.

Throughout this period, apart from the upheavals of 1641-1660 (the Great Rebellion, Civil War, Commonwealth and Protectorate, when it was driven underground), the Church of England remained, in every sense, as it had always been, the Established Church, the bastion of the social order whose function was cynically said to be:

To keep men in their proper stations
and bless the squire and his relations.

In a great many country parishes Church and Hall were in close proximity and alliance. The squire was often the patron of the living who appointed the parson, sometimes from his own family, the squire's pew prominent in the church, and other box pews, privately owned, and graded from front to back to accommodate the village's social hierarchy, with humble benches right at the back or up in a gallery for servants and the lower orders. Few Essex churches have preserved such interiors, which were anathema to busy Victorians bent on 'restoration', but Bardfield Saling and Little Warley are two such examples. In days when sermons were highly regarded, churches were re-ordered on 'auditory' lines with a three-decker pulpit, complete with sounding board or tester, in a commanding position (cf. Great Baddow, Thaxted and Wanstead). The holy table or altar was decently railed in and behind it on the altar piece or reredos were inscribed in letters of gold on black the standards of Christian belief, conduct and devotion, the Apostles' Creed, the Ten Commandments and the Lord's Prayer (as at Henham and Messing), occasionally flanked by large paintings of Moses and Aaron, representing prophecy and priesthood, (Gestingthorpe and Purleigh). The organ, if there was one, was on a western gallery (e.g. Bardfield Saling, Colchester St Peter, Wanstead and Harwich) where sat the parish musicians, as described by Hardy in *Under The Greenwood Tree*.

In these years between the reformation and the accession of Queen Victoria, particularly after the Toleration Act, 1689, there were the beginnings of another, allied but more democratic, tradition, the architecture of Dissent, of Protestant Non-Conformity. First in the field (architecturally that is) in Essex were the Quakers. Inspired by a visit from their founder, George Fox, Friends' meeting houses were built as early as 1674 in Stebbing and Earls Colne, domestic square brick boxes with pyramidal tiled roofs, as different from 'steeple houses' as could be. An example of a rural Friends' meeting house still in regular use is at Great Bardfield; inside and out it retains all the unselfconscious, unpretentious aura of austere Quaker integrity. Only slightly later (c.1700) are Independent (now United Reformed) chapels at Little Baddow and Terling, while Finchingfield URC (1779), Manningtee Wesleyan Methodist (1807) and the Baptists' Potter Street, Harlow (1756) and Eld Lane, Colchester (1834) all lay claim to genuine architectural distinction, even elegance. The tradition was continued into the early Victorian age as at Castle Hedingham URC (1842) – an impressive building still in the classical style, as are Coggeshall, Maldon, Ongar and Saffron Walden (all URC)

The Victorian period, 1837-1901, was marked by feverish activity in the field of church building, unparalleled since the Reformation. This was especially the case in Essex owing to the rapid population growth in the London area and Southend, and with it the supposed need to build new churches for new parishes in new suburbs. Unfortunately this activity was not confined to building *new* churches.

The Gothic Revival, heralded by the eccentric genius of A. W. N. Pugin (1812-1852) and his disciples, accompanied by the Tractarian and Ritualist (i.e. Anglo-Catholic) movements in the Established Church, and enthusiastically adopted by a whole generation of church architects and patrons, inaugurated a new fashion in what, disdaining mere 'repairs', was grandly *mis*called church 'restoration'. This usually involved the dogmatic and wholesale destruction of the church furnishings and decor of the preceding seventeenth, eighteenth and early nineteenth centuries, described above, and their replacement by encaustic tiles, pitch pine pews in the nave, and choir stalls in the chancel, large organs in specially built organ chambers, quantities of stained and tinted glass to give a 'dim religious light', vestries and all the paraphernalia to which we have become so accustomed in so many of our churches.

Not that it was all bad, all loss. Connoisseurs of nineteenth-century church 'restoration' in Essex should visit Ardleigh, Little Braxted, Foxearth, Halstead St Andrew, Littlebury and Radwinter. They will find much to admire, particularly in the first and second. (Foxearth needs the Little Braxted treatment – careful cleaning and expert conservation.)

Turning from 'restoration' to church building, most of the leading Victorian architects are represented in our county – the prolific George Gilbert Scott at Holy Trinity, Halstead (1843) and nearby Greenstead

18

INTRODUCTION

Green; Teulon in a surprisingly conventional early phase at Birch (1850) – sadly now redundant and falling down; his St Mark's Silvertown (1861) of which Pevsner wrote 'as horrid as only he can be' is now a semi-derelict shell; Burges in his 'fabulously insensitive' (Pevsner again) completion of Waltham Abbey east end (1861); Woodyer at Twinstead (much polychrome – 1860) and St Mary and St Hugh, Harlow (1878); St Aubyn at Widford (1862) and Galleywood (1873); Bodley (and Garner) at Epping St John (1889), G. E. (Law Courts) Street at Hutton (1873) and W. D. Caroe at Stansted Mountfitchet St John (also 1889). Finally Butterfield, most famous of all, built the chancel at Hadstock (1884), and rebuilt the nave and chancel at Ardleigh. Pearson over-restored Braintree, St Michael.

With the turn of the century and the advent of the opulent Edwardian era, ending abruptly with the Great War, fashions were changing again. William Morris' Arts and Crafts movement bore striking fruit in Essex in the *art nouveau* church at Great Warley (1904), designed by Harrison Townsend, architect, and lavishly decorated and furnished by Sir William Reynolds Stephens. Also outstanding is Temple Moore's great church of St James, Clacton on Sea (1913).

Spanning this period and that between the two wars is the work of a distinguished Essex architect, the prolific but essentially conservative Sir Charles Nicholson, who favoured a combination of Gothic and Classical motifs, as can be seen in his St Albans, Westcliff, an early work (1898-1908), as well as in two later churches, Frinton St Mary Magdalene (1929) and Leigh on Sea St Margaret (1931). More adventurous was another Essex architect, Laurence King, whose earliest work is St George's in his native Brentwood (1934).

After the Second World War, the planned development of New Towns at Harlow and Basildon and, later, South Woodham Ferrers, challenged Chelmsford Diocese to seize the initiative with, first, St Paul's, New Harlow (1959) and, in the 1960s, St Martin's, Basildon, flagships of a distinctively modern, functional, style, making frank use of contemporary construction technology. The Roman Catholics were equally quick off the mark. Their 1960 church of Our Lady of Fatima, New Harlow with its central altar and superb glass, entire walls of it, is outstanding by any yardstick. Another good example of this is St Paul's Clacton on Sea (1966). The county's first purpose built *ecumenical* church, Holy Trinity, South Woodham Ferrers, followed in 1982. Evidence that the post-war impetus is not yet exhausted is the Anglican church of Emmanuel, Billericay (1992) and the elegant new Roman Catholic Cathedral at Brentwood, designed by the leading neo-classical architect Quinlan Terry of Dedham and consecrated in 1991 – both shaped around a focal, centrally placed altar.

This rapid survey would be incomplete without a reference to the melancholy fact that in Essex, as elsewhere in recent years, a number of our historic churches have become redundant to pastoral needs or (a kinder description) have 'gone into retirement'. The most fortunate, such as Chickney and East Horndon, both historically important, are lovingly cared for and maintained by the Churches Conservation Trust, until 1994 called the Redundant Churches Fund. This admirable body, set up by statute in 1968, derives its income from both Church and State and discharges its duties to perfection. Others, less fortunate, have been turned into houses; yet others, including All Saints' and Holy Trinity, Colchester, have become museums and so remain accessible. Remote Tolleshunt Knights was handed over to the Orthodox Monastery nearby and, equipped with a simple but beautiful iconostasis, is regularly used by the Orthodox community, except in winter.

CONCLUSION

I conclude on a positive note. Thanks to the convergence or concurrence of a number of factors, the last quarter of this millennium has witnessed a spectacular advance in the care and condition of our heritage of historic churches, so much so that it can truthfully be claimed that the great majority of them are in better trim now than they have ever been. The main factors conducing to this happy state of affairs are (i) the compulsory regular five-yearly inspection of all Anglican churches by qualified architects, required to list necessary repairs in order of priority, (ii) conscientious compliance with such reports by the majority of clergy, churchwardens and parochial church councils, involving truly heroic and herculean fund raising efforts, (iii) supported and encouraged, as never before, by the (national) Historic Churches Preservation Trust, such county bodies as ourselves, the Friends of Essex Churches, *and* since 1977, most significantly of all, by long overdue State aid to historic churches which qualify for it (not all do). This is ongoing. Success must not breed complacency.

On top of that, much good modern art and craftsmanship can be seen in so many of our churches, ranging from the humble kneeler worked in a variety of colours and designs, to stained and engraved glass, wood and metal work; and, finally, two further signs of vitality. The first is the widespread, and necessary, building and equipping of extensions to existing churches to provide them with modern facilities, kitchens, lavatories, meeting rooms, creches and offices, usually on the less visible north side. This is often done with tact and panache as, notably, at Rivenhall, Lawford and St Mary's Maldon. Secondly, and closely allied to this – following the example of Chelmsford Cathedral's radical and successful 're-ordering' carried out by architect Robert Potter, and provost John Moses in 1983 – the better to adapt and equip churches for the needs of contemporary worship and liturgy. As with earlier drastic re-orderings in the sixteenth and nineteenth centuries, this has sometimes been achieved without due sensitivity to historic period furnishings and atmosphere. But where, as in most cases, it has been done with a due sense of historic continuity and in such a way that, with later changes in social needs and liturgical fashions, it can be reversed, it has brought new life to an ancient building.

Thus, in the cathedrals, churches, chapels and meeting houses of Essex, built, all of them, to the glory of God, their construction, enrichment and maintenance stretching over a period of thirteen centuries, we have an extraordinarily rich and diverse inheritance. It is surely up to our generation in this historic county to value, appreciate, enjoy, use and, at whatever expense, conserve and maintain it, intact, and where possible enhanced, for those yet to come.

NOTE: Little is said in the Introduction on the subject of *fittings* and *furnishings* and nothing about *brasses* and other *monuments* although all these features provide so much of the interest in churches. Attention is drawn to the Lists of Special Features following the Gazetteer.

ACCESS TO LOCKED CHURCHES

It will be readily understood that, sadly, for security reasons in these days of widespread sacrilege, theft and vandalism, many churches and all chapels are kept locked. Users of this book desirous of visiting Anglican churches listed here are recommended to buy a copy of the current Chelmsford Diocesan Year Book, obtainable from the Diocesan Office, Guy Harlings, 53 New Street, Chelmsford CM1 1AT. Before visiting a particular church, disappointment can often be avoided and time saved by a telephone call to the priest in charge or churchwarden listed in the Year Book, who, if the church is kept locked, will tell you where a key may be obtained. For non-Anglican churches etc., notice boards will often give the name and address of the caretaker.

Always remember when visiting a church that it is primarily a house of prayer. Also that it is in most cases expensive to maintain. A contribution towards the cost of upkeep put in the box provided is recommended and will always be welcome.

To assist readers in locating each church or chapel described, each entry is prefixed by a letter and a digit corresponding to the appropriate square in the county map printed on the first few pages (and reproduced by kind permission of Penguin Books).

THE GAZETTEER

Note: The scope of this book is the old, historic (i.e. pre-1974) county of Essex, now including five London Boroughs and co-terminous with the Anglican Diocese of Chelmsford. This is the area covered by The Friends of Essex Churches. Churches, chapels and (Quaker) meeting houses, regardless of denomination, are listed strictly in the alphabetical order of their parish or town. Where two or more parishes share the same basic name, e.g. the Sampfords and the Thurrocks, they will be found under that name, differentiated as Great, Little, Grays, West etc.

The reference after each entry records the location on the map.

ABBERTON (D3) *St Andrew*

A singularly plain, homely, unpretentious little country church, with a pretty Tudor brick west tower, fourteenth-century nave, and nineteenth-century brick chancel. Its charm lies in its simplicity and in its peaceful rural situation, well away from its village, overlooking the calm waters of the South East Essex reservoir. Sheep may, and do, safely graze the churchyard.

ALPHAMSTONE (C2) *St Barnabas*

This remote Stour valley church, in its pleasant sloping churchyard, has some vestigial Norman features (a blocked window and a large square Purbeck marble font with five blank arches on each face) but is mainly fourteenth-century with good sedilia and piscina and a three-bay south arcade of octagonal piers. The handsome domed font cover is of the seventeenth century.

The tower was damaged by a storm in 1728 and replaced by the timber bellcote the following year. When the three bells were inspected in 1970 an eighteen-foot jackdaw's nest was found. It took two men a whole day to remove the sticks the birds had carried in for thirty years.

ALTHORNE (C4) *St Andrew*

Its prominent site on a ridge above the river Crouch makes Althorne's flinty embattled East Anglian style tower a powerful landmark. A Latin inscription under the three-light west window bidding the reader pray for the souls of John Wylson and John Hyll leads one to suppose that they gave the cost of it, *c.*1500. The nave, too, has an embattled parapet (an unusual embellishment in Essex). There is a brass to William Hyklott (d.1508) who 'paide for the werkemanship of the wall of this churche'. The humbler chancel is of Tudor brick, patched with Victorian. Inside, the most notable feature is the fifteenth-century font, one of the best of its period in the county. On the eight faces of the bowl are carved the martyrdom of St Andrew, the patron saint, tied to a saltire cross, a baptism, a king and queen, a feathery seraph, etc., etc. An odd, but salutary feature is the strengthening of the chancel arch in modern brick to prevent collapse. There is a set of Hanoverian Royal Arms.

The Tudor south porch at Ardleigh.

ARDLEIGH (D2) *St Mary the Virgin*

Situated by the central crossroads in the village, in a churchyard with many mature trees, this church was rebuilt by the leading Victorian church architect Butterfield in 1882, with the sole exception of the late fifteenth-century west tower and south porch. The tower is built of flint and dark brown ironstone conglomerate, similar to puddingstone; its parapet and stepped battlements with simple octagonal pinnacles seems to have been rebuilt by Butterfield. The fine, elaborate porch is entirely in the East Anglian idiom, reminiscent of that of Woodbridge St Mary Suffolk, with its flint flushwork, niches and spandrels with St George and the dragon. It has a wooden roof, and the traceried inner doors to the church are original. Crowned lions couchant guard the entrance and there are animal pinnacles.

The body of the church consists of nave, north and south aisles and a large chancel with south (Lady) chapel. The walls of the nave are painted russet and the piers and stone dressings cream. Above the chancel arch (beneath which are the dados of the old screen) are painted the rood figures in bold relief, but it is in the treatment of the chancel that Butterfield really 'went to town'. The richly painted panelled ceiling and every available inch of wall space was decorated in a colour scheme the beauty of which is now fully revealed by a cleaning and conservation scheme costing £20,000, carried out in 1995/6 by the same firm which had worked so successfully at Little Braxted (q.v.). It has been stated that Ernest Geldart worked with Butterfield on this scheme, but on what evidence is not known. *See also plate 24*.

ARKESDEN (A2) *St Mary*
This church on its commanding site in the village centre is mainly of interest for its monuments. The west tower was rebuilt in 1855 and the rest of the church heavily 'restored', but the nave and chancel and the north nave arcade with octagonal piers and south arcade with cylindrical piers are all basically thirteenth century.

The monuments include a fifteenth-century brass of a knight, an effigy of a late medieval priest (cut in two!) in a two bay recess in the chancel north wall and a huge brightly coloured six poster with obelisks and strapwork on top to Richard Cutte (d. 1592) and his wife, with four children kneeling alongside the tomb chest below. This is at the east end of the south aisle. Best of all is the cool classical wall monument under the tower to John Withers (d. 1692) and his wife. The busts of husband in periwig, looking, with his little moustache, the spit and image of Charles II, and his handsome wife are by Edward Pearce. *See also plate 46*.

ASHDON (B1) *All Saints*
It stands on higher ground to the south of the main part of the pretty village. The big square plinths on which the piers of the north and south nave arcades stand, and those beneath the chancel arch responds, may possibly be evidence of a Saxon predecessor on this site. All Saints, with its massively buttressed west tower of *c.*1370, is mainly fourteenth century though the chancel walls are earlier. The best feature is undoubtedly the south or Tyrell chapel, higher and broader than the chancel, from which it is divided by a two bay arcade. It has a fine east window with reticulated (i.e. netlike) tracery typical of *c.*1325 and a later four-light south window, and its original roof. Indeed all the roofs are medieval. There is a nave clerestory with eccentric fenestration. The early sixteenth-century Tyrell

tomb (much heraldry but no effigies) now in the chancel may originally have been in the Tyrell chapel. There are a number of interestingly carved head stops, and bits of medieval stained glass collected in a north window. The Old Guildhall is on the south side of the large churchyard.

ASHEN (C1) *St Augustine*
The delightfully rustic porch leads through an original south door with thirteenth-century ironwork into an equally rustic nave and a good chancel built in 1857, faced with flint and brick and with three lancets in the east wall. The tower is of *c.*1400 with a Tudor brick stair turret. There is a crude monument to Luce Tallakarne, 1610, with caryatids, and two large handsome Baroque tablets in the chancel with long Latin epitaphs.

ASHINGDON (C4) *St Andrew*
Outside this delightful little church on its hill overlooking the Crouch estuary is proudly displayed a notice board which reads: 'St Andrew's MINSTER Built 1020'. This bold claim (dare one whisper it?) is a matter of opinion rather than a matter of fact.

What is not in dispute is that, on 18 October 1016, Cnut, king of Denmark, won a famous victory over Edmund Ironside, king of England. This battle, which won Cnut the crown of England, was fought at 'Assandun'. Many people, including the distinguished historian, Dr Norman Scarfe, author of the *Shell Guide to Essex*, identify 'Assandun' with Ashingdon and believe the battle was fought here. Others identify it with Ashdon near Saffron Walden. Further, it is a fact that four years after this battle, Cnut caused a 'minster' to be built 'of stone and lime' on the site of the battle, where prayer was to be offered for the souls of the slain, English and Danes alike. Its first priest was Stigand the Saxon, later archbishop of Canterbury, but no saint. Those who put up the aforesaid sign maintain that, even if, as seems certain, the present church is no earlier than *c.*1300, it is the successor of the minster built by Cnut (here?) and therefore has some claim to be itself called a minster. An alternative possibility (no more than that) is advanced in the article on Hadstock church near Ashdon (q.v.). Both views are tenable. One interesting and possibly significant fact is that a silver coin of Cnut was found in Ashingdon churchyard; it is now in Prittlewell Priory museum. But even that does not amount to proof positive. The fact of the matter is that no one knows for certain *what* the fact of the matter is!

That aside, Ashingdon church in itself has much to commend it. It consists of nave and chancel built of flint rubble with some Roman brick, and Tudor brick in the chancel east wall, and a small west tower of Kentish rag heavily buttressed. The tower wears a slightly comical little 'hat', the 'brim' of which overlaps the tower walls all round. The medieval roof survives. Besides brass candelabra, there hang in the church two gifts presented by a twentieth-century Prince George of Denmark in support of the aforementioned claim. One is a beautiful scale model of a Viking longboat, the other is the Dannebrog, the Danish flag, a white cross on a red background. The only other such in an Essex church is at Hadstock!

AVELEY (B5) *St Michael*

The church stands behind the shops between the corner of High Street and Ship Lane, and is entered through the north porch. It is of considerable architectural interest as it reflects a mixture of building periods. The nave was built in the early twelfth century, the south aisle added *c.*1160, the north aisle *c.*1220. In the mid thirteenth century the north chapel was added and the chancel rebuilt. The west tower is of about the same date. The south aisle was altered in the fourteenth century and in the fifteenth century the north aisle was extended westwards, the upper part of the tower rebuilt, with a low spire, and the north porch added. A number of interesting features include a twelfth-century font in the north aisle, a twelfth-century pillar piscina with a fourteenth-century recess sunk into the chancel wall, a late thirteenth-century coffin lid with a raised ornamental cross in the floor by the pulpit, and an unexciting fifteenth-century screen. The Jacobean pulpit dated 1621 has an hexagonal sounding board high above it. Between them as a kind of backboard is a nice Baroque monument to Dacre Barrett-Lennard of Belhus, d.1724. Finally there are several good brasses including a fine Flemish plate of Ralph de Knevynton d.1370. The Latin inscription refers to the Dominical number F, a great rarity. The knight is depicted in armour with strangely long waist and short legs, under an intricate canopy.

BADDOW, GREAT (C3) *St Mary*

The church lies in the village; its early sixteenth-century brick clerestory with crowstepped embattled parapets, corbel frieze and pinnacles looks very fine. The contemporary north and south chapels and early seventeenth-century porch are also of brick, but the main body of the church is built of flint rubble. The chancel dormers, originally brick, were rebuilt in 1896. The chancel, nave and north aisle were erected in the mid thirteenth century. The aisles were widened and the west tower added in the fourteenth century; the tower has an octagonal spire. The most notable feature of the interior is the tall finely-carved pulpit (1639) in Jacobean style with back standard and sounding board. Brass to Jane Paschall (1614); monument to the Gwyn sisters (Cheere, 1753). Royal arms (1660); 8 hatchments.

BADDOW, LITTLE (C3) *St Mary*

The church stands a mile away from the village, on a slight rise overlooking the valley of the river Chelmer. The early Norman church is represented by the north wall of the nave, with Roman brick used for quoins and walling in herring-bone pattern. The nave was widened on the south side *c.*1330 and the tower was added later in the century. An unusual feature of the latter is that, owing no doubt to the uneven lie of the land, the north west buttress is diagonal while to the south-west there are two right-angled buttresses. Early in the fifteenth century the chancel was rebuilt. The bright and spacious interior has a number of treasures. The large wall painting of St Christopher, *c.*1375, is opposite the south door and adjoins recently uncovered earlier work: a twelfth-century devil and the thirteenth-century double-line masonry pattern. Built into the south wall of the nave are a piscina and two canopied recesses, *c.*1330, containing fine oak effigies of a man in civilian dress and a woman; the man's head shows a sensitive appreciation of the texture of the wood. The chancel has glass fragments of *c.*1400, including St Michael slaying the dragon, and the elaborate monument to Sir Henry Mildmay (d.1639) and his two wives. There is a seventeenth-century communion table in the nave.

Victorian drawing of the Old Meeting House, Little Baddow.

BADDOW, LITTLE (C3) *United Reformed Church*

Appropriately situated at the junction of Church Road and Chapel Lane. One of the earliest non-Anglican churches in Essex, its origins are traced back to a Puritan school established in this village before the Civil War by one Thomas Hooker, who, with John Eliot, later crossed the Atlantic to become 'Apostles to the Red Indians'. Its first minister was Thomas Gilson, rector of nearby Boreham under Cromwell but ejected from his living in 1661 for refusal to conform to the re-established Book of Common Prayer and Act of Uniformity. His Presbyterian congregation met at Cuckoo Farm until, in 1707, the Barringtons, sympathetic local landowners, gave the site and money for building what was long called the Chapel. It is a plain red brick gabled parallelogram and externally, apart from a small porch, there has been little or no alteration since it was built. Its distinctive 'period' features are two pairs of tall round-headed windows, each with one mullion and two transoms in the longer east and west walls, and one such window and two high circular windows in the end walls. Inside there was originally a dominant pulpit, probably dignified with a sounding board, in the centre of the west wall and facing it a three sided gallery. All this has now gone and the rostrum is at the north end. The adjoining manse, for the resident minister, dates from 1794 and there is still some original stabling for the horses of the gathered congregation. This chapel, or church, became Congregationalist earlier this century, later merging in the United Reformed Church.

BARDFIELD, GREAT (B2) *Friends' Meeting House*
In the middle of the village but modestly hidden from site, this old meeting house, built, it is said, in 1804, has all the plain austerity of the Quakers. It has three large casement windows looking over the graveyard and a hipped tiled roof, and is divided inside into two compartments by a wooden screen, a bit like an Orthodox ikonostasis minus its ikons! The worship or meeting room is simply furnished with benches on four sides surrounding a table.

BARDFIELD, GREAT (B2) *St Mary the Virgin*
Its church is on the southern edge of the unspoilt little market township, on steeply rising ground next door to Great Bardfield Hall. The stocky, unbuttressed, unsophisticated west tower, with its later recessed lead spire and its small lancet windows, is surprisingly dated 'early fourteenth century' by Pevsner. It certainly looks earlier, as does the plain pointed tower arch. The church itself, nave, north and south aisles, chancel and south porch, is by contrast a sophisticated building of the late fourteenth century. It is believed that the nave and the beautiful stone screen, so obviously influenced by its slightly earlier neighbour at Stebbing, were built in memory of his young wife Philippa by Edmund Mortimer, Earl of March (d. 1381), grandson of Edward III (1327-1377), whose likeness and that of his consort, Philippa of Hainault, may be intended in the crowned

heads on the south and north ends of the screen. Less elaborate than that at Stebbing, its straight lines, like the straight headed three-light nave windows and the clustered piers of the four bay arcades, are characteristic of the developing early Perpendicular.

The church is darkened by much late nineteenth-century and early twentieth-century stained glass, but in the north aisle the tracery lights of two windows contain late medieval glass, including the arms of Edmund Mortimer aforesaid. The tomb of Serjeant William Bendlowes (d. 1584) and his wife Alienor, bearing her brass effigy (but not his) forms sedilia in the chancel. He was a great local benefactor, and a copy of his portrait hangs on the west wall above the tower arch. Finally, the stone rood figures were certainly, and the pulpit possibly, designed by G. F. Bodley, and the organ case possibly by Pugin.

BARDFIELD, LITTLE (B2) *St Katherine*
In park-like surroundings near Little Bardfield Hall this church has a very late Saxon tower and nave. The unbuttressed tower is in five slightly recessed, i.e. diminishing, stages and none of its small round headed windows have dressings either to the jambs or cills, giving it a rough, unfinished appearance. It is built of flint and pebble rubble with a little Roman tile and brick. The chancel is fourteenth century, much restored. What is of great interest is the exquisite little organ, said to be by Renatus Harris and from a Cambridge college, possibly Jesus. Positioned in a Victorian organ chamber it has a *most* beautiful late seventeenth-century organ case, and a lovely mellow tone.

BARDFIELD SALING (B2) *St Peter and St Paul*
Far off the beaten track, this church is full of interest and atmosphere. Consisting of a small round tower (the youngest of six in Essex), nave, south aisle and short truncated chancel, it is basically all fourteenth century, predating the Black Death, 1348, with the exception of the chancel which itself must have been completed before the consecration of the whole church in 1380. The chancel seems to have been drastically shortened in the seventeenth century or later and further suffered by enemy action in World War II. A three bay arcade separates the nave from the south aisle (St Margaret's Chapel), which has a piscina and sedilia. The piers, especially the westernmost one, have graffiti, including a Tudor figure in doublet and hose. The furnishings include a good fourteenth-century screen, not in its original position, a handsome pulpit with arched panels in perspective, probably *c.*1600, and cut down box pews. Plaster ceilings, a west gallery of *c.*1780 with on it an eighteenth-century chamber organ, brick and tiled floors, oil lamps on standards (still in occasional use) and some intricate late nineteenth-century straw plaiting intended to

29

decorate the Lord's Table, complete the agreeably old-fashioned decor. The churchyard, rich in flora, is entirely in keeping. *See also plate 33.*

The Elizabethan pulpit and panelling at Bardfield Saling.

The seventeenth-century font at Barking.

BARKING (A5) *St Margaret*

This church stands in what is effectively an urban park, separated by roads from the busy town centre to the east and modern warehouses to the west. This is because it stood at the edge of the precinct of Barking Abbey, a nunnery founded in 666 by St Erkenwald. The entrance to the churchyard is through the fifteenth-century gatehouse known as the Firebell Gate, and the foundations of the mainly twelfth-century abbey church can be seen in a great hollow to the north. The church is surrounded by boundary walls of stone plundered from the abbey at the Dissolution.

St Margaret's is a spacious and well-lit church, its size and fittings reflecting the importance of Barking in the middle ages when it was the biggest town in Essex after Colchester. Today the way in is through a busy parish room and community centre on the south side designed by the K. C.

White Partnership and opened in 1991. The structural history of the church is one of bewildering complexity. The oldest part is the east end of the chancel, which has lancet windows. Much of the rest is fifteenth century in appearance including the west tower and the nave roof, but much is nineteenth-century restoration. In 1770 the interior of the church was remodelled on classical lines to resemble a city church; the roofs were ceiled, the windows replaced, and the nave arcades altered. Less than a century passed before tastes changed and a vicar decided to restore it to the Gothic building it had been before. Of the eighteenth-century work, the main survivals are the clerestory windows, the chancel ceiling, and the reredos, elegant but rather dark.

An unusual feature of the church is the outer north aisle, the successor to an earlier mortuary chapel with a crypt for bones disturbed and removed from the churchyard. This aisle is separated from the inner north aisle by an arcade of four-centred Tudor arches. Its crown-post roof was restored after a fire in 1994. A curiosity are the Norman drum piers separating this aisle from the organ chamber. These were plundered from the abbey buildings, and their scalloped capitals are made of cement. Apart from the unusual seventeenth-century font with its elaborate stem of twinned scrolls and octagonal bowl, the most interesting of the internal fittings are the monuments, most of which celebrate seventeenth- and eighteenth-century gentlemen who lived on estates in the parish when Barking was becoming a prosperous suburb to London. An exception is a fourteenth-century slab with an incised portrait identified by an inscription as 'MARTINUS VICARIUS', an early vicar of Barking. This was found in excavations on the abbey site and is now in the chancel. Of the later monuments, two of the more outstanding are that to Sir Charles Montague (d. 1625) in the chancel, a beautifully carved depiction of him in his tent in an army encampment, flanked by musketeers, and one in the outer north aisle to Captain John Bennett (d. 1716) with ships and nautical instruments of the period. *See also plate 25.*

BARLING (D4) *All Saints*
The west towers of this church and that of Little Wakering are so much alike as to be almost identical. They must both have been designed and built by the same master mason. The differences are minimal but interesting. Whereas Little Wakering has a flint and stone chequer pattern on its parapet and battlements, Barling has a chequer band above its three-light west window. The windows and diagonal buttressing are identical. The recessed spires, however, do vary slightly, but were probably added later. Pevsner does not notice this similarity but describes the Barling tower as 'stately'; that at Wakering (paid for by Bishop Wakering of Norwich, d.1425) as 'proud'.

31

Barling boasts a north aisle with particularly elegant, tall, slender, concave sided piers, late fifteenth century; and an octagonal font of the same period with shields and quatrefoils. Also a handsome Georgian pulpit with a large sounding board. Despite these assets, the interior strikes one as rather sad and drab. A final thought: another neighbouring Kentish rag tower, though larger and still grander, and with all the same characteristics, is Canewdon. From the same stable?

BARNSTON (B3) – dedication unknown
A charming little church of great character in a country lane some distance from the main road village. There is no porch: the church is entered through a plain Norman south doorway and three Norman windows survive. The Early English chancel has a good south window with stained glass by Burne-Jones, and a very fine double piscina with intersected round arches, identical with others at Jesus and St John's Colleges, Cambridge and Leighton Bromswold, Cambs. There is a nice eighteenth-century west gallery and in it a barrel organ, at the time of writing not in working order. The west end is graced with a belfry with an eighteenth-century cupola.

Detail of Norman doorway at Barnston.

BASILDON (C4) (including Laindon, Pitsea and Vange)
Basildon New Town was planned and developed very slightly later than its Essex counterpart Harlow, in the 1950s and early 1960s. It comprises most of the area of seven old, once rural, ecclesiastical parishes, each of which had its own church. Of these, three, Laindon St Nicholas, Basildon Holy Cross and Nevendon St Peter, all small, continue in use, but only the first is particularly notable.

BASILDON (C4) *St Martin*
Consecrated 1962 (architect: Mrs A. M. Cotton), this is the 'show' town church, and as such comparable to Harlow St Paul. It stands within the town centre and forms part of a homogeneous complex of church buildings. It is built of dark reddish-purple brick, but the north, south and west walls are largely of glass. Inside, the eyes of worshipper and visitor are drawn to the great elongated cross which forms the sole feature of the otherwise plain, windowless east wall above the high altar. Stained glass in the north and south walls by Joseph Nuttgens, *c.*1991, brings strong colour to the

Glass by Joseph Nuttgens in the Lady Chapel at Basildon, St Martin.

otherwise austere and lofty interior. Particularly striking is his Lady Chapel window, depicting 'the whole created order of the heavens taking the theme of Our Lady, Queen of Heaven'. On the south side, as approached from Town Square, is a tall portico of two stages with the majestic gilded and rayed bronze figure of the Risen Christ above the south doors. It is by T. B. Huxley-Jones, whose distinguished work may also be seen at Chelmsford Cathedral and Lambourne church. It is proposed to build a glass campanile west of the church, for which the bells wait in the vestibule. The fine organ in the west gallery was originally a Hill organ, enlarged by Hunter at the turn of the century and by Noterman in the 1950s. It was formerly in St Erkenwald's, Southend, now demolished.

BASILDON: LAINDON (C4) *St Nicholas*
Picturesquely perched on top of its steep knoll surrounded by a sea of twentieth-century housing, it incorporates within itself the stout original timbers of its fourteenth-century(?) belfry, with broach spire, weather-boarded outside in true Essex style. It has a thirteenth-century font, fourteenth-century chapel south of the nave, and fifteenth-century nave and chancel roofs. Curious primitive carvings in the porch spandrels include a dragon. West of the tower, but attached to it, is a two storey seventeenth-century wooden building, known as 'the Priest's House', much restored. *Illustrated overleaf.*

BASILDON: PITSEA (C4) *St Gabriel*
Consecrated 1962 (architect: John Corder), it forms part of Pitsea community centre. It is duodecagonal i.e. twelve sided (symbolising the Twelve Apostles?); emphasising togetherness in worship. The font is in the centre of the church facing the altar, thus linking the two main sacraments.

Basildon, Laindon St Nicholas, with the 'Priest's Room' on the left.

As a ground plan this is less novel in Essex than might appear, harking back to the fourteenth-century round church at Little Maplestead and the early Victorian (1838) octagonal one at Rowhedge, and looking forward to Billericay Emmanuel, 1992.

BASILDON: VANGE (C4) *St Chad*
Conspicuous at the south end of Clay Hill Road, it was consecrated 1959 to replace as parish church of Vange the old All Saints', now (1995) almost derelict. It was designed by architects Humphrys and Hurst, who, in that same year, designed St Paul's New Harlow (q.v.). It is of red brick with a tall thin tower. The tall windows south and west are now (1995) permanently boarded up due to vandalism, dimming the intentionally light, airy but plain interior. Stained glass in the baptistery survives, and a pretty blue and white pulpit.

BECKTON, London E6 (A5) *St Mark*
(Church and Community Centre) Sandwiched between the vast sewage outfall works and the famous (former) gas works to the east, London City Airport and the Royal Albert Dock to the south, and Canning Town and Custom House to the west, with Newham Way (the A.13) to the north cutting it off from East Ham, is Beckton, not exactly a beauty spot but humming with multi-racial, multi-cultural life – and problems. In the Tollgate Road, right in the centre of Beckton, is this large multi-purpose modern complex – with an ecumenical church in the forefront, dedicated in 1989 by the then Archbishop of Canterbury, Robert Runcie.

The whole enterprise was jointly planned and built in response to local need as a 'Local Ecumenical Project' by the Anglican, Roman Catholic and Free Churches with powerful financial backing from the London Docklands Development Corporation and the Church Commissioners, and up to the time of writing (1995), has been generously grant aided by the London Borough of Newham, as well as by numerous local and charitable concerns and individuals.

The community centre is well used; in 1994/5 an average 2,000 local people of all ages, races and religions passed through its doors in the course of a week. Its activities are manifold, ranging from youth provision through neighbourhood social work, family and children support and care for the elderly and mentally handicapped to communal fun and games, but here we are concerned with the church at the heart of it, used by a wide spectrum of different denominations.

It is a plain, somewhat austere functional brick building with a central altar/communion table and lectern behind and above which is a plain wood Cross draped with the Crucified Saviour's linen grave cloth, eloquent symbol of His Death and Resurrection for all mankind. There is a simple font in a recess backed by clear glass from floor to ceiling. Opposite is a large mural on the north wall – a 'hunger cloth' from Haiti, showing Christ in the world as it is – and as it might be.

At the time of writing, this remarkable Christian enterprise is under threat of closure. May that threat be lifted by the time this is in print is the urgent prayer of many, that it may continue to serve God's people in Beckton.

BELCHAMP OTTEN (C1) *All Saints and St Ethelbert*

An intensely lovable little church, its beautifully kept churchyard adjoining the (old) rectory garden. We enter by an impressive Norman doorway of two orders of various mouldings. The simple fifteenth-century font is under a tiny early nineteenth-century timber belfry in the form of a square tower, rendered, and perched on two much earlier carved posts. Together they form three west arches of disparate size and shape. Through them we behold a totally rustic whitewashed nave and chancel, furnished with box pews, miniature north west gallery ascended by a ladder, seventeenth-century pulpit, small chamber organ, communion rails of *c.*1700 with nice twisted balusters, brick floor in chancel, with a medieval priest's stone coffin lid set in it, and a good plain oak reading desk *c.*1970: no unnecessary clutter. The Royal Arms 1816-37 are cast iron. Under the belfry at the back is an effective modern painting of the Annunciation, signed D. Morton. Nothing whatever here to offend the eye – everything to please and conduce to prayer, worship and admiration.

ESSEX CHURCHES

BELCHAMP ST PAUL (C1) *St Andrew*

This Belchamp was given by King Athelstan to the Dean and Chapter of St Paul's in 930 – hence its name. Behind the church, at some distance from the village, is Paul's Hall with its ancient timber framed barn. The church is a fifteenth-century rebuilding by the St Paul's Cathedral Chapter, completed in 1490 when the tower was finished. It consists of nave and north aisle with three bay arcade, chancel with five-light east window (of clear glass), south porch and west tower with six bells. The south side of the nave is heavily buttressed. There is a simple fifteenth-century octagonal font. The chancel arch is of timber. In the chancel are fifteenth-century stalls with misericords, together with those at Castle Hedingham the only ones in Essex. There is a good brass, or rather two on one slab, of William Golding (d. 1587) and his second wife. His son Arthur, who died in 1606 and was also buried here, was a distinguished scholar, translator and poet, a friend of Shakespeare. There is, too, a series of mural monuments to Pemberton vicars who held the living from 1701 for over 150 years continuously.

BELCHAMP WALTER (C1) *St Mary the Virgin*

To visit this remote church is a richly rewarding experience, taking one back to a bygone age epitomised by the juxtaposition of church and stately Georgian Hall in a secluded country lane half a mile from the village. Externally the substantial fifteenth-century tower, with its tall transomed west window, stair turret and battlements, its eight bells and eighteenth-century clock, and the lofty wide nave of *c.*1325 (dated by its windows with intersected cusped tracery) overshadow the squat narrower thirteenth-century chancel. Entering by a pretty timber south porch, we are at first struck by the strident colours of the uninhibited High Victorian glass in east and west windows, the splendid old tortoise stove (still in regular use!) and the plain tie beam and queen post nave roof. The tub font is Norman, i.e. from an earlier church. There are two notable monuments (i) in the nave, an elaborate canopied affair of *c.*1325 to Sir John de Boutetort and (ii) in the chancel, one of 1720 (the year the Hall was built) to John Raymond (who built it and whose descendants, squires and patrons, still reside there). It is by Robert Taylor, sen., and is adorned by Baroque cherubs, but no effigy. But the church's most exciting treasure is its wall paintings in the nave, dating, it seems, like the Boutetort tomb, from the time it was built. Mostly discovered and conserved in the 1960s, they include on the north wall, left to right, a crowned Virgin suckling her Child, the martyrdom of St Edmund, Christ entering Jerusalem, the Last Supper and Feet Washing, a large pelican in her piety (symbol of the Eucharist, Corpus Christi) and, perhaps, the Three Living and Three Dead. For details see the guide. Finally, the panels of the Victorian pulpit were painted, 1865, by G. W.

Brownlow with the four evangelists – a good period piece. There are also some good medieval graffiti – if you can find them!

BENFLEET, SOUTH (C5) *St Mary*

This church, built from Kentish ragstone and flint, stands proudly in an attractive setting overlooking Benfleet creek. The tree shaded churchyard is on the site of Haesten's camp, where Alfred's men defeated the Danes in 893; according to tradition, a church was built on the site in the following year. The existing church has Norman features in the west wall of the nave. The tower, now crowned by a little white painted spirelet (1706), and the south aisle date from the fourteenth century. The chancel was extended and the embattled north aisle and timber framed south porch, of high quality, built during the fifteenth century. The interior is bright and colourful and has a feeling of space; much of the work was designed by Sir Charles Nicholson between 1890 and his death in 1949. He spent part of his life in the area and was buried just south of the tower. Older features in the nave include four great tie beams and the fifteenth-century stone corbels, carved with the signs of the evangelists, under the clerestory windows. The chancel roof has four Perpendicular octagonal crown posts; there is a black-and-white marble floor, *c*.1730. There are rood stairs in the north aisle and a timber staircase with an octagonal newel in the tower. Nicholson's work in the nave includes the organ loft (1927) and the rood screen, loft and rood (1927-33); there are twelve painted figures of saints in the panels at the base of the screen. The altar, reredos and communion rails were also by Nicholson. Most of the glass was designed by his brother, A. K. Nicholson; the subjects are saints and people from English church history.

BENTLEY, GREAT (D2) *St Mary the Virgin*

Modestly tucked away out of sight behind the Red Lion at the west end of the enormous village green, this church exhibits a mellow texture of rust coloured puddingstone with a little buff septaria, laid herringbone fashion in courses characteristic of Norman church building. This dating (*c*.1130) of the nave and all but the east end of the chancel is confirmed by the good Norman doorways of the nave, north and south, and a little Norman window in the north wall of the chancel. The fine south doorway is masked by the large red brick extension built in 1987. The chancel was extended in the fourteenth century; the two ogee headed niches date from that period as does the west tower.

Inside, as well as the simple octagonal late medieval font with shields, notice the interesting set of medieval (*c*.1300?) slip tiles formerly in the chancel floor, some with animals, others with heraldic devices, and the rood loft stairs on the north side. The pseudo-Norman chancel arch is, in fact,

37

Victorian. The altar stands well in the middle of the wide uncluttered chancel and there is some pleasing twentieth-century glass.

BENTLEY, LITTLE (E2) *St Mary*
This handsome church stands close by the roadside accompanied by the charming Victorian mixed school by Joseph Clarke, now the church hall. Remarkably unrestored, the exterior displays a felicitous combination of textures and colours from shiny knapped flint to mellow deep red brick and crumbly caramel septaria, to which cling traces of ancient lime render; the overall effect being softened and united by the patina of age.

Twelfth-century in origin, the nave and chancel were extended in the thirteenth century with a smart triplet of stepped lancets to the east wall and by a north aisle with an arcade of cylindrical piers. In its present form the north aisle is of fourteenth-century character, heightened in the sixteenth century, at which time an attached Priest's House was removed, leaving a noticeable scar about the north door. Next came the fine fifteenth-century west tower and the early sixteenth-century remodelling of the south nave wall in red brick and the addition of a south porch.

Internally, it is the elegant verticality of the proportions and the good hammerbeam roof with angel carvings which raise this parish church above the ordinary. Other pleasures include the gault brick and mellow pamment floors; a set of (restored) poppyhead nave benches and an eighteenth-century altar rail with twisted balusters; a splendidly sculptural iron bound and studded chest and a pretty wall memorial of 1741 to Elizabeth Lidgould and Jane Spencer with drapery swags and cherubs' heads. The rood stairs survive and a sturdy octagonal font bearing the Pyrton arms; Sir William Pyrton (d.1490) and his family are commemorated by a brass, now sadly half covered by the organ.

BERDEN (A2) *St Nicholas*
Close to the Hertfordshire border, this delightful country church is set well within its village off a lane signposted to Little London.

It is cruciform. Although there are indications in the nave of a Norman origin, the church as it stands beautifully exemplifies the Early English style of the thirteenth century. There was a Victorian 'restoration' in 1868, but although the east window was totally, but sympathetically replaced, the church escaped lightly and the side windows in the chancel, north and south, both consisting of two lancets with a cusped circle above, and carefully dated by Pevsner *c.*1260-70, are intact inside. Both windows have shafts close to the window surface and stronger shafts, all with stiff leaf capitals, in the outer arches. There is nothing else of the period as sophisticated as this in Essex; they are precious and very lovely. Also, both transepts, probably originating as private family chapels, are also thirteenth century, the north transept slightly the earlier of the two, and similar features, with engaged shafts, to the two chancel windows and arches are to be found in both.

The tinted glass in small leaded squares in most of the windows in this church is quite unusual and distinctly pleasing to the eye. The pulpit is mid seventeenth century and has some interesting geometrical patterns in the panels. In the north transept there are some good small brasses to William Turnor d.1473 and his wife. Finally, the organ, under the fifteenth-century tower, dates, with its case, from c.1790, and is said, but on what evidence is not known, once to have belonged to Samuel Sebastian Wesley, the organist and composer grandson of Charles, John's hymn writer brother.

BILLERICAY, Laindon Road (B4) *Emmanuel*

With the town and the church congregation expanding, St Mary Magdalen's was increasingly found to be cramped and inadequate for present day needs. As early as 1930 a far seeing lady, Miss Archer, gave land in Laindon Road as a site for a new parish church, but funds then would only run to a church hall. With the Second World War and its aftermath intervening, it was not until the 1980s that plans were agreed to build a new church on this site and to raise funds to pay for it.

John Marsh, himself a Quaker, of the Marsh, Eddison, Brown Partnership of Sevenoaks was appointed architect. After 10 years of planning and fund raising, during which it was decided to go for a building 'in the round' on an octagonal ground plan, the bishop of Bradwell laid the foundation stone in June 1991. The building was completed, to be consecrated a year later by the same bishop. The total cost was £800,000, all to be raised locally and it is hoped that this will be paid off in full by the end of this century.

The walls are of honey coloured brick. The weight of the roof structure is borne by pillar joists of laminated Norwegian spruce, and light is admitted through eight large triangular fanlights – a kind of clerestory – between the walls and the roof. The building is given unity by a central steeple on top of a glass lantern resting on the octagonal roof. The worship area is entered through a large, open foyer with a glass screen and glass doors. Between the foyer and the worship area is an engraved and enamelled window, depicting the Communion cup and bread between consecrating hands with the inscription 'I am with you always. Emmanuel'. It was designed and made by the artist Jenny Clarke who also designed and made the glass chandelier depending from the central lantern and symbolising the wind and fire of Pentecost – the Holy Spirit. The main body of the church has seating for 400 (or more if the glass doors of the foyer are folded back) in a semi-circle towards the Lord's Table, the altar, of plain oak. The wooden fittings and furniture (all in grey and blue) were made by James Chase of Kelvedon. The total-immersion baptistery in the sanctuary, used chiefly at Easter, has edging tiles made by a local potter, Harvey Bradley, a member of the congregation. A one-way window looks from the church into the creche. Incorporating modern electronic sound and video systems and some meeting rooms, this is a church for the twenty-first century.

BILLERICAY (B4) *St Mary Magdalen*

This thriving town began life as a hamlet in the mother parish of Great Burstead, to which its church was a chapel of ease. The red brick Tudor tower of 1490 is all that remains of the second chapel on the site. With its tall polygonal pinnacles and stepped battlements between, resting on an arched corbel frieze, it is reminiscent of the tower of East Horndon church, possibly designed and built by the same man. Its effect, though, was completely spoilt when in the late eighteenth century a new two storey chapel, in matching red brick, was built on to it with its pitched roof rising to the height of the tower's parapet. The result is that, approached from the north, occupying as it does the angle between Chapel Street and High Street, it looks curiously hunchbacked! Inside there are three galleries, nice eighteenth-century communion rails and font and an east apse with two Georgian windows filled with Victorian glass.

BIRDBROOK (C1) *St Augustine*

The church is in the village, next to the hall. Though much restored, the early Norman date of nave and chancel is evident from the herringbone masonry of the north wall, and that it was extended at both ends in the thirteenth century is equally clear from the three lancet windows in the east and west walls. The timber belfry houses three bells. Apart from the nice communion rails (*c.*1700), the furnishings of the chancel are all good craftsmanship of the second half of the twentieth century. The same applies to the interesting stained glass. One of the north windows commemorates the life and interests of G. E. Unwin of Baythorn Hall, churchwarden here for seventy years up to 1971. The tiny octagonal font, given in 1763, incorporates in one of its panels a miniature painting of the Baptism of Christ. There are several gentlemanly eighteenth-century mural tablets, mostly to Walfords, in the nave, and under the belfry one to Martha Blewitt of The Swan at Baythorn End who had nine husbands before she died in 1681. The Royal Arms are of William IV.

BLACK CHAPEL, see FORD END

BLACKMORE (B4) *St Laurence*

What we have here is, basically, two almost completely separate buildings. First in time the nave, aisles and chancel, which began life *c.*1160 as the church of a then newly founded Augustinian Priory, and was eventually,

Blackmore, timbers of tower structure.

following the Priory's dissolution in 1527, remodelled minus its choir, for continuing use as Blackmore parish church. Secondly, the prodigious three storey timber tower, built c.1480 adjoining and masking the Norman west facade of the then Priory church and described by no less an authority than Sir Nikolaus Pevsner as 'one of the most impressive, if not the most impressive, of all timber towers of England' (*Essex*, p. 88).

To return to the church itself. The west front as seen from inside the tower is built of flint rubble and consists of a west doorway of three orders of columns, surprisingly plain, with two large tall round headed windows above and a circular window above these. Inside, the first bay of both north and south arcades is also Norman, with plain piers and arches. Thereafter the north arcade is early fourteenth century (Decorated) with quatrefoil piers, whereas the south arcade piers are of Tudor red brick, octagonal, indicating a rebuilding after 1527 when the monks had gone. Two blocked thirteenth-century doorways east of the south aisle survive. Presumably they led to the cloister. There is the upper half of a civilian brass of c.1430 and an Elizabethan monument with two large effigies to Thomas Smyth (d.1597) and his wife.

Now back to the tower, which naturally invites comparison with Norwegian stave churches and Chinese pagodas. Outside, the ground floor has lean-to roofs on three sides, then a square of vertical weather-boarding, with four lean-to roofs, then the square bell stage with straight weather-boarding and finally a shingled broach spire. Inside there are ten huge posts with the tower standing on the middle six. Above is a complex forest of arched braces and cross struts, a tremendous feat of late medieval carpentry.

Blackmore House, the large square building east of the churchyard, now early eighteenth century externally, was often visited 'for pleasure' by Henry VIII and then nicknamed Jericho – hence the phrase 'gone to Jericho'. *See also plate 45 and picture on front cover.*

41

BOBBINGWORTH (B3) *St German*

Confusingly for the stranger, this parish seems undecided whether to call itself Bobbingworth or Bovinger.

It has a most curious church, found 'disappointing' by Pevsner. The exterior is certainly unprepossessing, with its overlarge white brick north west tower of 1841 incorporating the porch; its chancel of 1840, and nave, said (by Scarfe) to be of 1680, refaced in red brick in 1818. After this it comes as a welcome surprise to find inside box pews, an interesting pulpit with seventeenth-century decoration, some agreeable mural tablets and several hatchments 'skied' up in the roof.

BOCKING (C2) *St Francis*, Convent Lane

This is the church of the Roman Catholic Franciscan convent transplanted here from Portobello Road at the end of the nineteenth century. Designed by J. F. Bentley, architect of Westminster Cathedral, it is built of red brick with stone dressings and has a little polygonal turret. There is a south-east lateral arm originally for the lay public. The chancel has a handsome panelled ceiling and the stone altar is faced with a mosaic in turquoise blue with three angels, the design of Bentley himself.

Bocking, St Mary.

BOCKING (C2) *St Mary*

Bocking is unusual in having been an archbishop's 'peculiar' – i.e. like its Suffolk counterpart, Hadleigh, directly under the jurisdiction, not of the bishop, but of the Archbishop of Canterbury, who not only appointed the rector (styled the dean) but delegated his judicial authority to him locally. At the north extremity of the town this handsome church stands in its spacious churchyard partly surrounded by an old retaining wall several feet above the outside level. The churchyard has regrettably been denuded of its tombstones which are arranged along the wall, leaving the church adrift in a sea of green. It is basically a fifteenth-century building but the chancel is fourteenth century. The tower with its ten bells and prominent stair turret and battlements is fifteenth century but the porch and clerestory were not added until 1520. Internally the chancel and its north and south chapels are effectively partitioned off from the nave by the great twentieth-century rood screen, the church's most conspicuous feature, stretching right across it. Begun in 1905, it owes its completion in the 1950s to Sir Ninian Comper, who also designed the rood figures and the Christ in Majesty over the tower arch. The roofs of the nave and aisles are fifteenth and sixteenth centuries with some good carving and there are some interesting brasses. The south door with its fine ironwork is much earlier than the church. There are some good, but modest, monuments.

BOCKING (C2) *St Peter*, St Peter's Road, Bocking End

One is surprised to find this large late Victorian church, tucked away almost out of sight on the very border with Braintree. It was designed by J. T. Micklethwaite (1843-1906), a pupil of Scott. It was to be on the grand scale with north and south aisles and a south tower but funds did not run to its completion. The arcades of the intended aisles are seen inside but blocked up. There are five-light east and west windows (the latter with characteristic glass by Leonard Walker) and a good wooden pulpit and screen, all very seemly.

It is aptly characterised by Pevsner as 'competent and sensitive'.

BOCKING END, BRAINTREE (C2) *Congregational Chapel*

This chapel near the centre of Braintree was founded in 1699 with Thomas Shepherd, who died in 1739 and is buried in the adjoining graveyard, as its first minister and, it is said, 800 'hearers'. The first meeting house was erected in 1707 but was much enlarged and rebuilt at a cost of £2,500 in 1818, since when its external appearance has changed little, apart from the replacement of intersecting glazing bars by large paned window frames in the late nineteenth century. The front wall is of white gault brick dating entirely from 1818. The side and rear walls are of red brick and incorporate part of the original building. There is a hipped slate roof surmounted by an octagonal lantern, again of 1818. The front wall has five bays of round arched windows in two heights and square headed doorways in round arched recesses.

The feature of the interior is the domed plaster ceiling rising from a large square base to the glazed octagonal lantern. Most of the fittings were renewed in the late nineteenth century. These include the gallery fronts, pulpit, rostrum and pews. There is a large graveyard at the rear.

BOREHAM (C3) *New Hall, Roman Catholic Chapel*

In 1798 the canonesses of the Order of the Holy Sepulchre at Liège, refugees from the French Revolution which had by then overrun what is now Belgium, acquired the extensive remains of what had once been Henry VIII's summer palace at New Hall and re-established their convent school there. Their Order had been founded in 1642 for Catholic refugees from Protestant England: so the wheel had come full circle. New Hall was in fact one of the first nunneries to be established in England since the Reformation.

The canonesses adapted the great banqueting hall, or to use the correct eighteenth-century term, saloon, for use as their chapel, retaining much of its previous character and decor. Wright's description in his 1836 *History of Essex* (vol. 1, p. 107) substantially still holds: 'On the ceiling there is a splendid display of stucco work, representing cherubim supporting the chandeliers, with the arms of the Waltham family (previous owners) in the centre ... this capacious apartment has been conveniently and elegantly fitted up as a chapel for ... the use of a community of nuns ... besides their religious occupations usefully engaged in superintending the education of a limited number of young ladies'.

Apart from the austere modern altar and tabernacle and the plain but handsome classical reredos with a large crucifix, the decor is still that of an elegantly panelled early eighteenth-century hall, with a gallery for organ and choir (added by the nuns in 1799) and a spectacularly exuberant ceiling painted in blue, stone and gold. To all this there is one surprising exception. High on the wall over the door are the superbly carved arms of king Henry VIII in bold relief and colourful blazonry. They were placed there in the eighteenth century in a finely carved surround when most of the palace was destroyed: the very last thing one would expect to find in a Roman Catholic chapel!

Although it must be understood that this is essentially a private chapel, the Reverend Mother the Prioress says that anyone is welcome to attend any of the chapel services and that for other visits, permission, preferably with prior warning, is readily given.

BOREHAM (C3) *St Andrew*

This is one of the most complex churches in Essex – its building history not easy to unravel. There was undoubtedly a Saxon church on the present site, of which interesting evidence remains. It is believed that at this period the walls of the original Saxon chancel were thickened and raised to form the present central tower; the ground floor stage has Saxon work, possibly including the windows. The brick parapet of the tower was erected by the 3rd (Radcliffe) earl of Sussex in the mid sixteenth century. The present nave was built in the thirteenth century; later in the century a chapel was built into the east end of the south aisle. The piscina and hexagonal font, to which quite pleasing Victorian tiles have been added, date from this period. The tall Saxon chancel arch of Roman brick is visible above the pointed arch erected in the late fourteenth century when the Norman chancel was rebuilt. The north aisle was widened during the fifteenth century; the windows have interesting sculptured heads forming the ends of the dripstones; the porch is also fifteenth century. Its sixty feet prolongation as a covered way right down to the pavement was originally built by a Colonel Tufnell Tyrell of Boreham House for the wedding of his daughter c.1843. This was subsequently demolished and the present tunnel erected as a memorial to Canon Hulton d.1923. The Sussex chapel was completed in accordance with the will of the 3rd earl (d.1583) to contain the magnificent monument with alabaster effigies of the first three earls, made by Richard Stevens of Southwark at a cost of £240. The chapel was reduced to its present size in 1860. The brass to Alse Byng (1573) and her six named children is a palimpsest; there is a copy of the mid fifteenth-century Flemish reverse.

BORLEY (C1) dedication unknown
An unpretentious little church on top of a long hill, approached through spectacular topiary in the churchyard. The west tower and the chancel are probably sixteenth century, the nave possibly eleventh century. There are two fonts, the uninteresting Victorian one in use, and another of uncertain age (seventeenth century?) with a stone cover, in the vestry. There is an overpoweringly large six poster monument to Sir Edward Waldegrave (d.1561) and his wife (d.1599) on the north side of the nave and a big clumsy mural monument with effigy to Magdala Southcott d.1592 in the chancel.

BOWERS GIFFORD (C4) *St Margaret*
The large sprawling nondescript 'village' adjoins Basildon but its church is entirely on its own and remote at the end of a long lane on to the marshes, overlooked by the embankment of the busy Southend railway line. Externally its highly distinctive feature is the huge diagonal buttress propping the west tower and weather-boarded spire at its south-west corner. There is a notable military brass of c.1350 (Sir John Gifford?), headless.

BOXTED (D2) *St Peter*
Snugly surrounded by a picturesque cluster of old houses at the north end of its extensive parish, St Peter's is best approached from the Colchester-Sudbury road (A.134) at the marked turn-off to the east about 1 mile north of Great Horkesley.

The core of the church, viz. its west tower and nave, dates from the twelfth century. The tower, built largely of puddingstone, was topped, embattled and given diagonal buttresses in Tudor brick in the early sixteenth century. The plain Norman chancel arch opens into a chancel

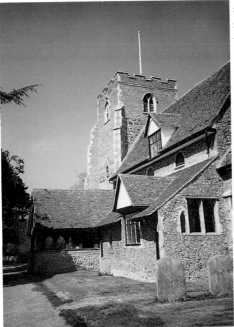

Boxted, St Peter.

apparently rebuilt also in the sixteenth century. The way in which the Norman nave was enlarged in the fourteenth century is that, as at Fingring-hoe, the thick walls were roughly cut through on both sides to make the crude, pointed north and south arcades and aisles. The whitewashed walls are lit by large clear glass dormer windows as well as those of the small clerestory, giving a pleasingly light interior. There is a west gallery of 1836 on cast iron columns, and a set of late Hanoverian Royal Arms, in cast iron painted, on the north wall. An interesting mural in the chancel commemorates Sir Richard Blackmore, poet and royal physician (d.1729).

BRADFIELD (E2) *St Lawrence*

With its stocky west tower of thirteenth-century rubble with a much later brick top, it stands well on a corner of the Manningtree-Harwich road, once overlooking the broad Stour estuary. To the thirteenth-century nave and chancel transepts were added in 1840, making the church cruciform. The cement covered exterior walls are whitewashed and in consequence look delightful. The thirteenth-century octagonal font of Purbeck marble has two blank pointed arches on each face of the bowl. The handsome eighteenth-century pulpit incorporates earlier carved panels. There is a brass of 1598, a funeral helm and Grimston family ledgers, and in the nave two good two-light stained glass windows by Rosemary Rutherford *c.*1965, commemorating Dunnings (cf. Broomfield and Clacton St Paul).

BRADWELL JUXTA COGGESHALL (C2) *Holy Trinity*

This delightful little, basically Norman, church right away from its village abounds in wall painting and much else besides. Until 1932 it was *completely* unrestored (box pews, pulpit with sounding board and west gallery). But though, sadly, these have gone, a lot remains. Externally there is a typically Essex timber bell turret and low shingled spire and much puddingstone and some Roman tile in the walls giving a lovely warm texture. You enter through a fourteenth-century timber porch an interior still lit by oil lamps

Bradfield, St Lawrence.

and with a brick floor with some medieval glazed tiles near the plain (Norman?) font on its Tudor brick base and with a seventeenth-century pyramidal cover. The fifteenth-century screen tracery is surmounted by a most unusual survival: the boarding which formed the back of the original rood loft and serves as a tympanum completely separating chancel from nave. Behind the altar is a double monument to the Maxey family with two pairs of kneeling figures – erected 1592. On the north wall are other Maxey tablets recording family loyalty to Charles I (epitaph must be read). Wall paintings are mostly in window splays: subjects include the Trinity (God the Father holding a Crucifix) and the Incredulity of Thomas. Arms of Charles II.

BRADWELL JUXTA MARE (D3) *St Peter on the Wall and St Thomas*

The tiny church of St Peter is the most ancient of the churches of Essex and an evocative monument to the earliest years of Christianity in England. This simple stone box stands in a remote but bleakly beautiful spot beside the North Sea, approached only by a footpath. The wall upon which it originally stood was the west wall of one of a chain of shore forts erected by the Romans to protect the east coast from Saxon raiders. Little trace of the fort now remains, but taken from it were materials to build the church; Kentish ragstone, honeycombed volcanic tufa, septaria and brick.

Eventually many of the shore forts were taken over by Saxon settlers as strongholds, later becoming monastic sites. In AD 653, Sigeberht, king of the East Saxons, having received the faith from his Northumbrian overlord Oswy, installed as bishop the saintly Cedd of Lindisfarne. The Venerable Bede recorded how the bishop 'built churches in several places, ordaining priests and deacons to assist him in the work of the faith, and the ministry of baptising, especially in the city which in the language of the Saxons is called Ythancestir'. This has been identified with Bradwell, which became for a short time the site of the first cathedral in Essex.

Now only the nave survives of a church with an eastern apse separated from the nave by a pair or triplet of arches turned in Roman brick, remains of which may be picked out on the east wall. It was flanked on each side by a small chamber known as a *porticus*, a feature of early Saxon churches, and at some time had a west porch. Large areas of rebuilding, dating from the restoration and reconsecration of 1920, are evident in the side walls where wagon doors had been punched through around the late seventeenth century to convert the church to a barn.

The similarity of the plan form to the Kentish group of early Saxon churches has led to the suggestion that this church may only have been built after the death of Cedd, when Archbishop Theodore reunited the diocese with London in 669, thereby returning it to the influence of Rome rather than the Celtic Church. However, it is questionable whether the site

which was thus demoted would have warranted the building of a stone church, and this speculation remains uncertain.

The monastery belonging to the church was destroyed during the Danish invasions of the ninth century but the church continued in use until the sixteenth century as a chapel of ease to the church of St Thomas in the village, which should also be seen. It has a nice red brick tower of 1706 and an extraordinary font, dated fourteenth century by Pevsner who aptly describes the 'four big ugly heads reaching up from the stem, as if their shoulders carried the bowl'.
See also plate 1.

Detail of the font at Bradwell-juxta-Mare, St Thomas.

BRAINTREE (C2) *St Michael*
St Michael's is a prominent landmark on the south side of the town, marooned in an expanse of greensward which has the lack-lustre quality of a public open space. Braintree's former citizens have been ruthlessly evicted from the churchyard; all that remains of them are a few stones lined

48

up against the east boundary wall. A small knot garden commemorates the seventeenth-century naturalist John Ray, Braintree's – or more accurately, Black Notley's – most famous son. The church dates from the foundation of Braintree as a new town with a market charter in 1199 by the bishop of London. The unsympathetic, uniform appearance of the church is the result of a drastic but much-needed restoration by J. L. Pearson in 1864-66. The red brick patterns in the flintwork probably replicate decoration originally executed in reused Roman brick. The original church probably had a chancel, nave and tower of the same dimensions as those that exist today. Only the tower preserves the lancet windows which would have been a characteristic feature of that building. Aisles were probably added in the thirteenth century, only to be rebuilt wider in the fourteenth century and then in the sixteenth century, when the Jesus chapel was added to the south side of the chancel. The north chapel is fourteenth century, extended in 1886 to accommodate the organ. The church is invariably locked, but it has a plain airy interior surmounted by Pearson's hammerbeam roof. Of note is the Jesus chapel, which has a roof with carved bosses, and a spiral stair in an octagonal turret which led to the rood screen. The window embrasures are carried down to serve as seats, and there is a piscina.

BRAXTED, GREAT (C3) *All Saints*
Essentially the 'estate church', set among lovely trees overlooking a lake, its churchyard surrounded by iron railings with a notice by a double padlocked gate 'STRICTLY PRIVATE KEEP OUT'. The public entrance is from the west where there is a car park. Having penetrated these defences, we find a long narrow building constructed of septaria mixed with flint, freestone and Roman bricks, possibly from the villa at nearby Rivenhall. The northwesternmost window in the chancel betrays its Norman origins, and it seems the Norman chancel ended in an apse. It was extended and straight ended in the thirteenth century and given lancet windows – three of them slightly stepped in the east wall. A tower was begun but left unfinished until the Victorians added an incongruous spire. The fifteenth-century porch has a king post roof.

In 1761 the Du Canes of Braxted Park added a north transept in brick with vaults beneath and fitted it up as a family pew. It was later Victorianised as was the rest of the church, very thoroughly, and so it remains. An 1844 window by Warrington in the transept is admired by some. There is no accounting for taste!

BRAXTED, LITTLE (C3) *St Nicholas*
Next to the hall and with the picturesque water mill and the mill pool nearby, but far from the village, this tiny Norman church (originally only 45 x 16 feet), with apse and timber bell cot, is built of rubble with a good deal of puddingstone. Date *c*.1120. There is a brass, William Roberts and two

wives 1508. But what everyone comes to enjoy is its transformation by the Rev. Ernest Geldart (1848-1929), amateur architect and decorator, its Tractarian rector 1881-1900. First he enlarged it by adding a north aisle which he called 'the children's aisle', re-using a door and windows from the old north wall, so that from the south the appearance of the church was unaltered. He also installed a new altar, reredos, altar rails, pulpit, choir stalls, low chancel screen, with rood and rood beam above, and font. 'Practically every available surface, from the dado rail to the roof timbers, is covered with decoration and apart from the stencilling it all has symbolic meaning' (James Bently, in *Country Life* 15 April 1993). There is not space here to describe it: it demands to be seen. Let one example suffice. On the south wall is the Apostles' Creed with Christ in the centre holding an open book. The church was expertly cleaned and restored between 1989 and 1992 at great but justifiable expense, with funds raised locally and grants from many sources including the Friends of Essex Churches. It had become shabby, dingy and depressing; now to enter this little church is an overwhelming experience, not to be hurried over.

BRENTWOOD (B4) *Roman Catholic Cathedral of St Mary and St Helen*
This magnificent church, commissioned by Bishop Thomas McMahon and designed by the well known neo-classical Dedham architect, Quinlan Terry, was built between 1989 and 1991, when it was dedicated in the presence of Cardinal Hume. It replaced an altogether inferior and inadequate Gothic Revival building of 1861, later enlarged. At the preliminary planning stage a conscious, but inevitably controversial, decision was taken to incorporate part of the old church, including its spire, as the south aisle of the new cathedral, where it serves as the Blessed Sacrament Chapel. Though purists will probably disagree, most unprejudiced visitors will feel that this expression of continuity has been brilliantly (and inconspicuously) achieved.

The architect took his inspiration from two sources, the Florentine Renaissance exemplified by Brunelleschi and the English Baroque of Sir Christopher Wren, as seen especially in his London City churches, e.g. St Stephen, Walbrook. The building materials chosen were Kentish rag for the main structure with dressings, piers and pilasters in Portland stone, hand-made brick for the clerestory and slate for the roof. They blend together surprisingly well. The ground plan is a parallelogram for the new building turned almost into a square by the incorporation of the old.

The cathedral is entered from the north though a tall Doric portico and the exterior derives its unity from its culmination in a handsome domed octagonal lantern. Seen from inside in the centre of the plain but gilded coffered ceiling, it sheds dramatic light onto the central altar. The gloriously light and spacious oblong interior within its four arcades of

Tuscan columns, with its multiplicity of elegant brass chandeliers and its large clear glass round headed Wren style windows, is wonderfully conducive to calm reflection and prayerful receptivity.

Space does not here permit more than a glancing reference to the furnishings, stoup, font, altar, cathedra (bishop's throne), ambos, organ case, all architect designed and carefully detailed. Everything here has its appropriate symbolism and significance: all clearly explained in the excellent Pitkin guide written by the Bishop himself. It is essential reading for a full appreciation of this fine church.

One outstanding feature deserving special mention is the Stations of the Cross, roundels above the arcade, designed and made by Raphael Maklouf (who designed the Queen's head on the current coinage).

A distinguished architect has written: 'The exterior which faces on to a large forecourt rather than on to the road has added enormously to the townscape of Brentwood. Despite its controversial elements it is an exciting building which well repays a visit'. It does indeed. *See also plate 67*.

BRENTWOOD (B4) *St George*

About this suburban church, built in 1934, its architect Laurence King, a local man, wrote years later: 'This brick church is characteristic of the modern movement of that time. Free standing stone altar in large apsidal sanctuary. Good contemporary fittings', in *John Betjeman's Guide to English Parish Churches*, Harper Collins revised edn 1993, p. 205. But King wrote in the original edition 1958. There is not much to add, save that though now still more of a period piece, St George's should stand the test of time. The best of the 'good contemporary fittings' designed by King are the font and its cover flanked by big standard candlesticks. In one respect St George's, King's first church, has fallen victim to passing liturgical fashion. The present skimpy nave altar, standing in front of the dignified apse altar designed by King, inevitably detracts from the latter: a pity.

BRENTWOOD (B4) *St Thomas*

The present church was built between 1881 and 1883 on the same site as a smaller church constructed in 1835 to replace the medieval chapel dedicated to St Thomas of Canterbury, the ruins of which can still be seen in the High Street. It was designed by Ernest Lee in the Early English style, using flint with stone dressings. The church is large with chancel, Lady chapel, nave with aisles and clerestory. The north west tower and spire, added in 1886, is visible from a considerable distance. The design of the church was influenced by the Oxford Movement. Betjeman described the interior as 'big boned and stately'. The eye is naturally drawn to the east end with its high brightly decorated ceiling and impressive reredos, added in 1896 and coloured during Laurence King's redecoration of the chancel in the 1950s. There is now a nave altar, surrounded by steps on three sides. The stained glass is good: a series of Old Testament figures and saints; the martyrdom of St Thomas in the west window; that by John Hayward commemorating the centenary of the church and the life of Laurence King. The small brass plate to John Parker (1673) came from St Thomas' chapel. The Stations of the Cross in the aisles were formerly in the nearby Roman Catholic Cathedral and were given to St Thomas' in appreciation of the use of the church during the remodelling of the cathedral in 1974. A church centre was added on the south side in 1988; the use of flint with stone dressings successfully echoes the materials of the church itself.

BRIGHTLINGSEA (D3) *All Saints*
The first sight of the noble 97-foot flint tower of All Saints' silhouetted against the sky as you approach Brightlingsea from Thorrington is unforgettable; a landmark too from far out to sea. Completed in the 1490s in four stages, the ten foot thick base decorated with shields in quatrefoils, with its great windows and diagonal buttresses with empty niches most of the way up, it ranks with Dedham and the finest flint towers of East Anglia. The crenellated parapet and pinnacles were added late in the nineteenth century and it may be doubted if they are an improvement. The fine south porch is part of the opulent late fifteenth-century rebuilding; the east parts of the north and south arcades are much earlier, *c.*1300. The nave was lengthened to join the tower and a north chapel and south vestry were added *c.*1520. Disaster struck in 1814 when the nave roof fell, bringing the clerestory with it. The clerestory was not rebuilt, with the result that the interior sadly lacks height.

There is a good fifteenth-century font, many niches and a splendid collection of fifteenth- and sixteenth-century brasses of the Beriffe family of Jacobes and, in the chancel, a great Baroque monument to a wealthy German marine insurance magnate and squire, Nicholas Magens (d.1764). By Nicholas Reed, it displays a globe (showing California as an island) but no effigy.

Round the nave will be found 212 individually inscribed tiles commemorating Brightlingsea men lost at sea from 1872 until the present day. This poignant custom, unique in England, was initiated by Arthur Pertwee, vicar 1872-1917, a devoted priest greatly loved and revered. Good modern art is represented by a pleasing blue window in the Lady Chapel by Caroline Swash and Celestial Mary carved in walnut by John Doubleday. The town is a 'limb' of the Cinque Port of Sandwich and its deputy (mayor) is elected annually by the Freemen meeting in church.

A daughter church of *St James'* in Victoria Place in the town, a good mile from All Saints, was designed in white brick by William Mason of Ipswich (architect of St Botolph's Colchester and Rowhedge) and consecrated by Blomfield, bishop of London in 1836. *See also plate 30.*

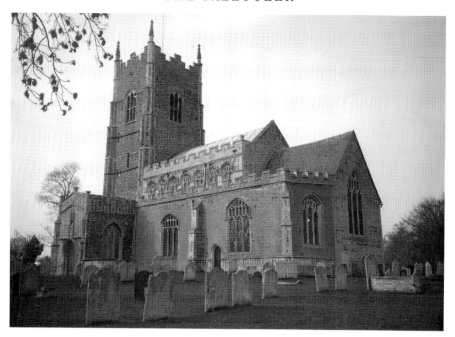

Great Bromley, St George.

BROMLEY, GREAT (D2) *St George*

A handsome church, the compact nave with its flushwork clerestory and porch dominated by the big puddingstone west tower. The chancel, nave and south aisle date from the early fourteenth century, refenestrated around the mid fifteenth century, when the north aisle and south chapel were added. The chancel is over-restored, as is much of the window tracery throughout. In the south chapel is a fine brass of 1432 to William Bischopton, with a figure of a priest under an ogee canopy. Both arcades have octagonal piers, but the capitals to the south are carved with seaweed foliage and vigorous grotesques, which is unusual in this area. The hood-mould of the south door of *c.*1400 also has fine foliate carving, with reset figures of Adam and Eve above.

A major phase of rebuilding commenced in the late fifteenth century with the tower. Following on, around 1500, came the elaborate flushwork porch with its spandrel figures of St George and the dragon. The tall clerestory, with its closely-set windows, forming seven bays above the three bay arcades, was added about the same time. It is crowned by a magnificent double hammer beam roof, lavishly carved and painted, with wall posts terminating in figures under canopied niches. Finally, a curiosity: a row of bell-ringers' hats is seen high above the inside of the tower arch. *See also plates 28 & 29 and illustration on p. 213.*

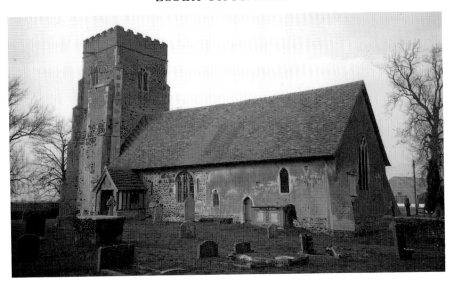

Little Bromley, St Mary the Virgin.

BROMLEY, LITTLE (D2) *St Mary the Virgin*

This lonely little church far from the village has a rich texture from large lumps of rust coloured puddingstone in nave and west tower, the latter topped in mellow red brick. Nave and chancel are under one continuous tiled roof. Rustic south porch. The church is now 'in retirement'.

BROOMFIELD (C3) *St Mary*

The village still retains its identity though Chelmsford draws ever closer. The church at the top of the village green, half hidden among trees, has one of Essex's six round towers, Norman with much re-used Roman brick and, as at Great Leighs, crowned with a (later) shingled broach spire. Until 1870, when a north aisle was added, the church simply consisted of nave and chancel, both Norman, but with later windows inserted. There is a Victorian stone reredos of the Last Supper, in low relief.

But what gives this otherwise not particularly remarkable building peculiar distinction, is the work of Rosemary Rutherford (d. 1972), daughter of a former vicar. She was an artist in glass and paint whose achievement has yet to be sufficiently recognised. The east window and three in the south wall are by her. The two single-light windows, Christ washing His disciples' feet (given in memory of her mother) and the Raising of Lazarus, may be judged outstanding. (Her later masterpiece is at St Paul's, Clacton on Sea.) But what must not be missed is the fresco in the tower ground floor, Christ stilling the storm, painted in collaboration with her brother John, while the plaster was still wet. It is a powerful composition of which Broomfield should be proud.

BROXTED (B2) *St Mary*

Quite apart from its village, this church consists of a nave and chancel, both basically thirteenth century with three lancets in the east wall, and Tudor brick windows in the nave, to all of which a north aisle was added in the fifteenth century, and a typically Essex belfry on the usual four posts. Features include a fine Jacobean pulpit and a handsome altar with triptych reredos, east window and tester of 1961 in the north aisle, all designed by Francis Stephens. But what gives this church peculiar distinction and topicality is the remarkable pair of two-light 'hostage' windows by John Clark at the west end, symbolising Captivity and Freedom. They were put in in 1993 to commemorate the long, cruel captivity and eventual release of journalist John McCarthy, an active churchman, whose home before his kidnapping was the big house next door (now the Whitehall Hotel), and of his fellow Beirut hostages, Brian Keegan and Terry Waite. Also, a hatchment designed by John's herald brother Terence, in memory of their mother Sheila who died while John was still held hostage, was dedicated in 1991.

BULMER (C1) *St Andrew*

The church overlooks the village from rising ground to the south. It has two notable features: (i) the exceptionally large, light, spacious fourteenth-century chancel, if anything longer than the nave. Notice its roof, the sedilia, and on its north wall a plain mural tablet to two of Gainsborough's (of nearby Sudbury) most memorable early sitters, Mr and Mrs Robert Andrews of Auberies: and (ii) the fifteenth-century font, especially the Bacchanalian Green Man sprouting vine leaves and bunches of grapes, on one of its panels – a pagan fertility symbol.

BULPHAN (B5) *St Mary*

As Pevsner says, 'The interest of this church is entirely its timberwork, the tower, the porch, the screen.' The tower, picturesquely tile-hung, together with the nave east wall above the chancel roof (in the nineteenth century presumably), is in the same category as Blackmore, Navestock, Magdalen Laver, Margaretting *et al*, with 'aisles' projecting to north, west and south. Inside it is supported by six great posts with cross beams and diagonal braces. The south porch of *c.*1500 has ornate barge boards. The screen is a handsome piece with two bays each side of the centre arch and elaborate tracery.

BUMPSTEAD, HELIONS (B1) *St Andrew*

An attractive church in its shady hilltop churchyard in the centre of the village. Basically medieval with a thirteenth-century (Early English) chancel, nave and fourteenth-century south aisle with five bay arcade with octagonal piers, and clerestory, it underwent a major restoration in 1812,

Helions Bumpstead, St Andrew.

when the west tower was rebuilt in red brick with pointed windows and battlements, the nave and chancel ceiled, and most of the south wall rebuilt including the three-light windows with wooden frames and mullions. Apart from the fifteenth-century font with pleasing modern cover, most of the furnishings – pews, pulpit and organ case – appear to date from this time (1812). They have all been painted cream, with occasional splashes of scarlet, as on the pulpit sounding board. This, with the whitewashed walls and ceilings and almost complete absence of stained or tinted glass, makes the church agreeably light. Brick and pamment floors and absence of clutter complete the effect.

Surprisingly there are eight bells in the tower, regularly rung, and with bright scarlet sallies. Colour in the nave is supplied with embroidered kneelers one of which near the pulpit commemorates a recent hunting parson depicted in action! Among tablets on the chancel north wall is one to Devereux Tallakarne, killed 1627 in Buckingham's disastrous Rochelle expedition.

BUMPSTEAD, STEEPLE (B1) *St Mary*
The church is in the centre of the village. In the lower part of the west tower and the quoins of the chancel east wall is evidence of an early Norman church on the same site. The present building, dating from the late fourteenth or early fifteenth century, has extensive red brick repairs in the aisle walls, clerestory, south porch and upper stages of the tower, giving

it a not unpleasing patchwork texture. Inside, first to be noticed is the sixteenth-century poor box, ironbound and panelled, and the fifteenth-century font. The nave has four bay arcades to the north and south aisles, the roofs of which are finely carved. Numerous medieval graffiti, cut into the soft clunch of the piers and chancel arch, include two dragons, some musical notation and a collect for St Erkenwald. Otherwise the chief interest is in the monuments and the five Gent family hatchments. In the north aisle are monuments and glass commemorating the Bendyshes of Bower Hall (demolished 1926). The largest, signed by Thos. Stayner, is splendidly Baroque and shows an almost life-size Sir Henry (d.1717) with peruke and double chin, with his infant son beside him, reclining between barley sugar columns and beneath an elaborate pediment with mourning putti and coat of arms. Those of the Gents of Moyns Park in the south aisle are more modest.

BURNHAM ON CROUCH (D4) *St Mary*
A good mile north of the little town, in its large churchyard adjoining a farm, this church is basically fourteenth century, though its long row of seven standard three-light south windows, seen as we walk up the path to the handsome sixteenth-century embattled flint south porch, are fifteenth-century Perpendicular. The west tower of Kentish rag is clearly fourteenth century but had to be partially rebuilt after damage in the famous gale of 1703. The windows of the north aisle are mostly fourteenth century and there is a Tudor brick north porch. There is no structural division between nave and chancel and a run of no fewer than nine bays, all rather narrow, from west to east. There is no clerestory and the central (nave and chancel) roof, ceiled inside, is lit by three small dormers each side.

Apart from the plain Norman font on its central pillar and four corner shafts, there are no early furnishings, due to a bad fire in 1774, and the replacement of the Georgian pulpit, altar piece etc. put in afterwards in the Victorian 'restoration'. However, there is a fine chandelier and the old brick floor happily survives. The impression is one of light and warmth.

BURSTEAD, GREAT (B4) *St Mary Magdalen*
This was until the nineteenth century the parish church of Billericay. Its urban connection explains its relatively large size. Its fourteenth-century Kentish ragstone tower with a shingled steeple makes it a conspicuous landmark.

Unusually, it has two porches. Enter by the north porch and in the stonework of the fifteenth-century door note the heads of a king and queen, and a scene depicting the Annunciation. There is a stoup in the porch. Take care over the steps down into the church where the floor level has been lowered, and the first impression is of white walls and a large and spacious interior beneath a wonderful array of crown-post roofs supported by heavy tie beams. Each part of the church – nave, chancel, south chapel and south aisle – has a separate roof of slightly differing date, though all are fifteenth and sixteenth century.

The oldest part of the building is the narrow Norman window in the north wall of the nave. A late fifteenth-century arcade of five bays separates the nave from the south aisle. Curiously, the wall of that aisle is older than the arcade, being datable to the fourteenth century on the evidence of its windows and of the wall paintings which were discovered during the redecoration of the church in 1989. The series of cartoon-strip representations comprise a variety of subjects, including St Catherine, the Nativity, the Annunciation, and the Weighing of Souls.

In the south chapel, there is a piscina and close by on the wall is a sixteenth-century painted altar curtain. In the south aisle are ten fifteenth-century pews. Other interesting examples of medieval woodwork are the south and north doors, the latter now at the west end of the nave adjacent to a twelfth-century chest believed to have been used to collect money for the Crusades. In the sixteenth-century south porch, note the medieval scratch dials on the stonework of the doorway. The parish registers record the marriage of Christopher Martin, one of the leading 'pilgrims' in the Mayflower.

BURSTEAD, LITTLE (B4) *St Mary*
Very much a country church still despite the inroads of Billericay. Its typically Essex belfry, topped by a shingled spire, looks out over rolling country. The nave is of Norman origin, witness one north window. Both nave and chancel retain their medieval roofs.

BUTTSBURY (B4) *St Mary*
The church is out in the country at the junction of three lanes between Ingatestone and Stock. It is small, alone and lovely with long views over fields across the Wid valley. It has a short late fifteenth-century nave, which may once have extended further to the west. The chancel was rebuilt in brick (now cemented) in the late eighteenth century, at the same time as the brick west tower with a weather-boarded belfry with one bell. The two aisles have east windows with excellent reticulated tracery. The well-maintained interior is bright with white walls and plain glass; it is candlelit at night. The nave roof is high; the crown-post roof in the chancel must have been retained when it was rebuilt. The doors are of particular interest: the north door has been identified by Cecil Hewitt as of Anglo-Saxon construction, with characteristic rivetting round the circular inner ledges, partly obscured by late Norman planking of the same date as the serpent-type ironwork of high quality; the door must have been altered to fit a pointed Gothic arch. The south door is fourteenth century; both doors have small grilles 'for the inspection of would-be entrants'.

CANEWDON (C4) *St Nicholas*

'Considering the part of Essex where it stands, an unusually stately church' (Pevsner). It has a grand fifteenth-century west tower of ragstone in four stages, crowned with a parapet and battlements faced in flint and stone chequer pattern, as on the south porch, also fifteenth century. The tower, which has five bells, has wide angle buttresses, adding to its impressive appearance. The south door is original. Inside notice the tie beam and king-post nave roof, the octagonal piers of the four bay north arcade and the thirteenth-century font brought here from demolished Shopland church. There is an exceptionally fine late seventeenth-century pulpit, carved in Grinling Gibbons style with cherubs' heads and swags. Royal arms of George II and two hatchments are in the nave, and a pre-Reformation altar stone, two niches and a piscina in the north aisle. The handsome electroliers were formerly in Westminster Abbey. At the east end of the churchyard is the village 'cage' and stocks – disused!

CANFIELD, GREAT (B3) *St Mary*

In its quiet rural setting close to the site of the Norman motte and bailey castle, this little church is richly rewarding to the discerning visitor. Its timber belfry with recessed spire and embattled stone porch, both slightly incongruous and both added in the fifteenth or early sixteenth century, do little to disguise its essentially Norman character. The handsome south doorway has three distinctive features: (i) a tympanum with flat concentric zigzags 'probably meaning the sun' (Pevsner); (ii) the left hand capital carved with two birds (ibis?) pecking a bearded face; (iii) the left hand reveal with squares carved with swastikas (Sanskrit – good luck). The Norman chancel arch is impressive. It incorporates as abacus on the south side a carved Saxon grave slab. (The 'bullseye' above it is not original.) But what people come from far to admire is the east wall above the rather good Victorian alabaster reredos. Two deeply splayed Norman round headed windows flank a round arched recess. In the recess is one of the most tenderly beautiful thirteenth-century wall paintings in England. Above a plain consecration cross is the throned, crowned Madonna offering her breast to her Child who is seated on her lap looking at the spectator, His right hand raised in blessing. It is strongly reminiscent of the work of the brilliant St Albans monk/historian/artist Matthew Paris and can confidently be dated *c.*1250. The east wall above the nineteenth-century arcading has the characteristic masonry pattern and the window splays and the surround of the central painting have stiff floral decoration; all is in red and yellow ochre. All this was revealed in an excellent state of preservation when, in the course of 'restoration' in 1877, the fine monument of Sir William Wyseman (d.1684/5) and his second wife Arabella (shown frontally holding hands) was moved from its original position behind the Holy Table to the south wall of the nave. *See also plate 51 and frontispiece illustration.*

CANNING TOWN (A5) *Mayflower Family Centre* Vincent Street, London E16

The Mayflower, Canning Town, is a vigorous centenarian. It began in September 1894 as the Malvern College Mission. After World War One it changed its name to Docklands Settlement, while retaining its Malvern link, and flourished under the energetic leadership of Reginald Kennedy Cox, attracting widespread fame and financial support. Its chapel in Vincent Street in one of the East End's roughest neighbourhoods was built in 1930, replacing makeshift tin tabernacles, and was dedicated in honour of St George and St Helena in the presence of Queen Mary.

Designed in Tudor red brick in conscious imitation of the dining hall of Lincoln's Inn, with a central cupola topped by a weather vane of St George, it is a wide, spacious building with a hammerbeam roof, an attractive rose window above the altar and a large seven-light west window. There is some heraldic glass in the side windows and one, composed of jumbled fragments, commemorating the chapel's survival in the blitz – also a pulpit with tester given by Malvern College.

To the south the chapel opens upon a pleasant garden surrounded by residents' houses in the form of a courtyard in the midst of a complex of buildings in which the community work is carried on.

The Docklands Settlement went through a bad patch after World War Two and in 1956 was faced with imminent closure. It was in these circumstances that it was taken over by new management under the strongly evangelical aegis of Hugh Gough, bishop of Barking and David Sheppard, already renowned as a cricketer. In 1958 he was appointed warden of what was then renamed the Mayflower and, with his wife Grace, stayed there twelve years building up its work and witness on solid foundations. Despite inevitable ups and downs it continues to bear faithful Christian witness in this tough environment, with the chapel as its spiritual centre.

CHAPPEL (C2) *St Barnabas*

As you come down the hill from Great Tey, the first sight of this diminutive church with its white four-sided timber spire/bellcote, grouping perfectly with all its neighbours, is indeed memorable.

It gave the village its name. It was originally a chapel of ease to Great Tey for the hamlet of Pontisbright, a name now vanished. Although there is some evidence of an earlier chapel on the site, the present building was consecrated by the then Bishop of London in 1352, shortly after the Black Death. It is a single cell, nave and chancel under one roof with no structural division. The interior does not disappoint. Although the pitch pine benches are Victorian, there is a Georgian west gallery, altar rails and Royal Arms (on canvas, dated 1742) and a good Jacobean pulpit. The rustic south porch

60

is eighteenth century and the door itself with strapwork hinges, contemporary with the timber framed south doorway, probably seventeenth century. There are two bells in the belfry.

CHELMSFORD (C3) *Cathedral Church of St Mary, St Peter and St Cedd*

Lying near the centre of Chelmsford, the cathedral, built in the fifteenth and early sixteenth centuries, is essentially the parish church of the prosperous medieval town. From the outside the most important features are the fine late fifteenth-century west tower with its eighteenth-century 'spike' on top and the early sixteenth-century south porch with flint flushwork. Alterations in the nineteenth century included the north aisle (1873) and the raising of the chancel roof (1879). After the creation of Chelmsford diocese in 1914, two bays, designed by Sir Charles Nicholson, were added to the east end, together with north vestries. In 1802, following the collapse of the nave due to gravediggers undermining one of the piers, it was rebuilt by John Johnson, with a pretty 'Gothic Tracery Ceiling' and the use of Coade stone for the south piers and clerestory windows.

The interior owes its present appearance to the major reordering of 1983 (architect, Robert Potter): bronze and steel pulpit and lectern (*ambos*), Westmorland slate altar, bishop's throne and font. The two small ikon-like paintings behind the ambos are by Sister Petra Clare. A multi-coloured patchwork hanging, comprising 1520 individual pieces and designed by Beryl Dean to symbolise 'Glory', fills the width of the east wall below the east window.

The chapels of St Cedd and St Peter are at the west end of the north and south nave aisles respectively. Both are effectively enclosed by steel screens designed by Giuseppe Lund (who also designed the ambos). St Peter's Chapel commemorates all who have given their lives for their country. Central in it is George Ehrlick's bronze, 'The Bombed Child'. St Cedd's Chapel is used for daily worship and has as its focal point T. B. Huxley-Jones's Christus; near it is an aumbry in which the Sacrament is reserved. The window in St Peter's Chapel, depicting the saint, was engraved by John Hutton, famous for his great west window in Coventry Cathedral. There is, incidentally, on the south east corner outside, a fine stone carving of St Peter, in modern fisherman's boots and holding a Yale latch key. It is also by Huxley-Jones.

There are two outstanding Mildmay monuments: Thomas Mildmay (1571) and Earl Fitzwalter (by James Lovell, 1756). Unusual features are the fifteenth-century fan arch on the north side of the chancel and the banner cupboards in the buttresses between the tower and the nave.

The nave organ by N. P. Mander was installed under the tower in 1994 and is said to be the first new organ built in an English cathedral for 150 years. There is a peal of thirteen bells in the tower.

Finally, in the room over the south porch is the nucleus of the Cathedral Library. Dr Knightbridge gave the 600 volumes of his library to what was then Chelmsford Parish Church in 1679 and others have been added since. There is a similar library at Hatfield Broad Oak church. *See also plate 22.*

CHICKNEY (B2) *St Mary*
This delightfully remote little church is now 'in retirement', well cared for by the Churches Conservation Trust, and abounding in interest and character. Its asymmetrical nave and the west half of the chancel are Saxon, i.e. pre-1066, and remain much as they were before the Norman Conquest, with small, deep set, double splayed windows (as well as others inserted later). The chancel probably originally ended in an apse. In the early thirteenth century it was extended and given a square east end. A century later the charming little tower with its pyramidal spire was added. The rich fourteenth-century octagonal font with its four carved ogee crocketted canopies, each containing a shield, is also approximately of this date. It is unique in Essex. There are two fifteenth-century bells in the tower. The larger one is inscribed in Latin, 'To heaven from Sinai lead us Katherine'. (St Katherine of Alexandria, martyr, is buried in the famous monastery on Mount Sinai.) There is a medieval stone altar, one of only two in Essex. It was found beneath the floor in 1858. Also a nice plain late Georgian pulpit, possibly from Terling. Philemon Whale, rector 1578-1620, christened one of his sons Jonas (=Jonah)! Jonah succeeded his father as rector but only for a year.

CHIGNAL SMEALEY (B3) *St Nicholas*
Set in an attractive churchyard in the middle of the village, this church is unusual in that it was built of Tudor brick in the early sixteenth century. The north aisle was added in 1847 in brick of a reasonably good match. Even the font is of Tudor brick. There was almost certainly an earlier church on the site and it is believed that the bell, fragments of stained glass and the indent of a brass come from the earlier building. The chancel screen and six benches on the south side of the nave are sixteenth century. There is an early seventeenth-century pulpit and a late seventeenth-century communion table. The beautifully carved wooden altar comes from the closed church at Chignal St James, where it formed a World War One memorial. The reredos and screen by the door are early twentieth century. There are seventeenth-century armorial ledgers to the Lucking and Clopton families. The Essex historian, Philip Morant, held the living from 1735 to 1743.

Brass of Samuel Harsnett at Chigwell.

CHIGWELL (A4) *St Mary*

This church is in the ancient village of Chigwell, occupying a hilltop position with extensive views. It is indeed worthy of a visit because it represents a true village church which developed over the years to serve the ever-growing community. On the south side is the entrance porch which shields the fine Norman doorway with its typical chevron moulding and scalloped capitals. This leads into the church, which was remodelled in the fifteenth century. As the village was in Epping Forest, it is natural that much use was made of local timber. The wooden belfry is supported by massive oak posts, and the nave has a magnificent crown-post roof, all this work dating probably to the early fifteenth century. However, by the nineteenth century the church had become too small for the community, and in 1880 there was built on the north side of the original building a larger flint-faced church which dominates the older structure. The new chancel was lavishly decorated by Bodley, who also designed the reredos and the pulpit. The east window is by Kempe.

Of particular note is the fine brass in memory of Samuel Harsnett (d.1631), one time rector of the parish and founder of the school, who ended his career as Archbishop of York. Note also the numerous funeral hatchments on the north pitch of the roof of the old church; these were displayed at the house when the owner died and then hung in the church. Here is a church which retains its village character even though so close to the metropolis.

CHINGFORD (A4) *St Peter and St Paul*

This, the parish church of Chingford (then still a village, now a London suburb), was built on Chingford Green in 1844 to replace the old church of All Saints which had long been increasingly ruinous, and picturesquely overgrown with ivy. It remained in this state until restored and largely rebuilt in 1929 (see the next article).

The rector in 1844 was also squire and patron of the living, wealthy Robert Boothby Heathcote. He himself commissioned and paid for the new church. His architect was Lewis Vulliamy and the total cost over £5,000. It is a large building of white brick with panels of chequer flint flushwork and originally comprised a tall west tower and spire, a wide aisleless nave, and a shallow chancel with apse. In 1903 it was greatly extended eastwards by Sir Arthur Blomfield. The extension was aisled in three bays and terminated in three five-light windows replacing the apse. The twelfth-century square Purbeck marble font and the fine eighteenth-century pulpit with sounding board were brought here from the old church, together with communion rails, parish chest and nine hatchments.

CHINGFORD OLD CHURCH (A4) *All Saints*

It stands high on top of Merry Hill, surrounded by twentieth-century housing. After more than a century of neglect, decay and disuse, it was restored and largely rebuilt in 1929/30 by C. C. Winmill, architect. It is mainly Perpendicular in character but the south arcade is of thirteenth-century cylindrical piers. The fifteenth-century west tower is of Kentish rag, the south porch of Tudor brick. A few minor monuments, mostly to the Leigh family of the seventeenth century, have survived.

CHRISHALL (A1) *Holy Trinity* (formerly St Mary the Virgin)

One cannot fail to be impressed by the calm tranquillity of this isolated church on its ridge so far from the village. The parish name in its earliest form of Christhale, the home of Christ, suggests an early Christian origin. The present church, mainly of *c.*1400, is a spacious building with north and south aisles and porches and a chancel with a broad five-light east window. The embattled west tower with chequer parapet is a century earlier than the rest. Because there is little stained glass the church is beautifully light.

There is a stone recumbent effigy of a fourteenth-century lady in a tomb recess in the south wall but the main feature of the church is its fine collection of brasses near the (plain) font. Pre-eminent among them is that of Sir John de la Pole in armour hand in hand with his wife Joan (Cobham from Kent). They are under a triple arched canopy, his feet on a lion (for valour), hers on a dog (fidelity). The date is *c.*1375 and the stone lady is probably his mother. The powerful de la Poles, originating as merchants in Hull, were seated (the main branch) at Wingfield Castle, Suffolk and at Ewelme, Oxon. They married into the royal family.

CLACTON, GREAT (E3) *St John the Baptist*

Although increasingly engulfed in a sea of Clacton suburbia, St John's, the mother church of the whole conurbation, is still one of Essex's most impressive Norman *parish* churches. And this despite the facts that its original chancel was replaced in the fourteenth century and that its massive, unfinished tower, now (1996) in such a parlous state, was added in the fifteenth century. Also, it was singularly unfortunate in its Victorian 'restoration' by Hakewill in 1865. Pevsner may have somewhat overstated the case when he wrote that it was 'badly ill-treated' by Hakewill and that 'due to him', the east front 'is even more painful inside than outside'. In his defence it seems likely that when Hakewill replaced the, doubtless worn, Roman brickwork of window arches and quoins, he was at least trying to be faithful to the original. Further it must be acknowledged that the yellowy septaria of which the church is largely constructed is not particularly sympathetic to most modern eyes. Nevertheless the north and south doorways of the nave still impress. The big flat buttresses made Pevsner wonder if there was an original intention to vault the wide nave, as at Copford (q.v.).

Unhappily, at the time of going to press, St John's has been out of action for some nine years, as a dangerous structure. But discussions are proceeding between the parish, the diocese and English Heritage with the firm intention that it will eventually be repaired and, as needful, reordered and re-equipped to make it once again an active centre of Christian worship and evangelism in the twenty-first century.

CLACTON, LITTLE (E3) *St James*

It stands in the middle of the village, nave, chancel, timber south porch and typically Essex weather-boarded belfry. There is some evidence of Norman work in both nave and chancel and the font is of the square Purbeck type, plentiful locally. The furnishings, which include a west gallery, are all modern but entirely traditional in design.

CLACTON ON SEA (E3) *St James*

The unprepossessing appearance of this church gives little indication of its splendid interior. Built during 1912-13 to the designs of Temple Moore (1856-1920), it is obviously unfinished: two further bays and a west tower were intended. The proportions of the simplified Perpendicular exterior are inevitably uneasy, and the severity of its cement render is hardly relieved by Bath stone tracery or the forbidding Calvary on the east wall.

The interior comprises a dramatic sequence of interlinked volumes culminating in the greatly elevated sanctuary, in the glorious colours of the reredos, a purely Gothic work by Sir Ninian Comper. The nave has an elemental Romanesque character, but the curious asymmetrical choir arcades are Romanesque to the south and mildly Moorish to the north; the sanctuary windows are Decorated Gothic. This stylistic diversity is secondary to the spatial quality of the church.

The play of light and dark is essential. In the nave, light is soft, filtered through the aisles. The choir is lit only by a clerestory, an effect intensified by the deep shadows of the side chapels; beyond it the sanctuary is drenched in light.

The materials are spare: brick, plaster and stone, employed with the honesty and feeling for texture of the Arts and Crafts movement. Their simplicity is subtly enriched: the plaster is contrasted with minimal red tile bands and voussoirs, and the stone piers have self-consciously coarse tooling. The sculptural exaggeration of the stone mouldings accentuates the monumental scale of the building. There are unexpected quirks like the cat-sized wall passages, the high timber galleries and the tiny window at the top of the east wall of the north aisle.

The muscular originality of the architecture is a brilliant expression of the last great period of the Gothic revival; an extraordinary fusion of traditional and modern sensibilities. *See also plate 63.*

CLACTON ON SEA (E3) *St Paul*

When Clacton began to be developed as a popular seaside resort in the 1870s, its first church, St Paul's, was built as a chapel of ease to Great Clacton at the east (Holland) end a little behind the seafront. It soon acquired independent parochial status and had to be much enlarged to cope with increasing congregations. But it was an inferior building, especially when compared with the fine Anglo-Catholic St James', built 1913, and between the wars a fund was started and plans made for its replacement by something better. These plans did not finally come to fruition until 1966 when, with Roy Gould as architect, the new St Paul's was built and consecrated. Although admirably functional, unfussy, and full of light, it is not strikingly original – a rectangular nave, deliberately built to suggest an upturned boat, with a nice Lady Chapel to the south and a triangular campanile with one solitary bell. But what lifts it high above mid twentieth-century mediocrity is the superb nine-light east window, the *chef d'oeuvre* of Rosemary Rutherford (d.1972), some of whose earlier work may be seen at Broomfield. With pieces of thick stained glass cut by the artist herself from 10 inch by 8 inch slabs and set in panels of concrete, French fashion, its theme is the Conversion of St Paul, who 'is seen in the centre light, half kneeling with arms raised above his head, struck by shafts of light from all sides and with the brilliant figure of the glorified Christ above him'. The artist also intended to suggest his great vision in Romans 8, of the whole created universe awaiting its redemption with eager expectation. Intensely dramatic, it is an inspiration to all who worship here. *See also plate 64.*

CLAVERING (A2) *St Mary and St Clement*

This fine large Perpendicular church, built *c.*1400, and entirely East Anglian in appearance, is set in a lovely village and the lane by which it is approached from the south is memorable. Built of flint rubble, the entire church, west tower, clerestoried nave, north and south aisles, chancel and south porch, is embattled. The font and the knight's effigy in Purbeck marble in the north aisle are from an earlier church. It has been carefully restored in recent years and there is much to enjoy. Notice particularly: (1) the cambered tie beam nave and aisle roofs; (2) the chancel screen of *c.*1450 with its delicate tracery and remains of painted saints on the dado panels (Anthony with pig, Lawrence with gridiron and Agnes with lamb, among them); (3) the good Jacobean pulpit with earlier base; (4) much fifteenth-century stained glass in north aisle; (5) carved stone corbel heads; (6) brasses; (7) monuments, especially in chancel to John Smith, vicar 1592-1616 and in north aisle to Haynes Barlee and his two wives – notice especially the way the children of one are depicted, living and dead, at the base of her monument. *See also plate 27.*

COGGESHALL, GREAT (C2) *Christ Church* (formerly United Reformed), Stoneham Street

As recorded in a worn inscription in the entrance loggia, this church owes its origin to the powerful preaching of the outstanding Puritan, John Owen, who under the Protectorate was the intruded minister of the parish church, and later dean of Christ Church, Oxford and one of Cromwell's chaplains. On St Bartholomew's Day, 24 August 1662, when the Restoration Act of Uniformity was enforced, Owen's supporters left the parish church and set up a separate Puritan congregation, meeting in private houses. Later, land was given and an Independent (Congregationalist) chapel built on the site in 1710. This was replaced by a larger building, 'still of a clumsy late neo-Classical, four bays with a pediment and a Tuscan porch' (Pevsner) in 1865. With its three sided galleries it then had seating for 850. A few years ago the local Baptists and Methodists joined forces with the United Reformed congregation, renaming this chapel Christ Church. By partitioning the interior north to south, they reduced the seating capacity to present day requirements, and gained a hall for other purposes. *See also plate 59.*

COGGESHALL, GREAT (C2) *St Peter Ad Vincula*

Built to one plan at the time of the little town's maximum prosperity in the late fifteenth century, this large lofty town church (120 feet long, 62 feet wide) was severely damaged by a German bomb in 1940 – the north aisle destroyed and the tower having to be demolished. After the war it was beautifully restored and, where necessary, rebuilt by Stephen Dykes Bower, architect (cf. Quendon). The eight bells salvaged from the old

Great Coggeshall: interior of the church of St Peter in Chains

tower were re-hung in its replacement which, however, is regrettably too small and painfully unworthy of this splendid church. Tower and two storied vaulted porch apart, St Peter's is a parallelogram.

Pausing in the porch to glance up at the centrepiece of its vaulting, the 'Pelican in its piety' feeding its young with its own blood (thus symbolising Corpus Christi, the Eucharist), on entering the church you cannot fail to be impressed by its sheer size and spaciousness, the width of its aisles and nave, the elegance of its tall slender piers and the light pouring through the ample clerestory windows. Do not miss the Paycocke brasses in the north aisle: it was their wealth and generosity which were largely responsible for the church being built, and you should visit their fifteenth-century house in the town (National Trust). Notice too (i) the two windows by L. C. Evetts put in in the north aisle in 1974 ('Peace' and 'The Martyrdom of St Catherine') and (ii) the wood carving of Mary the Second Eve in the south aisle – both good examples of traditionalist modern art and craftsmanship. This is one of the few churches in Britain dedicated to St Peter in Chains; another is in the Tower of London.

COGGESHALL, LITTLE (C2) *St Nicholas*
The abbey founded here by King Stephen in 1140 became Cistercian in 1148. There are some remains of the monastic buildings but none of the abbey church. Standing in a meadow by itself is the former gate chapel of St Nicholas, a rectangular box with lancet windows and a steeply gabled roof, built *c.*1225, and comparable therefore in date as well as in origin (but not in sophistication) to Tilty. What gives it peculiar interest is the use of some of the earliest medieval bricks in the quoins and the dressings of the lancets, notably the group of three forming the east window. This church for many years served as a barn but is equipped for worship by the inhabitants of the hamlet.

COLCHESTER (D2) *Baptist Church*, Eld Lane

Standing well back from the narrow lane, this church with its two twentieth-century wings forms an impressive architectural ensemble, all in a cool, classical idiom. The church itself, built in 1834 in white brick, is still entirely in the late Georgian tradition. It has two storeys with three round headed windows in the upper storey to give light to the spacious gallery inside, and a plain doorway with pediment in the centre. On either side of the church are two wings added 1923 and 1990 respectively, and almost identical, well designed to harmonise with the church's facade.

COLCHESTER (D2) *St Botolph*

This frankly unprepossessing neo-Norman church was, to quote Pevsner, 'with the curious assertiveness that belongs to the Victorian age', built in 1837 in then fashionable white brick, cheek by jowl with and in deliberate imitation of the gaunt but tremendously impressive ruins of St Botolph's priory church. To put this in broad historical perspective, the priory, founded *c.*1100 and dissolved by Henry VIII in 1536, was the first house of Augustinian canons to be established in England, but even before its foundation, there seems to have been in Saxon times a church dedicated to St Botolph on this site just outside the south east gate of Colchester's Roman wall, a position so often associated with churches with that dedication, e.g. Cambridge and the City of London (which has no fewer than three, still in use). Following the dissolution the nave of the priory church continued in use as the principal parish church of the town until savage bombardment in the siege of 1648 reduced it to a ruin. Thereafter, rather than rebuild it, the parish was united for nearly two centuries with nearby All Saints' until the building of this remarkable church in the year of Queen Victoria's accession.

Its architect was W. Mason of Ipswich, who the following year built an equally curious church at Rowhedge – also in white brick. Neo-Norman, as a variant of the Gothic Revival then coming widely into fashion, was here particularly in vogue: the Roman Catholic church of St James the Less was built close by in Priory Street in the self same white brick neo-Norman, also in 1837 but by another architect, J. J. Scoles. Which, one wonders, came first? Rivalry there must have been.

St Botolph's exterior is just as the architect left it, apart, that is, from its century and a half's accumulated grime, and is very much a townscape feature of that part of Colchester. Inside it is much more cheerful, broad and spacious under a plain central tunnel vault and retaining its (Norman!) north and south and west galleries partly supported by two tier 'Norman' arcades – again echoing the two tiered arcades of the ruins next door! It has a strong musical tradition and, with excellent acoustics, is often used for concerts, as well as regular worship.

COLCHESTER (D2) *St James the Great*

It stands as proudly on top of east hill as St Peter's on north hill, as High Church as the other is Low. The chancel and chancel chapels, all parapetted and faced with black knapped flint, are typically late fifteenth century or early sixteenth century, handsome and opulent in the East Anglian fashion. The nave, aisles and tower are earlier, with traces of a Norman predecessor at the north west angle (Roman bricks) and a bit nondescript. The unimpressive tower (in comparison with the chancel) is given more dignity with its see-through spire of uncertain age. Inside, the church is tall, spacious and light, especially as you move east. There is a nineteenth-century rood (but no screen) and six tall candles on the high altar. Some pleasing heraldic glass is in the east window of the north chapel and there are some sixteenth-century brasses. Near the north west entrance is an elegant black and white marble monument to Arthur Winsley Esq., alderman and J.P. (d.1727). He reclines, holding a book. The monument is unsigned. Could the statuary have been Thomas Dunn?

COLCHESTER (D2) *St Peter*

It stands proudly at the top of north hill, its Georgian (1758) red brick tower topped with white brick battlements, not improved by its projecting Victorian Gothic bracket clock – a Georgian 'frying pan' would have been fine. The entrance is through the tower, past a staircase leading up to the west gallery, into a long gloomy interior heavy with the atmosphere of Low Church civic piety, evoked too by the, wisely retained, gas lamp fittings. It is dark even on a sunny day, not because of stained glass (mercifully there isn't any) but thanks to smallish windows and great late Georgian north, south and west galleries on Tuscan columns behind the surviving fifteenth-century arcades – giving it a seating capacity of around a thousand (cf. Harwich). Apart from the incongruous nineteenth-century Gothic east window with its opaque, greenish glass, all the windows were classicised *c.*1700 with clear glass and plain round headed frames with keystones, but the surrounding buildings and chestnuts in the churchyard also conspire to shut out light. Banners lodged by the Worshipful Company of Farriers and the Royal Arms of William and Mary give a welcome touch of colour. The *chef d'oeuvre* is the noble pulpit of *c.*1700 with garlands of fruit down the angles and a fine contemporary staircase. There are a few brasses and small memorials. A walk round the outside is recommended, to see the fine ironwork on the south door and the entrance to the bone hole of *c.*1520 under the chancel and to admire the varied texture of the wall.

COLNE, EARLS *see* EARLS COLNE

COLNE ENGAINE (C2) *St Andrew*

It stands high in its village looking to Earls Colne across the valley, its handsome embattled Tudor brick tower top (the base is of rubble with some puddingstone, earlier) and equally handsome south porch with stepped battlements, dominating the scene. The nave seems to be originally Norman with much Roman brick, the chancel Victorian. The furnishings are unremarkable, Victorian mostly, but the interior is redeemed from dullness by some good twentieth-century stained glass – notably the 'fishers of men' window in the chancel commemorating Canon R. H. Jack, rector 1953-61 and 'sowing and reaping' in memory of Katharine Courtauld, 1935.

COLNE, WAKES (C2) *All Saints*

It stands back beside the A.604 but looks south across the Colne valley to Chappel. The tall nave is Norman, twelfth century, with its original doorways both north (with scalloped capitals and roll moulding) and south (plain) and windows very high up in the thick walls, again both north and south. There are also fourteenth-century windows and an early sixteenth-century three-light brick window in the south wall. The chancel was rebuilt in the fourteenth century and there must have originally been a Norman central tower which would account for the extreme thickness of the walls at the chancel arch. In the fifteenth century a large timber belfry with a pyramidal roof was erected on posts at the west end with crossbeams and arched braces and a tie beam further east. The font is octagonal with three blank arches each side. The screens and furnishings are modern. The faded painting on the east wall is Victorian.

COPFORD (D2) *St Michael and All Angels*

Now known as St Michael and once as 'Our Lady at Copforde', the medieval dedication of this church remains unknown. This exceptional building, dating from about the second quarter of the twelfth century, was originally vaulted and contains an unparalleled contemporary scheme of wall paintings. These rare features would be difficult to explain but for the connection with the Bishop of London who, as lord of the manor, may have built the church as his private chapel.

The twelfth-century plan was a three bay vaulted nave with single bay chancel and apse. The tall nave was lit by unusually large shafted windows placed high in the walls between the wide pilaster buttresses reinforced in Roman brick, designed to support the vault. A south aisle was pushed out in stages from the late twelfth century and the vault presumably fell, to be replaced by the existing fifteenth-century crown-post roof.

The paintings have suffered numerous indignities from destruction by architectural alteration, successive covering and rediscovery, restoration and

71

partial repainting of 1872 by Daniel Bell, to waxing in the 1930s. Nevertheless, they remain impressive and recent conservation has further revealed their exceptional nature. The nave walls are adorned with an elaborate painted architectural framework into which narrative scenes and symbolic armed figures are set. Biblical scenes ran up into the vault, the only complete example now being the miracle of the Healing of Jairus' daughter on the north wall above the pulpit. Bands of geometrical patterns converge upon the focal point of the Christ in Glory on the apse vault, repainted by Bell. In subject matter and style the Copford paintings are complex and sophisticated with rich colouring, in striking contrast with most parish church decoration of this period in England, having their closest surviving parallels in the apse of St Gabriel's Chapel, Canterbury Cathedral.

Besides the main features described above, the plain Norman font, the fifteenth-century rood screen and timber belfry, and a handsomely carved and gilded Hanoverian Royal Arms are to be seen.

For a full appreciation of this remarkable church the masterly guide by A. J. Wright, 1993, is essential reading. *See also plate 50.*

CORRINGHAM (C5) *St Mary*

This church, on the edge of the old village centre, could well have been begun before the Norman Conquest. The evidence for this assertion, oddly ignored by Pevsner despite the Royal Commission, is the herringbone pattern of the rubble masonry in the chancel south wall – this is always taken to indicate an early date. The tremendously impressive early Norman west tower, unbuttressed, with its pyramidal roof and two tiers of large blank arcading below the parapet, the middle niche of the top row on each side pierced, with a central colonette, was evidently built on to an earlier, existing nave and chancel. The plain, low, narrow tower arch is surmounted by a small keystone carved with a grim little face looking towards the reordered sanctuary and modern altar. The church was enlarged in the fourteenth century and there is a good wooden screen of that period in the north aisle. The building materials in this aisle are laid in alternate layers of colour. There are two medieval brasses in the chancel, one to a fourteenth-century priest with a bristly chin. The church was restored by G. G. Scott in 1843/4. *See also plate 5.*

CREEKSEA (D4) *All Saints*

This remote little church is chiefly notable for two things. The first is its setting. Approached via the drive to its elegant Georgian neighbour, Creeksea Hall, it, or rather its car park (in front), commands superb views over the Crouch and across to its opposite bank. Secondly its external texture. When Frederick Chancellor all but rebuilt it in 1877 he used an extraordinary medley of stone, flint, brick and tile. The interior is quite pleasing with its unusual if not unique effect of two identical but quite separate two-light windows side by side in the east wall. From the old church there survives the curious rather shapeless font with its saltire crosses and what might be a coiled serpent; and a brass to Sir Arthur (not 'Bomber'!) Harris, d.1631, with an epitaph which repays the effort of finding and reading. (Cheats will find it in Pevsner.) For good measure there is a second medieval font.

CRESSING (C2) *All Saints*

A small, two cell, church but full of interest. The nave is basically Norman and the chancel thirteenth century (Early English), but when the nave floor was renewed some years ago, evidence of a still earlier building was found. The timbers supporting the belfry/spire, probably fifteenth century, are impressively complex. There is a small stone carving over the north (vestry) doorway, the significance of which is a matter of conjecture. (See the church guide.)

The monument on the south wall of the chancel commemorates Henry and Anne Smith, 1607, and shows them kneeling with a kneeling daugher and a baby in swaddling clothes in the predella below. There is a good brass to Dorcas Musgrave who died in childbirth 1610; it shows her in her farthingale with an hourglass, pointing to her baby. The colourful heraldic banner is that of a famously heroic soldier son of a vicar, Field Marshal Sir Evelyn Wood V.C., K.C.M.G., 1838-1919. It had hung over his stall in the chapel of St Michael and St George in St Paul's Cathedral. By the door is a Jacobean (former communion?) table given to the church by Dorcas Smith, 1610, and so inscribed.

DAGENHAM (A5) *St Peter and St Paul*

This, the original village church of Dagenham, stands endways on to the approach road. The visitor is thus confronted with a stocky west tower and nave built *c.*1800 in 'the most ignorant and entertaining Gothick' (Pevsner). This tower of rubble, with lavish quoins and dressings of red brick, has curly brick battlements only paralleled in Essex by those of Toppesfield, a century older and at the opposite end of the county. Entrance is through the tower under a tall semi-circular portico with Gothick quatrefoil stone shafts and shaft rings. The aisleless nave has a bow fronted west gallery beneath which is an elegant classical marble font. After all this, it is a surprise to discover that the chancel, entered through an arch 'of fancy detail' and a light wrought iron screen, is pure Early English of about 1225, with an east window of three stepped lancets, a Reckitt's blue plaster ceiling and Low Church decor. On a tomb chest is a brass to Sir Thomas Urswick, d.1479, Recorder of London, his wife and children. In the north chancel chapel, mentioned as new in a will of 1475, is the Baroque tomb of another judge, Sir Richard Allibon d.1688, justice of the King's Bench. He stands bewigged in judicial robes on one side of an inscribed pedestal surmounted by an enormous urn, his wife on the other. Below them is a skull and crossbones and a plinth. The parents of George Carey, present Archbishop of Canterbury (1995), are buried in the sizeable churchyard. *See also plate 39.*

DANBURY (C3) *St John the Baptist*

The church stands on top of Danbury Hill, 365 feet above the river Chelmer, with a further 120 feet to the top of the spire. The churchyard and green lie within an Iron Age hill fort. The north aisle is late thirteenth century and the remainder fourteenth century, apart from the south aisle dating from G. G. Scott's restoration (1866) and the south chancel aisle rebuilt in 1951-2 (A. Garden) after war damage. The interior is spacious, nave and aisles being wider than they are long. The north aisle has a contemporary roof with fifteenth-century panelling and carved head corbels at the east end. The three fine oak effigies of knights may be members of the St Clere family. The benches with poppyheads are based on four fifteenth-century originals at the back of the nave; some in the north aisle commemorate regiments serving locally in 1914-18.

DEBDEN (B2) *St Mary the Virgin and All Saints*

A church for the connoisseur! First, its setting. It lies at the end of a narrow leafy lane from the village, all by itself on a gentle slope: Debden signifies 'deep valley'. It is not known for certain who landscaped the grounds of the Hall (demolished 1935) and church, but it could well have been Repton. Whoever it was knew his job.

The church so charmingly situated is a sophisticated blend of medieval and late eighteenth-century romantic Gothick, such as would have appealed to the author of *Northanger Abbey*. The medieval nave, sprinkled with Gothick battlements and pinnacles in 1786, and entered through the fourteenth-century south porch, is impressive, with its thirteenth-century four bay arcades of stout cylindrical piers, the two westernmost on the south side having simple foliated capitals. There is a flat plaster ceiling and above the chancel arch are the Hanoverian Royal Arms, nicely modelled and framed. From the back of the church the eye is led up the five steps to the chancel, past the well dressed altar, to the dark mysterious 'chapel' or mausoleum beyond, with its dimly perceived ribbed plaster vaulting and forest of pretty cusps and pendants. (Remember to take a torch.)

Before going up to the chancel, pause to admire the celebrated Coade (artificial) stone font and cover in its railed enclosure at the west end of the south aisle, its sharp lines and crisp pseudo-medieval detail. It was

Early nineteenth-century print of Debden church.

designed by Richard Holland, kinsman of the famous architect Henry Holland, and after being shown to, and approved by, the king, George III, installed here in 1786.

By that time the former central tower had twice collapsed and the chancel was in ruins. Fortunately there was no shortage of money or taste at the Hall. In 1792 the wealthy tycoon R. M. T. Chiswell commissioned the antiquary/draughtsman John Carter to design, and Holland to build, an octagonal Gothick 'chapel' with vault beneath, in white brick with two Coade stone medallions bearing his arms and initials. This is linked to the medieval nave by a broad passage or chancel.

In the 'chapel', Chiswell, who had changed his name on inheriting a fortune, erected neat monuments either side of the east window to his uncle and his parents, Peter Muilman, merchant, author of *A Gentleman's History of Essex* (1769-72) and Mary, née Chiswell. After a financial disaster Chiswell committed suicide in 1797. His elegant Gothick tomb chest and canopy in the 'chapel' was probably also designed by Carter.

Before leaving, be sure to inspect the attractive west front, completed in 1930. It complements the rest admirably. *See also plate 15.*

75

DEDHAM (D2) *St Mary*

This stately church dominates the heart of Dedham, an enduring monument to the wealth and piety of the cloth merchants who were responsible for its complete rebuilding between 1492 and 1520. This great work coincided with the period of utmost prosperity for the cloth producing area of the Essex-Suffolk border which saw the rebuilding of some of the finest Perpendicular parish churches in England, including Stoke by Nayland, Long Melford and Lavenham. The principal donors here were the Gurdon and Webbe families, the latter being commemorated by their 'merchant marks' on shields in the tower vault and, more emphatically, by their solid *bourgeois* tomb at the east end of the north aisle.

Civic pride was undoubtedly a motivating force, particularly for the magnificent tower rising to 131 feet, which the townsfolk of neighbouring East Bergholt aspired, but failed, to outdo as the region sank into economic decline. The tower remained the most prominent feature in the landscape in the Dedham Vale paintings of Constable, who wrote of this area 'I associate my careless boyhood with all that lies on the banks of the Stour. Those scenes made me a painter.' Dedham's external show is mostly in the tower, with its lavish display of finely knapped and squared flintwork, clasped by polygonal buttresses topped with spiky crocketed pinnacles which are echoed in the flushwork of the embattled parapet. At its base is an open processional passageway with a panelled vault adorned with quatrefoils, Tudor roses and portcullises.

The chaste grey render of the body of the church is entirely in the spirit of the austere Perpendicular style with its finely-drawn lines and hard edges. The repetition of identical windows gives the nave a homogeneity, which becomes severe, and a trifle dowdy, on the south side with its eighteenth-century brick buttresses and no parapets. The chancel halts the eastward progression and injects a change of rhythm, with its tall narrow bays and vertical emphasis.

The fancy flushwork two storey north porch protects fine original carved doors with pairs of decapitated saints. Dignified Perpendicular elegance returns inside; the light and airy nave opening into the aisles between the slender piers of the arcade. Finely moulded, low-pitched timber roofs have, in the nave, a hint of decoration along the wallplates and crown-post-like timber shafts descending to meet stone shafts rising from the arcades. The chancel's contrasting sense of contained enclosure is largely due to the set of early twentieth-century Kempe stained glass.

Medieval glass there is none, save the sixteenth-century fragment in the 'Sherman' window above the Webbe tomb. The same family gave their name to the most delightful house in the village, the little Baroque masterpiece of *c.*1730 opposite the church, as well as to the less delightful Sherman tank, named after a descendant of emigrants to New England of the 1630s. Monuments are plentiful, notable amongst which are the Rogers and Burkitt memorials of *c.*1605 and 1703 respectively, to celebrated preachers and holders of the Dedham Lectureship (for more information on which see the church guidebook). *See also plates 23 & 31.*

DODDINGHURST (B4) *All Saints*

This church was heavily restored and largely rebuilt by the Victorians. The timber belfry with vertical boarding and shingled spire stands on six posts with arched braces and trellis strutting. Cecil Hewitt thought it could well date from the early thirteenth century. The unusually long late medieval south porch has ten unglazed openings each side. The south doorway into the church is believed to date from *c.*1220 and has characteristic dogtooth decoration. The font is fourteenth century; and the rood figures, Christ crucified with Mary his mother and St John, are evidently ancient but their provenance seems to be unknown.

DONYLAND, EAST, see under ROWHEDGE

DOVERCOURT (E2) *All Saints*

Originally the mother church of Harwich, All Saints in Upper Dovercourt consists of a substantial fifteenth-century west tower, Norman nave, fourteenth-century chancel, south porch and a modern extension on the north side. Perhaps some time in the 1920s the church authorities were so ill advised as to cover the whole exterior with roughcast pebbledash. Not only did this, together with harsh red roof tiles, ruin the church's appearance, but it had the effect of preventing the rubble walls from 'breathing' and trapping rising damp behind the render. It is excellent news that, at very considerable expense, this unpleasant render has now (*c.*1994) been stripped off the tower, which below its (Tudor?) brick top stage has been limewashed and looks fine, and that it is proposed to do the same to porch, nave and chancel as soon as funds permit. FEC will certainly help all it can.

Inside, the church is very dark on account of so much stained glass. Notice particularly (1) the massive poor box, dated 1596, near the door; (2) the plain fourteenth-century font; (3) one small Norman window on the south side; (4) beneath the classical style woodwork of the (Edwardian) chancel arch, and above the twentieth-century screen incorporating the pulpit, the great carved rood beam and console brackets dated 1615 – a very rare feature; (5) the small Hanoverian Royal Arms over the entrance to the vestry and extension. In the latter is a fine modern tapestry of the Holy Family by Elizabeth Rumble.

DOWNHAM (C4) *St Margaret*

Its substantial hill top west tower is late fifteenth or early sixteenth century; built of red brick with black diapering, it commands wide views over

Basildon and Wickford. The body of the church, with the partial exception of the timber south porch, was completely rebuilt in 1871 by the famous Victorian architect G. E. (Law Courts) Street; he did a similar job at nearby Hutton. Apart from the walls (those of the nave of flint rubble, of the chancel of big lumps of rust coloured ironstone conglomerate), Street's church was destroyed by fire, started by an arsonist in 1977. It has been well rebuilt and refurnished with modern facilities, including a kitchen in the tower ground floor, in an unfussy traditional style and is beautifully light. Part of the condition of the rebuilding was that it should be dual purpose, to serve the needs of the growing community, so the seating is moveable chairs and there is neither pulpit nor fixed font.

In the churchyard is the largest pollarded field maple in the British Isles, sixteen feet in girth. By the lychgate is an eighteenth-century dovecote, moved brick by brick to this site in 1991, and former stables now serving as a meeting room for church and Sunday School.

DUNMOW, GREAT (B2) *St Mary the Virgin*

Great Dunmow, St Mary the Virgin.

A large town church though a good mile from the town centre in the quite separate settlement of Church End, on the edge of the country. As Pevsner points out, it looks 'externally all of a piece', i.e. fifteenth-century Perpendicular. In fact the chancel is earlier, *c.*1340, with a distinctive five-light east window with elaborate geometrical tracery, culminating in a foiled circle at the top. The west tower, in three stages with angle buttresses ending in polygonal turrets or pinnacles above three-light straight headed bell openings, and the two storied south porch, both embattled like the aisles and clerestory (with opulent three-light windows), all combine to assert late medieval prosperity.

Inside, the wide nave with north and south aisles and four bay arcades leads up to the

78

spacious chancel and south chancel chapel. A thorough-going mid-Victorian 'restoration' (1872) under G. E. (Law Courts) Street left no old fittings except a large fifteenth-century gallery over part of the south aisle (once used as a family pew) and a handsome eighteenth-century candelabrum in the chancel. Some medieval glass fragments are assembled in a south window. The nineteenth- and twentieth-century glass is mostly of good and pleasing quality. There are no major monuments, but plenty of minor ones.

DUNMOW, LITTLE (B2) *St Mary the Virgin*

The parish church of this attractive little village was originally the south chancel chapel (or Lady Chapel) of the church of a priory of Augustinian canons founded in 1106. It acquired its present status when the priory was dissolved by Henry VIII and the rest of its church demolished. Truncated fragment though it be, it is a building of immense interest, and some distinction. Externally it has five splendid windows, four in the south wall (three-light and four-light alternating), all with wonderfully intricate tracery, and the east window of five lights, restored by F. Chancellor *c.*1875. Those in the south wall all had their stonework carefully renewed in 1988. These windows date, it seems, from an opulent remodelling of this part of the priory church *c.*1360, though the two four-light windows are a remarkable foretaste of the Perpendicular style only then coming into being. Entering through the west door, pausing to glance at what Pevsner calls the 'silly' thin north west turret of 1871, we are at once impressed by the beauty of the five bay north arcade, of *c.*1200, which originally divided the south chapel from the chancel of the priory church. Stop to admire the carving of the capitals and the richness of the arch mouldings. The south and east walls between and below the great windows have blind arcading, niches etc. with intricately carved leaves and little animals – easily overlooked!

So much for the architecture. The furnishings are all (with one exception) of the 1870s restoration, but quite pleasing. But the monuments are outstanding, especially the exquisitely carved alabaster effigies of Walter, Lord Fitzwalter (d.1431) and his wife Elizabeth, and in the sanctuary, a complete contrast, the typically eighteenth-century Hallet monument by T. Adye, a female holding a medallion portrait of Sir James (d.1703). In front of it is the historic fifteenth-century flitch chair, used to carry couples in triumph who had successfully proved to a jury that they had lived in marital harmony for a whole year without once regretting their marriage.

This is one of the very few Essex churches still lit by oil lamps (cf. Bardfield Saling, Bradwell by Coggeshall and Fobbing) and how nice they look. Do try and choose a bright sunny morning for your visit, with light flooding in through the south windows.

79

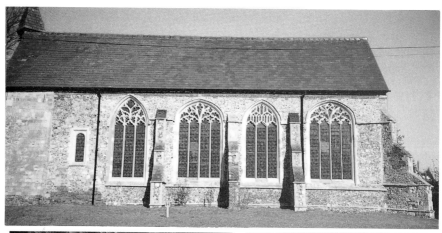

Little Dunmow: (top) general view of the church; (centre) two capitals of *c*.1200; and (bottom) the tomb of Walter, Lord Fitzwalter (d. 1431) and his wife Elizabeth.

EARLS COLNE (C2) *Friends' Meeting House,* Burrows Road
This modest little meeting house may well be Essex's oldest surviving non-conformist place of worship still in use. It was built by John Garrod in 1674, following George Fox's fourth visit to the county the previous year, as a result of which several 'nests' of Quakers were established. Although considerably altered externally in 1986 when a (later) porch was pulled down and the original front entrance bricked up, to be replaced by a side entrance communicating with a new, harmonious annexe by a short corridor, the original meeting house is basically a square red brick box with a pyramidal tiled roof. Inside it is plainly furnished with long benches in three tiers – nothing more – true Quaker austerity. The only concession to decoration is the simple diapering of the exterior – black headers, red stretchers.

This feature, diversified by a chequer pattern below, is also found in the contemporary and almost identical former Quaker meeting house at STEBBING. Here the date 1674 appears over the entrance porch. It seems at least probable that John Garrod was the builder (and designer) here too. It is only fair to add that Pevsner (*Buildings of England: Essex* 1st edn, p. 337) says that this date 'cannot refer to the house in its present form, with segment headed windows and a small porch ... probably the (meeting) house was remodelled early in the eighteenth century'. In view of the Earls Colne parallel, the striking similarity, and the coincidence of the dates, Pevsner may well be mistaken, though he has the support of the leading expert on nonconformist meeting houses, Christopher Stell. *See illustration on page 216.*

EARLS COLNE (C2) *St Andrew*
The notable feature of this large and prominent church is its fine west tower. It is strongly East Anglian in appearance as seen from south, west and north, with its flint flushwork dated 1534, bearing the De Vere arms and mullet (star) on the parapet. (They founded and were mostly buried in Colne Priory nearby.) The east face of the tower, however, is of red brick, as are the top parts of the stair turret, crowned with an eighteenth-century weather vane. The church, apart from the tower, was almost entirely rebuilt, nave, chancel, and north and south aisles, in 1884 and calls for no comment. Monuments remain from the previous building including a tablet by Roubiliac with reliefs of Mercury and Justice.

EASTER, GOOD (B3) *St Andrew*
Travelling westwards along the A.1060, the Chelmsford to Bishop's Stortford road, a tall shingled spire can be seen to the north across the fields. It is that of Good Easter (said to mean Godwith's estre = sheep fold). It was built after two disastrous fires towards the end of the nineteenth century: its external belfry timbers are (unusually) vertical. The four

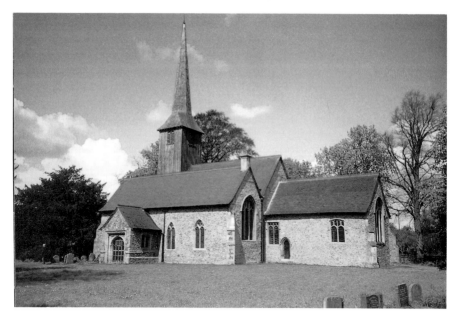

Good Easter.

massive posts on which, with their arched braces, it rests are seen at the west end of the thirteenth-century nave. The two half arches either side of the chancel arch must in their complete form have flanked a narrower, Norman, chancel arch, later widened when the thirteenth-century chancel was built and a four bay south aisle added to the nave, and later still, a Tudor brick porch added to that.

In medieval times this parish provided the principal endowments of four, perhaps five, prebends in the collegiate church of St Martin le Grand, London and herein may be the explanation of the unusual blank arcading on both sides of the chancel: did they form the backs of prebendal stalls? Notice (i) the small funeral helm and crest high up in the chancel, (ii) medieval glass fragments in tracery lights in the south aisle, (iii) a small incised medieval tombstone set in the chancel north wall, (iv) an early seventeenth-century brass in the south aisle, and (v) an eighteenth-century pillory.

EASTER, HIGH (B3) *St Mary the Virgin*
This fine church, in the centre of an attractive village, is approached through a narrow passage between two timber framed houses as old as its imposing fifteenth-century west tower. Outside, the only evidence that the nave and chancel are much older than they look, in fact Norman, is the Roman bricks (from a nearby villa?) re-used as quoins on the south east angles of both nave and chancel, and the absence of corner buttresses.

82

Before going inside, pause to admire the sophisticated brickwork of the embattled clerestory by which the nave was heightened in the early sixteenth century and notice the two three-light windows above the chancel arch at the east end of the nave, a most unusual feature. While you are about it, go round to the west of the massive tower to see the weathered angel at the apex of the west doorway and the carvings in the spandrels: what are they? Passing through the handsome embattled Tudor red brick south porch and the unusually plain Norman doorway into the nave, you are at once struck by its width, and looking up, by the splendour of its great dark low pitched, elaborately carved roof, contemporary with the clerestory.

The four bay north aisle was added c.1350. It has simple parclose screens at the east end. Look for St Valentine, with his (partner) St Dorothy in a pretty window: he is seldom met with in churches. Another rarity is the stone mortar discovered embedded in a wall during repairs in 1968. It is probably medieval and may have been used in making lead for stained glass. The font is fifteenth century and has the symbols of the evangelists on four of its eight sides. Finally, in the dark chancel, study the lovely three-light east window. Made by Martin Travers in 1931, it was given to commemorate two Edward Gepps, father and son, vicars between 1849 and 1916. Its subjects all relate to the Blessed Virgin Mary, the Annunciation, Nativity and Presentation of her infant Son in the Temple. *See also plate 11.*

EASTHORPE (D2) *St Edmund*
A small church, with nave and chancel under one roof, basically Norman but the chancel rebuilt in the thirteenth century with three handsome stepped lancet windows with dogtooth decoration in the east wall, a classic example of Early English. There are good sedilia with pointed trefoil arches. The chancel floor is handsomely paved with black and white marble. There is a panel of sixteenth-century stained glass showing Christ preaching, and some vestigial angels painted on the soffit of a south window. A west timber bellcote contains one bell. The moated Hall is next door.

EASTON, LITTLE (B2) *St Mary*
Set in a remote sylvan landscape, this church is full of historic interest and beauty, too full to describe in detail here. Entering through the fifteenth-century west tower, we are in a (far from obviously) Norman nave. On its north wall is a large and fine but faded late twelfth-century painting of a seated prophet or apostle. Opposite is an unusual fifteenth-century painting of six scenes from Christ's Passion. On either side of the chancel are two handsome medieval canopied tombs of the great Bourchier family. That on the north wall has a miniature recumbent effigy of a knight in armour, two feet long. On the south side is the grand tomb of Henry, first earl of Essex and his royal wife Isabel Plantagenet, their brass effigies on

ESSEX CHURCHES

top of the tomb chest. It was moved here from Beeleigh Abbey after the Dissolution. On the south side of the church, enclosed by elaborate seventeenth-century iron railings, is the Maynard chapel with numerous notable tombs of this family, which was seated at Easton Lodge from the sixteenth century until the death of Frances, countess of Warwick, beloved of Edward VII and a philanthropic socialist, in 1938. The most spectacular of these fills the east wall. It is by Charles Stanley, sculptor to the Danish court. Erected in 1746, it shows Charles, first viscount Maynard standing surrounded by seven portraits of his ancestors and siblings, in busts and medallions against an obelisk surmounted by the family coat of arms. The two south windows of this chapel each contain three separate panels of fine seventeenth-century glass depicting scenes from the Life of Christ. They were commissioned from Baptista Sutton in 1621 for Easton Lodge Chapel and transferred here in 1857. (Pevsner here is in error.) The space north of the chancel has recently been constituted a Memorial Chapel to the US Air Force stationed at Easton manor in the 1939-45 war. Two colourful windows by Gordon Phillips of Cleveland, Ohio illustrating, respectively, Crusade and Peace were dedicated in 1994. *See also plate 63.*

EASTWOOD (C4) *St Laurence and All Saints*
The church lies in a large churchyard beside Southend Airport and close to industrial development, but is well worth a visit. The chapel of Eastwood was granted to Prittlewell Priory in 1100, which may have resulted in the building of the present nave. The south aisle and the tower at its west end were added in the early thirteenth century, when the chancel was rebuilt. The north aisle was added in the fourteenth century, cutting through the Norman windows; its west end was partitioned in the fifteenth century to form a priest's chamber on the upper floor. The brick south porch is sixteenth century. The south aisle was raised and two gables constructed on the south side in the sixteenth or seventeenth century. The upper part of the tower was demolished and replaced with a timber bell turret before the mid eighteenth century. The chief treasures of the church are the late twelfth-century font and the original north and south doors, with elaborate ironwork. The north door may be late twelfth century and has been rehung as the entrance to the new choir vestry (1966); the south door is thirteenth century and has a worn Lombardic inscription on the strap, invoking peace on those entering and leaving the church. The fourteenth century nave roof has good octagonal crown posts of early type. The two ends of the rood beam cut off flush with the walls are visible below the late fourteenth-century chancel arch. The west window has glass (1978) depicting the life of Samuel Purchas (vicar, 1604-1614), editor of *Purchas His Pilgrimes*, a collection of travel narratives, including those of Andrew Battell of Leigh.

ELMSTEAD (D2) *St Anne and St Lawrence*

Next door to Elmstead Hall a mile north of the busy main road village, this church has a complex history but for most visitors its chief interest probably lies in its attractive period furnishings. The main entrance now is on the north side through the new (1983) wing. The actual door with its elaborate ironwork is an accurate replica of the original still preserved inside, probably dating from *c.*1100. The round arch through which you enter with its Roman brick surround is Norman and above it is what appears to be an even earlier, Saxon, stone arch. But the nave and chancel as they are now were rebuilt in the early fourteenth century: see the fine sedilia and piscina in the chancel. The stumpy little tower above the south porch is of this period too and the handsome south chapel with its two bay arcade is only a little later. The three low side windows (one in the chancel, two in the chapel) have long puzzled experts. (What is your explanation?)

There is a wooden effigy of a cross-legged knight, now thought to represent Sir Thomas de Weston who died in 1354. Compare this with similar effigies at Little Horkesley, Little Baddow and Danbury. There is, too, one remarkable fifteenth-century brass: two hands raised in prayer pointing to a heart and an inscribed scroll. Translation: 'I believe I shall see the goodness of the Lord' (Psalm 27 verse 13).

Period furnishings include seventeenth-century three sided communion rails, eighteenth-century pulpit with sounding board, Royal Arms and attractively written framed texts in the nave and early nineteenth-century west gallery, box pews, a 'dumb organist' and a magnificent scrolly wrought iron hatstand.

ELSENHAM (B2) *St Mary the Virgin*

A Norman church a long way from the village with a handsome fifteenth-century embattled west tower which looks more Suffolk than Essex. The Norman south doorway is striking and unusual. It has zigzag carved columns, curiously carved capitals (Pevsner thought they might represent sun and moon), a tympanum with stars and saltire (i.e. diagonal) crosses, and more of these on the outer arch. Still more saltires and zigzags appear in the chancel arch. There are three Norman windows. The pulpit is Jacobean. There is a remarkable medieval graffito on the west wall of the tower.

EPPING (A4) *St John the Baptist*

It comes as something of a surprise to learn that this 'prime site' in the centre of a flourishing main road small town with few signs of antiquity is in fact a truly historic one. For William the Conqueror, no less, built a chapel here for forest keepers and charcoal burners. This free chapel, having undergone all kinds of vicissitudes in the course of its long history, only became the parish church of Epping by special Act of Parliament in 1888, and was promptly demolished to make way for what we now see, a grand church which represents the apotheosis of the Gothic Revival in Essex.

Pevsner as usual got it right when he wrote that 'when it came to building a parish church of sufficient size, in 1889, the authorities were wise in the choice of their architects. They went to Bodley and Garner and got a church of remarkable dignity if not striking originality ... it is all very serious, and no light relief is permitted'.

The style chosen was fourteenth-century East Anglian and the arcades of the nave and aisles march purposefully eastwards amid a sea of chairs, not benches, up to the great rood screen, and beyond, through the spacious chancel, to the high altar with its six tall candles and behind and above them an enormous and richly carved triptych forming the reredos under the great seven-light east window filled with Kempe's lovely glass. It all combines to create an overwhelming impression of late Victorian and Edwardian opulence and prosperity. Astonishingly, the screen, the reredos *and* the superb four manual Wordsworth organ, their woodwork all meticulously designed by G. F. Bodley, were the gifts of one man, E. J. Wythes, and his wife, who, to crown their munificence, in 1908 met the entire cost of the 96 feet south east tower which dominates the High Street so effectively still. What would those charcoal burners have made of it all?

EPPING UPLAND (A3) *All Saints*

In a hamlet in fine rolling country a good two miles from the town stands what began life in the early middle ages as the mother church of Epping. So it continued until 1888, shortly before St John's was built and constituted the new parish church of the *town*, All Saints then becoming simply the parish church of *rural* Epping, known henceforth as Epping Upland.

It is a long narrow building, nave and chancel all under one continuous roof, their walls regrettably covered with rough cast shingle dash (like Dovercourt where it is due to be stripped off when funds permit, q.v.). This unseemly exterior is partly redeemed by a fine sixteenth-century Tudor brick west tower with diagonal buttresses, battlements, six bells and a clock installed in 1793. The lancet windows in the nave and chancel are patently Victorian 'restoration', probably taking the place of original ones of the thirteenth century, a date confirmed by the surviving nave piscina. There are two fonts, one with a Jacobean cover, eighteenth-century altar rails, an alms box dated 1626 and a fine brass of Thomas Palmer d.1621, Professor of Law at Cambridge.

FAIRSTEAD (C3) *St Mary and St Peter*

A 'fair place' indeed in its remote unspoilt rural setting in deep Essex among Lord Rayleigh's farms. A small, ancient 'atmospheric' church, beautifully kept and replete with interest. Nave and west half of chancel early Norman, chancel extended (see evidence in north wall outside) in thirteenth century with three stepped lancets as east window. Piscina and sedilia. West tower, also of rubble with some Roman brick, probably added at same time as chancel, topped by tall spire *c.*1600, contains four bells, earliest 1340. Plain fifteenth-century benches with linenfold ends. Superb 'dug-out' parish chest nine feet long, iron bound, and made of a single piece of oak, thirteenth century? Small eighteenth-century pedestal font. The most exciting feature is the well preserved wall paintings, albeit somewhat faded, especially the scenes from our Lord's Passion, above plain Norman chancel arch. At the top Christ on a short legged donkey rides past a tree (into Jerusalem?); below, the Last Supper, with feet washing (?), the Betrayal, Malchus' big ear cut off, and Judas (?) in hat. Also two series of consecration crosses, a prayer for king James I, and texts. There is a good relief of shepherds, angels and the star of Bethlehem (1934) behind the altar; and the Arms of George III.

FAULKBOURNE (C3) *St German*
Pronounced Fawb'n. Very much the estate church, dwarfed by the neighbouring magnificence of Faulkbourne Hall, and well away from the village. It consists simply of nave, chancel and belfry with a brick porch with crow stepped gable. The nave and chancel are Norman; see the tiny slit windows north, south and west, and the good Norman south doorway with one order of semipolygonal columns. The small belfry is on two posts. There are some late medieval benches in the chancel and a funeral helm. Also a barrel organ still in working order. There is a thirteenth-century effigy of a knight and several Bullock memorials of the eighteenth and early ninteenth centuries. (The church restoring parson of Radwinter (q.v.) was of this family.)

FEERING (C3) *All Saints*
Pleasantly sited just off the village green, its typically fifteenth-century square embattled flint rubble tower (with eight bells) contrasts delightfully with the rich Tudor red brick of the porch, and south nave wall and windows. The brick is diapered and the porch vaulted and embattled, and there is a terracotta bas-relief of Virgin and Child in the niche over the door, done in 1985. The chancel is older (fourteenth century) and humbler. Inside there is much to admire, thanks in part to the generous initiative and good taste of the present vicar, Rev Aubrey Moody. In the north aisle, side by side, are two treasures, a lovely Nottingham alabaster crowned Virgin and Child of *c.*1400 found at Earls Colne Priory (and no doubt originally made for the former priory church), and John Constable's fine painting of the Risen Christ, done by him for Manningtree church in 1822 and acquired, cleaned and reframed when that church was scandalously

demolished in 1965. (Constable used to stay at Feering with his friend W. W. Driffield who had baptised him, and who served as resident curate here for half a century.) The Victorian pulpit has inserted in it seventeenth-century carved panels of our Lord's Passion, and there is much else besides.

FELSTED (B2) *Holy Cross*

The church stands behind a row of medieval houses and shops on the village street. The main approach is through an archway set into the original school house. However, if you park in the car park, you are first struck by the lovely Norman doorway on the west side of the tall, unbuttressed tower and the wooden cupola and weather vane on top. The clock is by John Fordham of Dunmow, 1701. Before entering notice the south chancel chapel built *c.*1600 and faced with clunch. Inside, the south nave arcade is late Norman/Transitional, comparable to those at Castle Hedingham, the north arcade fourteenth century. Enter the south chapel to admire the superb marble, alabaster and bronze monument to the unscrupulous Richard, first Lord Rich of Leez 1496-1568. It was erected as a result of the third Lord Rich's will in 1621 and is believed to be the work of the great sculptor Epiphanius Evesham. Rich served Edward VI as Lord Chancellor 1548 and founded Felsted School in 1564 but otherwise did little to live up to the Virtues, Justice and Charity, symbolised on his tomb. Take time to study the details, especially the beautifully carved effigies of Rich and his son and the delicately engraved panels depicting him on his catafalque and on horseback. There are two brasses in the chancel, to Christine Bray and a knight, both *c.*1420 and two feet long.

FINCHINGFIELD (B2) *St John the Baptist*

Its picturesque setting above the village green, bridge and duck pond is one of the most photogenic sights in the country. Entering the churchyard through the archway under the former Guildhall, we behold the massive square west tower, basically Norman and originally unbuttressed, its top stage fifteenth-century embattled. (Pevsner pithily wrote: 'the one nineteenth-century diagonal buttress no doubt adds punch and the (eighteenth-century) cupola grace'). Note the west doorway with three orders and the curious, unexplained blank arcading on the ground floor inside. The church itself exhibits a complex building history. The chancel arch and the south aisle arcade's octagonal piers are thirteenth century, and contrast with the later, more graceful north arcade. Nave and, unusually, chancel both have clerestories. The fifteenth-century chancel screen is perhaps the most elaborate in Essex. At the east end of both aisles there are chantry chapels and both as seen from outside have high pitched domestic style tiled gable roofs in contrast to all the rest. The south or Berners chapel has a richly carved fourteenth-century screen. Take time to examine

Drawing of Finchingfield by Edward Bawden.

it in detail and note also the extreme (Decorated) elaboration of the window tracery.

Inside is the lovely tomb chest of Sir John Berners and his first wife, d.1523, with brass effigies. Look out for the monkey. At the east end of the north aisle is the Kempe chapel which, besides a monument to the Kempe (d.1652) who kept a vow of silence for seven years, has numerous memorials of the Ruggles Brise family which later occupied Spains Hall. In the chancel too are several good monuments, especially that to Thomas Marriott, 1766, with bust. It is by Wm. Tyler RA. Note, too, the font, and the fine Royal Arms of Charles II 1662 above the tower arch. There is much else to enjoy, including (if you can find them) some very peculiar medieval graffiti – one of a mask, on a pillar in the north chapel; others are on pillars of the south arcade.

FINGRINGHOE (D3) *St Andrew* (originally St Ouen of Rouen)

This is a delectable church. It is not surprising that both Pevsner ('visually quite exceptionally successful...') and Scarfe ('irresistibly beautiful, outside and in, for its colour, shape and above all texture') came under its spell. It has all they claim, including a memorable site above the Colne ferry opposite Wivenhoe, and more, especially through fascinating discoveries since they wrote. It is a veritable gallery of late medieval art – sculpture, wood carving and painting.

But first the building itself. The nave was basically the original Norman church. Then in the fourteenth century (as at Boxted) a south aisle was added by piercing the south wall, cutting two plain arches in it, and

89

The porch at Fingringhoe.

building a new south wall, for the Lady Chapel. The chancel was enlarged at the same time and the tower and south porch built, the latter apparently in two stages. The square west tower with three bells, is striped (cf. Purleigh) with bands of knapped flint and plastered rubble. The porch is dazzling. As it is now, it is faced with knapped flint, East Anglian fashion, with battlemented parapet of flint and stone chequer. The spandrels either side of the entrance arch are carved with the Archangel Michael, feathered, and a ferocious dragon, both incredibly sharp and well preserved. A modern bronze by Gerald Laing of the Virgin seated is in the niche over the entrance. The original fourteenth-century south door is in situ. First to meet the eye inside is the plain font with its three tiered, much crocketted fifteenth-century cover, well restored (invisible mending). Then in the nave look up to the fifteenth-century roof and the vividly painted and highly individual heads (of contemporary Finginghoe worthies?) male and female. (See the admirable guide for speculative identifications.) You will see traces of several large wall paintings discovered in 1884 and now very faded. The coloured sketches of them when discovered are on the west wall near the south door and show them to have been of great interest. Two exciting discoveries in the 1960s were, first, that made by the present (1995) vicar, Richard Handscombe, in the walled up piscina in the Lady Chapel. It was the Trinity Crucifix, dated c.1395, and now set on a bracket above the pulpit. Secondly three years later, the slightly damaged statue of St Margaret of Antioch with another ferocious dragon was found in the wall close to the niche to which it belonged and in which it has been replaced. Both are excellent examples of late medieval stone carving, presumably hidden during the Reformation years.

Nor is this all. On the north wall of the chancel is a distinguished monument with frontal head and shoulders effigy of George Frere, London 'merchant', d.1655. The Victorian east window in such a lovely church can only be described as regrettable. If it could be replaced with something quieter and more in keeping, the family commemorated would be better honoured. The Royal Arms of George III, 1763, have been well restored.

FOBBING (C5) *St Michael*
Its tall Perpendicular silvery-grey Kentish rag tower with its still taller staircase turret commands a dramatic panorama overlooking the marshes and the Shellhaven oil refineries. It served as a landmark for Thames navigators. A blocked late Anglo-Saxon window in the north wall betrays a pre-Conquest church on the site, but the present building dates from the fourteenth and fifteenth centuries. The four bay arcade separating the nave from the spacious south aisle is fourteenth century, but the roofs are all apparently fifteenth century. The large timber porch probably dates from *c.*1550; its spandrels have carvings of a dragon and (?) Father Neptune. There is a thirteenth-century octagonal Purbeck marble font of a common type, from the earlier church, and an inscription in Norman French of *c.*1340 commemorating Thomas de Craweden. Also late Hanoverian Royal Arms and oil lamps.

FORD END, North End (B3) *Black Chapel*
Despite its name, not in the least black, this quaint little timber framed late medieval wayside chapel, so unpretentiously domestic looking with its (contemporary) built-in chaplain's house, is a treasure indeed. Though its early history is obscure, it probably originated as an outlying chapel of ease of Great Waltham four miles away, and may possibly have been founded by a local well-to-do fourteenth-century family called Blecche or Blatch – hence Black. Possessing some useful endowments, it is run by trustees who keep it in excellent trim and, although completely independent of diocesan jurisdiction, provide regular, well attended Church of England services and a Sunday school for local children. Inside 'it is like being in an upturned boat' (Scarfe) with great timber tie beams holding it together. Quintessentially Church of England, it has everything it should: box pews, double decker pulpit, west gallery with eighteenth-century four-stop barrel organ with twenty tunes, traceried screen (probably fifteenth century), with a tympanum over it on which the arms of Queen Anne dated 1714 are displayed and behind the Jacobean Communion Table, the Lord's Prayer, Ten Commandments and Creed. *See also plates 26 & 52.*

FORDHAM (D2) *All Saints*
A light, fairly spacious church well within this extensive village. It is mostly fourteenth century although the north and south aisles were rebuilt, probably widened, *c.*1500 in unknapped flint with regular bands of brick, which gives it an unusual, somewhat restless texture. The tower was very

crudely repaired in red brick in the early nineteenth century. It formerly had a spire.

The pleasing chancel, which is ceiled and has a three-light Decorated window of clear glass and Georgian altar rails, contains a handsome Baroque marble monument to John Pulley, a rector's son, who died in 1715 aged 26, as a naval captain. There is a bust of him bewigged and a relief of men of war of the time.

FOXEARTH (C1) *St Peter and St Paul*

This remarkable building in its secluded sylvan setting in the village, exhibits throughout the exuberant romantic taste of high Victorian ritualism, all but smothering what little survives (in the chancel and north aisle arcade) of its medieval predecessor. It is thus, in north and mid Essex, in the same category as Little Braxted, Littlebury and Halstead St Andrew chancel, with all of which it has much in common. For stencilling and Victorian stained glass buffs it is a 'must'. Binoculars and a bright sunny day will help.

The tower was completely rebuilt in 1862, faced with flint and with groups of four lancets on each face as bell openings. It then had a spire, taken down in 1947. The rest of the church was thoroughly 'restored' in the 1880s with mostly rebuilt rood screen, much stencilling above it and throughout the chancel, a colourful new pulpit, and a vast array of most interesting stained glass, much of it, e.g. the east window, admirable. When leaving, notice the small windows in the porch, especially the Flood and Noah's Ark.

FRINTON (E3) *St Mary Magdalene*

When Frinton began to be developed as a highly respectable middle class seaside resort in the 1890s, its tiny old village church was bound eventually to become inadequate. But it was not until 1928/9 that a new church was built in Old Road, by which time both old and new had already been effectually upstaged by the highly conspicuous and ambitious Free Church, 1912, in Connaught Avenue. For the new church the prolific and safe Sir Charles Nicholson, with his strong Essex connection, was the natural choice as architect. One of his later churches, it is typical of his eclectic style blending late Gothic and Renaissance. The decidedly Perpendicular exterior, clothed in knapped flint with bands of red brick, suffers from the parish's failure to afford the lateral tower Nicholson had designed. Its cool, light, pleasing interior has arcades of Italian cruciform piers with round arches and a pretty blue ceiling.

FRYERNING (B4) *St Mary*

The church is almost surrounded by farmland; the countryside even extends into the beautiful churchyard, where parts are left uncut and wild flowers flourish. The nave, with its Norman doors and windows, and chancel are eleventh century, built of coursed puddingstone, flint and Roman brick. The handsome diapered red brick tower, with a stair turret, dates from the early sixteenth century. The interior was thoroughly restored by Chancellor in 1869. The twelfth-century Caen stone font, standing in front of the brick tower arch, is of high quality; its carvings include the Vine, the Sun, Moon and Stars and the Tree of Jesse. Similar fonts occur at Little Laver and Abbess Roding. The glass is of some interest; the east window is by Willement and modern glass in the nave includes the memorial to Airey Neave MP, who spent part of his early life here and was killed by an IRA bomb in 1979; the window was designed by Penelope Neave. In the vestry is a palimpsest brass: the figure of Mary Berners was engraved *c.*1563 on the reverse of part of a widow, *c.*1460.

FYFIELD (B3) *St Nicholas*
First its distinctive shape, an Essex rarity: a Norman church with a central tower, though a good deal rebuilt, much buttressed and unattractively cement rendered outside. The broad squat tower, its main feature, is surmounted by (i) a hipped roof, (ii) a square weather-boarded lantern, (iii) a low octagonal shingled spire.

Entrance through a fifteenth-century north porch. The wide nave, still basically Norman, was extended in the thirteenth century, first north, then a little later, south, with three bay arcades, cylindrical piers to the north, octagonal to the south. The chancel east of the crossing is fourteenth century with some good detail in the sedilia (note the head stops and the three balls for the patron St Nicholas), piscina and the carving in the splays of the east window. There was a bone hole, or crypt, below the chancel, but it was filled in and blocked in the nineteenth century.

GALLEYWOOD (C4) *St Michael and All Angels*
This handsome mid-Victorian Gothic church, surrounded though it is by tall mature trees, stands high for Essex, 277 feet above sea level and, its tower and spire rising to 131 feet (compare Widford 145, Thaxted 181 and Saffron Walden 193), it is a landmark for miles around.

It demands detailed comparison with Widford (St Mary) since both churches were designed by the same architect J. P. St Aubyn (who operated chiefly in Devon and Cornwall), and both were paid for by a wealthy brewer, Arthur Pryor (1816-1904) of Hylands; Widford in 1862, Galleywood in 1873. Galleywood is not an ancient parish. Until St Michael's was built, it was part of Great Baddow. Costing £6,300, competently designed in the then fashionable Decorated style, and built of (now mellowed) yellow brick with bands of red, with a tower with crocketted pinnacles, holding eight bells, and an octagonal freestone spire, St Michael's is much the larger of

Gestingthorpe, St Mary the Virgin.

the two, with north and south aisles to the nave with arcades of five bays, transepts and a spacious chancel with three-light east window by Clayton and Bell and tile and mosaic decoration below, by Burrow, otherwise plain. It is almost certainly unique in England in having been built *in the middle of* a former racecourse on the attractive Galleywood Common, where steeplechasing and, later, flat racing meetings were held twice a year from at least the eighteenth century until 1935.

GESTINGTHORPE (C1) *St Mary the Virgin*
This church, in the long village street, is dominated by its massive Tudor brick tower, 66 feet high, towards the cost of which William Carter left 40 shillings in 1498. Typical of its period in Essex, it has diapering in blue bricks on its north and south faces, large angle buttresses, and everything, even the window mullions, transoms, tracery and pinnacles, is of brick – no stone dressings. What an advertisement for the local brickyard which then and for long after existed in the village, and whose skilled workmen built it. It houses six bells, four of them cast by the famous bell founder Miles Graye of Colchester in the seventeenth century.

Entering the church through a plain brick south porch contemporary with the tower, we are immediately impressed by the double hammerbeam nave roof, built in 1493 at the expense of Peter Barnard and Thomas Loveday and their wives, as a contemporary inscription up there informs us. There is a cleverly restored screen to the chancel, which is flooded with light through the clear glass of the elegant and intricate fourteenth-century five-light east window. A handsome alabaster monument with kneeling effigy of John Sparrow, died 1626, is in the chancel and an eighteenth-

94

century one to John Elliston in the south aisle. In the nave are two good late Victorian stained glass windows, both commemorating members of the Oates family, generous benefactors of the church. The westernmost of these depicts St Francis of Assisi with the birds – twenty-seven of them. On the same north wall is a brass plaque commemorating Captain L. E. G. Oates, that 'very gallant gentleman' who perished in Scott's Polar Expedition of 1912. There are two church chests, and, displayed on the east face of the tower arch, large, good eighteenth-century paintings of Moses and Aaron, formerly part of an altar piece. The fifteenth-century font is octagonal, the bowl with shields and symbols of the four Evangelists.

GOSFIELD (C2) *St Catherine*

On the edge of the village but close to the Hall (seen across the park, with the great lake to the west) this is, or rather was, essentially an 'estate church', its story closely linked to that of the great house and its successive owners. The first church here was built *c.*1190 by a de Vere, earl of Oxford, but of this no trace remains. It was replaced by the beginnings of the present building *c.*1435, the benefaction of Sir Thomas Rolf, serjeant at law. The brass on his tomb in the sanctuary, depicting him in legal full dress, describes him, questionably, as a 'flower among lawyers'. The west tower was added *c.*1490. But the church assumed its present form *c.*1560 when the chancel was enlarged (note the two south east buttresses) and a north chapel added, all in Tudor brick, by the builder of the present Hall, Sir John Wentworth, who entertained Elizabeth I there, 1561. His tomb and that of his son-in-law Sir Hugh Rich, 1554, are in the north chancel chapel. The church's most unusual feature is the Hall family pew, the so called Nugent Room, added to the west of the north chapel *c.*1733 to commemorate John Knight and his wife, whose splendid monument by the famous sculptor Michael Rysbrack presides in the charming Georgian room, with its fine woodwork and plaster ceiling and its discreet window into the church. There are five hatchments, a Georgian pulpit and some good stained glass, both Victorian (in the tower) and of 1980 in the north chapel. Seventeenth-century Creed and Lord's Prayer inscribed on nave walls. There is also the Royal Arms of George III, carved, over the south door. Incidentally the Hall, now owned by Country Houses Association and run as service flats for elderly people, is open to the public on Wednesday and Thursday afternoons, May to September, and well worth a visit.

GREENSTEAD JUXTA COLCHESTER (B2) *St Andrew*

Submerged and almost lost to sight in a vast modern red brick housing estate with a population of around 20,000, this modest little (former) country church is a standing example of continuity with adaptability to revolutionary change. Even in Norman times when it was first built,

Greenstead, with three other peripheral villages, Lexden, Mile End and Berechurch, was within the borough of Colchester. During the terrible siege of 1648 it was in the centre of a Parliamentary army camp, Fort Whaley. When the parish population first began to rise with the late nineteenth-century expansion of the town, the Victorians added a south aisle to what was previously a simple nave and chancel with a small Tudor brick tower. Now, following the population explosion of the late twentieth century, it has two daughter churches, St Matthew's in Parson's Heath and St Edmunds, a dual purpose hall/church, and is the centre of a lively team ministry. Architect Tim Venn has recently (1995) reordered the old church, freeing the altar from Victorian chancel clutter and much enhancing its beauty, and there are plans for a two storey section at the west end of the south aisle to provide for junior church, hospitality and other modern needs.

GREENSTED JUXTA ONGAR (B4) *St Andrew*

St Andrew's is a unique church, the oldest timber building in Britain and probably Europe. It is of stave construction, built of split logs set vertically, their rounded faces on the exterior. Each log has grooved sides, and a tongue or fillet of wood is set in these grooves to form a weathertight seal between the uprights. The timber cill on which the logs stand is modern: originally the walls may have been set in slots in the ground. Excavation indicates that the chancel was narrower than it is today and was originally built in the same way as the nave.

Stave-built churches can be found in Norway, where they date from the twelfth and thirteenth centuries. The age of St Andrew's is uncertain. It has long been thought to date from 1013 when it is alleged that the body of St Edmund rested here on its journey back to Bury St Edmunds after being taken from London whither it had been temporarily removed. Edmund, king of East Anglia, had been martyred by the Danes in 869. But this tradition originated with an eighteenth-century antiquary, and there is no satisfactory evidence to underpin it. A date as early as 845 has been claimed based on an examination of the tree-rings visible in the ends of the timbers. More recently, the discovery of twelfth-century stave buildings in excavations in London has led some to think the church may be as late as that. (Since this was written the split logs have been tree-ring dated 1063-1100.)

Its tree-girt situation provides a beautiful setting for this charming building. The ancient walls of the nave are complemented by a red tiled roof with pretty dormers, a pleasant Victorian porch, and a very attractive white weather-boarded tower of the eighteenth century capped with a shingled broach spire. The chancel was rebuilt in brick in the sixteenth century, and its east wall again in the eighteenth century.

I

The fouth view of the *Church* drawn in 1748.

Greenstead church illustrated in 1748.

A Victorian restoration of 1848 was thorough and extensive as the church was very dilapidated, but did not seriously dilute the intrinsic qualities of this ancient building. The possible connection with St Edmund is featured in the roof dating from 1892, where in the spandrels there are carvings of a wolf guarding St Edmund's head and other symbols associated with legends of the saint. The importance of this unique building was acknowledged in 1972 when it was featured on a postage stamp in a series illustrating village churches.

HADLEIGH (C5) *St James the Less*

This little Norman church, in its churchyard crowded with tombstones, is marooned on a traffic island in the middle of the hectic A.13, the London to Southend road. The actual structure remains very much as it was built *c.*1140, with walls three feet thick, and consisting simply of nave and chancel terminating in an apse with flat 'pilaster' buttresses. It retains four of its original windows; the others were inserted later. On either side of the plain chancel arch are round headed recesses, each with a squint to enable the congregation to see the action at the altar.

In the north east window splay in the nave is a painting of Thomas à Becket, with mitre and pallium, inscribed 'Beate Thomas'. Becket was martyred at Canterbury in 1170 and canonised in 1174, so this inscription, calling him blessed, not saint, if genuine, would place this painting between these two dates, i.e. almost contemporary. Tantalisingly this and a later painting further west, of an angel, are all that survive of extensive murals discovered in 1856.

The weather-boarded belfry is said to be fifteenth century, and the equally charming weather-boarded porch late eighteenth century. The Royal Arms are those of Anne after 1707 (Act of Union with Scotland). The west organ gallery was erected in 1965, when the organ was installed.

HADSTOCK (B1) *St Botolph*

Some historical mysteries defy all attempts to resolve them. If we are honest, we must be content with a balance of possibilities, or at most, probabilities. So it is with this fascinating church (and its question begging dedication), on the Cambridgeshire border in one of our most unspoilt villages. Hadstock (ancient name Cadenho) is in a valley, twinned pastorally with its larger hilltop neighbour, Ashdon, two miles south east.

Its church is an immensely complex building. On a slope near the southern (top) extremity of its irregular shaped churchyard, it is approached gently uphill from the village green and entered through a plain fifteenth-century north porch, and an impressive late Saxon doorway with (no exaggeration) the oldest working door in England – both dating from *c*.1020. Note the so-called honeysuckle carving on the capitals, abaci and band round the arch. You will see it repeated inside the church. 'That unique thing, an Anglo-Saxon oak door' says Pevsner, 'is treated quite differently from the Norman way. It has plain oak boards and three long undecorated iron straps riveted through to circular wooden bars at the back.' The tradition is that a Dane was punished for committing sacrilege by being flayed alive and his skin nailed to the door. When the door was repaired a piece of human skin was found under one of the hinges; it is now in Saffron Walden museum.

The tall narrow nave you are now in is also late Saxon and was originally lit by six small double splayed windows high up in the walls; four survive. (Later you should go round to the south side to see the evidence, coursed rubble and windows, at close quarters.) The west tower was added in the fifteenth century. East of the nave are two transepts and a crossing originally surmounted no doubt by a central tower. The arch to the south transept, into which a fifteenth-century screen has been inserted (notice the fox preaching to geese in a spandrel on the door), is thirteenth century, but the abaci and base are Saxon. The north transept, which ends in a fine early fourteenth-century window, only has Saxon bases to its pointed arch.

(Presumably the central tower fell, partly destroying the tops of both Saxon arches.) The Danish flag in the north transept does not commemorate the Dane flayed alive but the link with St Botolph's Cathedral Aalborg. The chancel is a rebuilding of 1884 by the famous Victorian architect Butterfield. He copied the Saxon motif on his chancel arch.

Now for historical mystery number one. In 1016 the English king, Edmund Ironside, was defeated by Cnut the Dane at the battle of 'Assandun'. Afterwards he built a minster there of 'stone and lime' in memory of those slain and to commemorate his victory which won him the crown of England. If, as seems most likely, 'Assandun' = Ashdon, is this church Cnut's minster? It could well be.

Mystery number two concerns St Botolph, to whom the church is dedicated. Abbot Botolph with a reputation for holiness built a monastery at Icanho *c*.654, contemporary with St Cedd's missionary base at Bradwell. Icanho is generally thought to be Iken near Aldeburgh, Suffolk, where again the church is St Botolph's. There a Celtic cross was found embedded in the church tower in 1977. But three years before that, the floor of Hadstock church had to be relaid and the opportunity for archaeological excavation was seized. The excavation was conducted by Warwick Rodwell. He made two main discoveries. The most astonishing one was furnace pits, with Roman tiles, and what can only have been a bell foundry with charcoal remains. The other was a number of graves including a large one, with no skeleton, under the south transept, centrally against its east wall. There could be little doubt that this was the burial of someone of importance. In the twelfth-century Book of Ely (*Liber Eliensis*) there is a reference in 1144 to Hadstock 'as that place sanctified to religion in days of old by the Holy Botolph, there at rest' (*quiescento*). What was the connection between Icanho and Cadenho, Iken and Hadstock, and where *was* Botolph buried? His relics were scattered between Ely, Thorney, Peterborough and Bury St Edmunds. The mystery remains. *See also plate 2.*

HALSTEAD (C2) *Holy Trinity*
This fine early Victorian church, now 'in retirement', cared for and repaired (at great expense) by the Churches' Conservation Trust, is included in the gazetteer as an outstanding example of its style and period. With its 150 feet spire it is as prominent a Halstead landmark as its parent, St Andrew's at the top of High Street. Erected 1843/4 on or near the site of a medieval gild chapel dedicated to the Holy Trinity, to serve the growing part of the town south of the river Colne, it is one of the earliest works of that prolific architect Sir George Gilbert Scott, a leading spirit in the Gothic Revival. Built of gault brick faced with whole (i.e. unknapped) flints and partly dressed with Bath stone, it is in the Early English style throughout and its proportions are excellent.

This is a church for the connoisseur of good Victoriana. He will find a detailed description and history in the admirable guide by Roy Tricker.

HALSTEAD (C2) *St Andrew*

The large parish church of this busy little market town stands in a commanding position by the main crossroads near the top of the steep High

Street. Its tall pinnacled west tower, dating from a thorough-going 'restoration' and enlargement in 1850, is visible from afar. The church itself, very broad six bay nave, narrow north aisle, wide south aisle and long chancel, dates mainly from the mid fourteenth century, when Decorated was beginning to give way to Perpendicular. The north and south porches are fifteenth century. The chancel underwent much alteration in the nineteenth and early twentieth centuries: east window twice renewed; the, dated, roof of 1413 hidden behind a painted ceiling; ambitious late Victorian reredos erected; and the walls covered with sombre late nineteenth-century painting. In the south aisle is a series of tombs (one fine brass and two pairs of stone effigies, one under a canopy) of the powerful Essex family of Bourchier who in the fourteenth century resided at Stanstead Hall in the rural part of Halstead. The church suffered an arson attack *c.*1991. It has since been transformed by limewash and looks marvellous.

HALSTEAD, GREENSTEAD GREEN (C2) *St James*

Until 1845 when it became a separate parish, this quiet, unspoilt hamlet was simply known as Halstead Rural with no church. In that year a Mrs Gee of Earls Colne paid for this pleasing early Victorian church designed in Gothic Revival Decorated by the still youthful George Gilbert Scott, who had recently built Holy

Greenstead Green, Halstead.

100

Trinity, Halstead (q.v.) also largely funded by this generous lady. It is not hard to visualise its original congregation, top hatted and becrinolined. On a summer evening, seen from the far western corner of the pleasant shady churchyard, the slanting rays of the sun gild the slender square tower, become octagonal above and crowned with a tall, graceful spire. The interior, with nice furnishings of the period, culminating in the tiled reredos, in no way disappoints.

HAM, EAST (A5) *St Mary Magdalene*

This venerable Norman church stands in 9½ acres of churchyard, one of the largest in England. It was only closed to burials comparatively recently and is now beautifully maintained by Newham Council as a nature reserve, a haven of peace in the bustling East End. The church itself is of outstanding interest. Apart from its impressive west tower, it was built just as it now stands, *c*.1130, 'with masonry of large coursed rubble' (Pevsner), in three distinct compartments, wide aisleless nave, lower, narrower chancel, and still lower, narrower apse. It retains two of its original slit windows, deeply splayed inside; others have been much enlarged over the centuries. There is one low side window in the chancel. Apart from the heavily buttressed, slightly later (*c*.1230) tower, originally of puddingstone but embattled and partly rebuilt in the early sixteenth century, only the apse is buttressed. The walls are tremendously thick. The church is entered through the tower and a Norman west doorway of three plain orders. The font is a small bowl given by Sir Richard Heigham 1639; its pedestal is later. The chancel arch and screen have both gone but the rood loft stair remains with evidence of a priest's room above. There is Norman blind, intersected arcading in the chancel, and, under a seventeenth-century mural monument to Giles Breame and his wife, is the hatch of an anchorite's cell (cf Lindsell) in the thickness of the north chancel wall. The altar, under the Norman arch of the apse, with excellent iron cross and candlesticks of 1972, is free standing. Behind it is (i) a splendid Jacobean monument to Edmund Nevill, Lord Latimer (d.1613), and his wife and children and (ii) a fine thirteenth-century double piscina. The apse roof timbers remain as they were left by the Norman carpenters, with wooden pegs clearly visible. There are two seventeenth-century brasses. In the tower is a bell called Gabriel, cast in 1380. Finally, the churchwardens are equipped with a pair of 'prickers' dated 1805, useful for awaking sleepers during long sermons. (Two also survive at Little Maplestead.)

HAM, WEST (A5) *All Saints*

The ancient parish church of the former county borough is located near West Ham Park. The trees bordering the spacious well-kept churchyard protect the church from the noise of the busy surrounding roads. The original church was rebuilt in 1180 by Gilbert de Mountfichet who gave it

Engraving of West Ham church from 1832.

to the abbey of nearby Stratford Langthorne founded by his father. In marked contrast to its neighbour at East Ham, the story of All Saints is one of constant enlargement and alteration throughout the middle ages. It was extended both east and west in the thirteenth century and later by the addition of north and south aisles. The outlines of the original Norman windows can still be seen above the nave arcades. The tall, handsome west tower, 74 feet high, with higher stair turret, was built in the fifteenth century in Kentish rag. Finally, the north chancel chapel in Tudor brick *c.*1550 – from the proceeds of sale of the church plate at the Reformation. A notable feature is the long south porch – a tunnel reminiscent of that at Boreham.

There is one brass and a large collection of monuments, many of them outstanding, including the seventeenth-century Fawcit and Foot monuments and those of the Buckeridges and the James Coopers of the eighteenth century. The glass and most of the fittings are nineteenth century including the reredos by G. G. Scott. Until 1830 All Saints was the only church in West Ham, but with the vast increase in the population there were, by 1936, no fewer than 28 Anglican parish churches, one of the earliest and largest being Blore's great yellow brick church of St John the Evangelist, Stratford (1832-4) a landmark on the A.12 approaching Bow and the City (q.v.). *See also plate 36.*

HANNINGFIELD, SOUTH (C4) *St Peter*

This secluded little church approached up a private drive consists of nave, chancel and belfry with a broach spire, all pleasantly unassuming. The chancel and all the furnishings are Victorian. The south door is dated by the Royal Commission *c.*1400. The jambs of the fifteenth-century two-light south window have pretty foliage scrolls.

West Hanningfield.

HANNINGFIELD, WEST (C4) *St Mary and St Edward*

The church lies in the centre of the village and is dominated by the fine weather-boarded belfry, which differs in its cruciform plan from other Essex belfries of the same type with four vertical posts. The nave is probably twelfth century; the north wall, of flint, pebble-rubble, puddingstone and Roman brick, has evidence of coursing and one small Norman window. The south aisle and chapel were built in two stages in the early fourteenth century, possibly for Isabel Cloville, whose brass there was laid down in 1361. The position of the belfry in relation to the south aisle suggests that it must have been erected at a later date. A small semi-circular projection was built to house four bells by Miles Graye (1676); the spire was rebuilt in 1888. In the early sixteenth century the timber-framed south porch was added and the chancel rebuilt in brick on earlier foundations. There is a good brick window with mullions in the north wall, although most of the windows in the church have eighteenth-century Gothic window frames. The window at the east end was inserted in 1831 and has been reglazed in tinted glass with a central cross. There are remains of the tomb of John Cloville (1490), who may have begun the rebuilding of the chancel. Medieval features include the dug-out chest and the fourteenth-century font standing on a Norman base; a stoup outside the south door was discovered during restoration of the porch in

1994. Among interesting later fittings are an early seventeenth-century communion table and late seventeenth-century communion rails, eighteenth-century boards containing the Lord's Prayer, Commandments and Creed, a Royal Arms (1813) and Charity boards.

HARLOW (A3) *Baptist Chapel*, Potter Street

Built in 1756 this plain red brick rectangle has an impressive doorway under a scrolly pediment on brackets. Inside, the only original feature is the west gallery supported on Tuscan columns and painted in pleasing shades of blue. *See also plate 54.*

HARLOW (A3) *Our Lady of Fatima* Roman Catholic

This, like St Paul's, is a truly modern church of which all Essex Christians should be proud, regardless of denomination. Designed by Gerard Coalen, architect, and dedicated on its completion in 1960, it is a powerful expression in concrete, brick, glass and stone of contemporary insights in theology and liturgy and must be an inspiration to worship in.

Its ground plan is a cross with nave and transepts centring upon the altar. Like Coventry Cathedral it carries the fifteenth-century ideal of walls of stained glass forward into the twentieth century in terms of modern technology. The stained glass, made from one inch thick slabs of coloured glass joined by concrete instead of the usual lead cames (cf. Clacton on Sea St Paul), was designed and made by Dom Charles Norris at Buckfast Abbey, Devon, where he is a Benedictine monk. It is an amazing achievement. Beginning with the Tree of Jesse, our Lord's family tree, the mosaic of colour in the huge windows tells the Gospel story from the Birth of Jesus through His Passion, Death, Resurrection and Ascension to the outpouring of the Holy Spirit at Pentecost.

The statues, especially those in terracotta of Christ the King (above the altar) and of our Lady of Fatima, the processional crucifix, and furnishings are all works of art of a high order.

The church is surmounted by a thin, tapering rocket of a spire rising to 131 feet to the top of the cross. *See also plate 65.*

HARLOW (A3) *St Mary* at Latton

An outstanding example of Gibberd's brilliant landscaping, this good medieval church, although set well within New Harlow townscape, looks convincingly as if still in the heart of the Essex countryside. Seen from the south west, its exterior (west tower, diagonally buttressed; aisleless nave and chancel with a Tudor brick and timber south porch and original nail studded south door now blocked) appears fifteenth century, the date of most of its windows, but is in fact Norman, as appears from a small window high in the thick south wall. Entrance is now through the tower.

There are several good brasses and monuments to Ardernes, Franklins, Althams and Arkwrights, but the most distinguished feature is the little brick chantry chapel north east of the sanctuary. From this it is separated by the large stone tomb chest of Sir Peter Arderne, chief Baron of the Exchequer (d.1467), and Katherine his wife. This is under a triple carved stone canopy and is surmounted by the Arderne brasses and an iron grille. There are faint remains of wall paintings in the chapel, which has a squint looking to the original high altar. It is all faintly reminiscent of the lovely Clopton chantry in Long Melford church, Suffolk, though very much simpler.

After a serious fire in 1964 the church was splendidly restored and refurnished by Laurence King, architect. Its story is graphically illustrated on petit-point sanctuary kneelers worked by members of the congregation; they are among the finest in Essex.

HARLOW (A3) *St Paul*
When Harlow, the first Essex New Town, was being planned by Sir Frederick Gibberd in the 1950s, St Paul's, the new central parish and civic church, was assigned a prime site in The High (town centre). In College Square it is flanked north by the Playhouse Theatre and south by the College of Further Education. In designing the church the architects, Humphrys and Hurst, exploited the site to the full, using a sandy coloured brick, concrete and thick clear glass to create what later (1971) became a homogeneous cruciform complex including ancillary buildings behind the church. St Paul's itself consists of a high, wide nave, square on plan, north and south transepts, and a shallow recessed sanctuary, all surmounted by a tall thin copper fleche. A little to the south is a stocky bell tower with six bells and an outdoor balcony/pulpit. Instead of an east window the entire east wall behind and above the dignified Holy Table is taken up with John Piper's fine mosaic of the Risen Christ at Emmaus, mysterious against a black background, suggesting His presence with His people in worship and daily life. The organ is in the south transept and facing it is a gallery intended for the choir. Scarfe in his *Shell Guide*, p. 112, writes that 'the walls like lace' of clear glass and thin concrete tracery combine to achieve an 'almost dazzlingly light interior'. The only coloured glass, predominantly red, is in staggered slits in the west wall of the nave. The church was consecrated in April 1959 and cost £40,000. *See also plate 66.*

(OLD) HARLOW (A3) *St Mary and St Hugh*
This sizeable cruciform church with a tall stone spire was practically rebuilt by Henry Woodyer in 1878 and is the third church on the site. There are, however, several brasses and some unusual monuments from the earlier buildings in the north and south transepts, together with an exquisite fourteenth-century stained glass panel of the Virgin and Child in the vestry

and a five-light window in the north transept containing a quantity of interesting glass from the sixteenth century to the eighteenth century, much in need of conservation (1994). There is an admirable modern extension to the north west.

HARWICH (E2) *St Nicholas*
Originally this ancient seaport, borough and former naval base was a hamlet of Dovercourt. The medieval chapel of St Nicholas, having fallen into ruin, was demolished in 1819 and M. G. Thompson, architect, of Dedham was commissioned to design and build a new and larger church on the same site at a cost of £20,000, to be raised by public subscription. The new church, containing the monuments and font from the old one, was consecrated in 1822 by Dr Howley, bishop of London, whose coat of arms with those of the borough and the mayor adorn the three east windows. It is a large building in the Perpendicular Gothic style, built of Suffolk white brick with artificial Coade stone for the pinnacles. There is a west tower with recessed spire and eight bells. It was designed to accommodate huge congregations and all, including the great tiered, theatre-like, north and south galleries and the west organ loft, is on the grand scale. The side windows are in two tiers to give light both to the galleries and the groundlings. A possibly unique feature is the iron 'cage' for children at the west end high above the galleries, which are supported by the thin elongated piers of the nave. The immense ceiling is a plaster vault and the acoustics are excellent.

The splendid Gothic organ case, flanked by the cage, makes the centrepiece of the west end, with the Royal Arms of George IV, who contributed £1,000 to the building fund, on the front of the gallery. There is a Mayor's Pew at right angles to the nave pews, complete with red velvet cushions and a mace rest. The east end forms an apse with three large windows. Behind the High Altar is a painting of Moses giving the Law, purchased in 1700, with some affinity to Poussin, it is said.

HATFIELD BROAD OAK (B3) *St Mary*
In 1135 a Benedictine priory was founded here by Aubrey II de Vere, Lord Great Chamberlain. The priory church was then built on to the existing (pre-Conquest) parish church, to the east. The village people continued to use and worship in what then or later became the nave of the much enlarged building. Following a violent dispute in 1378 a dividing wall was built on the order of the young king, Richard II, permanently separating parish church from priory church. Thus when, following the dissolution of the priory in 1535, the monks' church east of the wall was eventually demolished, the parish church, splendidly rebuilt in the late fourteenth century and early fifteenth century, continued in use as before.

The noble Perpendicular west tower, rising in five stages with embattled parapet to 81 feet, has a peal of eight bells dating from 1782 and a clock of 1910, but the seventeenth-century machinery of its predecessor and its wooden dial still survive. The south porch, with double sundial, elaborate pinnacles with smiling carved faces and two external holy water stoups, is also fifteenth century. Inside, the five bay nave was handsomely re-roofed in 1843, replacing a hammerbeam roof of which the kneeling figure forming a litany desk is the sole survivor. The box pews and west gallery are also mid nineteenth century, surprisingly conservative for their date. Notice the vigorously carved corbels or headstops of the nave arcades and the handsome eighteenth-century candelabrum. In the chancel lies the weather-worn stone effigy of Robert de Vere, third earl of Oxford (d.1221), in chain mail and surcoat, and with sword and shield displaying the de Vere mullet (five pointed star). This effigy, made c.1270 to stand before the priory high altar, was left exposed in the churchyard following the dissolution and only put in its present position in 1891. The sanctuary received its sumptuous panelling, reredos and altar rails in the early eighteenth century, believed to be the work of John Woodward, pupil of the great Grinling Gibbons. Finally, in a room at the east end of the south aisle (access only by special permission, accompanied) is the parochial library, founded by George Stirling, vicar c.1684-1728, and consisting of some 300 volumes.

HATFIELD PEVEREL (C3) *St Andrew*

Invisible from its large village, this strange towerless church overlooks the extensive gardens of the Priory with its large fish pond created by the monks. As with the subject of the preceding article, the present parish church was the nave of the much larger church of a priory, in this case one founded by the Saxon Ingelrica, wife of the Norman Ranulph Peverel and mistress of William the Conqueror. She founded it to atone for her sins. The original priory church had a central tower destroyed by fire long before the dissolution, apart from its west arch which now contains the church's east window. The rest of the priory church to the east was destroyed after the dissolution. A north aisle was later added to the original Norman nave and a south aisle when the church was drastically restored in 1873. Thus, taking into account the impressive neo-classical brick church hall, built 1993 adjoining the south aisle to the south, what we now have is in plan something approaching a square. The Norman west door survives, together with some unusual medieval bench ends in the present chancel, an unidentified medieval effigy and an intriguing jumble of ancient glass in north and south windows, some of it foreign.

HAWKWELL (C4) *St Mary*

This pretty little church, still in the country between the built-up part of Hawkwell and neighbouring Ashingdon, consisted until very recently of a tiny fourteenth-century nave and chancel with a picturesque white painted timber belfry and spire, added, it is thought, in the fifteenth century, together with a rustic south porch. When visited in May 1996, it was in the process of being doubled in size by the addition of a north aisle built under a gabled roof to match the existing nave. So convincing was the new 'fourteenth-century' arcade that one visitor was completely taken in! This extension is to accommodate the swelling congregations due to the energetic evangelical ministry of the well known Tony Higton, the present rector. There is also a much larger modern church, Emmanuel, at the opposite end of this parish.

HEDINGHAM, CASTLE (C2) *St Nicholas*
After Waltham Abbey, this is the largest, most splendid Norman church in Essex. It stands in the centre of the village below the castle, stronghold of the immensely powerful de Veres, earls of Oxford, from the Conquest to 1625. They built the castle first and the church about fifty years later, c.1180, at a time when the round Norman arch was just beginning to give way to the stronger, pointed 'Gothic' arch. This dramatic development is seen in the (pointed) chancel arch and the easternmost arches of the nave; the rest are all round, as are the three doorways. The chancel outside is much as the Norman builders left it, with a (rare) wheel window above the three lancets in the east wall. As you walk from the churchyard gate to the Tudor brick south porch, notice (i) the fine early Norman (or possibly even late Saxon) churchyard cross, found in a nearby pub cellar and erected in 1921 as a war memorial, (ii) the Tudor brick battlements of the aisles and clerestory, all dating from a major rebuild of the exterior c.1500, with the de Vere badges of boar and five pointed star visible above the clerestory windows, and (iii) the grand Tudor brick west tower with the surprisingly late date 1616 (that of a repair?) below the west window.

Entering through the original (!) oak door admire the six bay arcades, the superb hammerbeam nave roof, the fifteenth-century screen, and in the chancel the carved misericords north and south and the splendid black marble tomb of John, fifteenth earl of Oxford (d.1539) and his countess. Before the late Victorian restoration this stood in the middle of the chancel. The effigies of the four sons on the north side are now unfortunately hidden in the wall. The four daughters are on the south side and their parents kneeling under their coat of arms, on the lid, in low relief. *See also plates 16 & 32.*

HEDINGHAM, CASTLE (C2) *United Reformed Church*
Built in 1842 to replace an earlier building of c.1700, of which there is a contemporary picture in the present chapel. Its architect may have been James Fenton. It is built of local white brick, with an impressive two storey facade of five bays still in a restrained Georgian idiom, with a plain

pediment, and recessed wings each of one bay and two storeys, the upper storey (gallery) windows all round headed.

Inside, apart from ugly lighting and heating fitments, it has undergone very little alteration since it was built: three sided gallery supported by the usual thin cast iron columns, and a complete set of box pews facing the handsome tall, early eighteenth-century pulpit, with its elegant staircase, retained from the original chapel. Dr Isaac Watts, famous hymn writer and divine (d.1748), is known to have preached from it. Unfortunately its sounding board went to form the roof of a little summerhouse in the manse garden next door. *See also plate 58.*

The pulpit at Castle Hedingham's United Reformed Chapel.

HEDINGHAM, SIBLE (C2) *St Peter*

It stands in a commanding position above the road to Wethersfield on an eminence in the unspoilt rural part of its extensive main road parish. The main body of this large church with north and south aisles, exceptionally wide nave and a clerestory, is Decorated, *c.*1335, but the south porch is Tudor and the massive, heavily buttressed, embattled west tower was evidently begun at the same time as the rest of the church (see its two-light west window) but completed or rebuilt later in the Perpendicular style *c.*1500. The feature of the church is the fine 'cenotaph' to the parish's most famous celebrity, Sir John Hawkwood (d.1394), son of a local tanner. He made his name and fortune in the military service of Florence, where he is commemorated in the cathedral by Paolo Uccello's famous painting of him mounted on a war horse. The 'cenotaph' in the south aisle has a big ogee arch decorated with hawks etc. There is a fine carved and painted coat of arms of king William III in the north aisle and a hideous medieval graffito of the Devil in the nave.

HEMPSTEAD (B1) *St Andrew*

The focal point of this attractive village despite being somewhat apart from it, St Andrew's only attained the status of a parish church in 1977. From the time of its consecration in 1365 until then it was merely a chapel of ease to Great Sampford. Its story reflects the vicissitudes of life. The dramatic collapse of the old tower in 1882 badly damaged much of the church, which was partially restored and re-opened in 1888. The tower, after several starts and delays caused by lack of funds and wars, was not finally re-dedicated until 1962, when it won a Civic Trust award.

The main feature of the church is its series of Harvey monuments. The most distinguished member of that family was Dr William Harvey (d.1656), chief physician to king Charles I and the discoverer of the circulation of the blood. He is commemorated in a wall monument with a bust by Edward Marshall, said to be a striking likeness, and his remains are in a large sarcophagus placed here by the Royal College of Physicians in 1883. Another Harvey monument to another William (d.1742) is by the famous Roubiliac. Admiral Sir Eliab Harvey (d.1830), who commanded the Fighting Temeraire, Nelson's support ship at Trafalgar, is commemorated both by a hatchment and a tomb.

There are several good brasses, too. Dick Turpin, the highwayman, was baptised in this church in 1705, having been born in the local pub. There is no monument to him!

HENHAM (B2) *St Mary the Virgin*
An attractive church with a pleasing, light interior gently restored in the nineteenth century, it stands surrounded by trees in an outstandingly well-kept, pretty village. Mostly fourteenth century apart from the thirteenth-century chancel, it has a nave with north and south aisles with four bay arcades, a west tower with short spire and south porch. With the exception of some excellent carving on the capital of the middle pier of the north arcade (Virgin, angels and a head) and on the fifteenth-century font (note especially the emblems of the Passion), the main interest is in the furnishings. These include the handsome fifteenth-century screen and pulpit, the altar rails, reading desk and small communion table in the north aisle, all of the seventeenth century, and the early eighteenth-century altar piece with nicely lettered Creed, Commandments and Lord's Prayer still fortunately in situ. Of the twentieth century there are some unusual altar candlesticks and a long altar table (which would probably look still better under a plain Laudian throw-over 'frontal'!). There are some hatchments and an unusual urn and obelisk monument to Samuel Feake, Indian nabob (d.1790).

HEYBRIDGE (C3) *St Andrew*
The church is almost complete Norman, the chancel and nave dating from the early twelfth century; the massive, squat tower, dedicated in 1181, was truncated at a later date. The north and south doorways both have diapered tympanums; the south door has a complete set of contemporary ironwork. The chancel was lengthened in the late fifteenth century. The nave roof has four tie beams and crown posts; this work and the insertion of clerestory

windows, now partly destroyed and visible only from inside the church, may have been carried out *c.*1518. There is a rood loft staircase. The roof of the chancel also has crown posts, terminating in a single hammerbeam at the east window. The chancel has communion rails with twisted balusters, *c.*1700, a large mural monument to Thomas and Sarah Freshwater (1638) and a small brass to John Whitacres (1627). The neo-Norman marble font (1897) has panels copied from old fragments.

HOCKLEY (C4) *St Peter and St Paul*

Hockley church's striking hill top position on the edge of this much built-up twentieth-century 'garden suburb' commands tremendous views especially northwards. Its extensive churchyard is all ups and downs. Its squat west tower, its lower stages heavily buttressed, continues above as an irregular octagon, embattled and crowned by a short recessed spire. The rest of the church, which includes a north aisle with a four-bay arcade on cylindrical piers, is thirteenth century, as is the large octagonal Purbeck type font. The nave roof seems a bit later. Scarfe's description of the interior as 'walls scraped and whitewashed and much bedizened in Anglo-Catholic fashion' still holds good.

HOLLAND ON SEA (E3) *St Bartholomew*

This austere but well designed modernish church cherishes its continuity with the more recent as well as the much more remote past. It proudly maintains its claim to represent the ancient but minuscule former parish of Little Holland, whose medieval church was 'beat down' by storms some time in the mid seventeenth century. The population was then so insignificant that no attempt was made to rebuild or replace it and the parish was merged with Great Clacton.

When at the turn of this century it started to grow in population, a corrugated iron 'tin tabernacle' was built in 1903 at a total cost of £80! This in turn was replaced by a more permanent building, dedicated to St Bartholomew by Bishop Henry Wilson in August 1928. With Little Holland growing fast as a satellite of Clacton to be known as Holland on Sea, the present church was built to replace it on the site in Frinton Road in 1971 and dedicated by Bishop Trillo in 1972, the parish becoming finally independent of Great Clacton in 1979.

St Bart's is built four square on a central plan with a many gabled roof and an open central spire terminating in a cross. It is well endowed with useful ancillary buildings. Altogether it provides a valued focal point in what otherwise might seem a somewhat formless and characterless seaside development.

HOLLAND, GREAT (E3) *All Saints*

Yet another great Tudor red brick tower, plainer than its cousin at Thorpe, but with the usual diapering and octagonal buttresses and a west window of four lights. The rest of the church was completely rebuilt in 1866 by Sir Arthur Blomfield who, as Pevsner remarks, 'shows himself already tamed ... He is now competently and dully E. E. (Early English) with circular piers and geometrical tracery.' Nothing more to be said!

HORKESLEY, GREAT (D2) *All Saints*

A pretty church reposing attractively in its secluded, arboreal churchyard, so remote from the village and almost invisible from the Sudbury-Colchester road. At first sight it looks all of a piece, fifteenth century; but in fact it incorporates masonry of a Norman predecessor, and the handsome tower with its six bells, though elegantly topped in the fifteenth century with battlements, pinnacles and two-light bell openings, is basically thirteenth century with tell-tale lancet windows and no buttresses. The north aisle was added in the fourteenth or fifteenth century and the arches of the three bay arcade separating it from the nave are decorated (as is the chancel arch) with carved fleurons and other devices – bells, chalices and heads. The good fifteenth-century nave roof rests on big head corbels. A nice timber porch was added in the fifteenth century. The Elizabethan pulpit was brought here from St Margaret's Ipswich in 1848 and the following year a new font was provided. This is crowned by a handsome cover with many pinnacles and much crocketting which looks convincingly medieval, fifteenth-century style, but is apparently largely, if not wholly, Victorian.

HORKESLEY, LITTLE (D2) *St Peter and St Paul*

The old church was totally destroyed by a parachute mine in September 1940. Its successor, of conservative design, on the site and lines of its predecessor, comprising west tower, nave, chancel, south aisle with Lady Chapel and vestry, was consecrated in 1958. What is so remarkable is the survival from this carnage of the splendid collection of medieval monuments, terribly damaged but with infinite skill and care restored, and replaced in the new church. They comprise three wooden effigies of the de Horkesley family – two cross-legged knights and a lady of *c.*1300; two magnificent military brasses, with canopies and an inscription in old French, of Swynbornes, father and son, who died in 1391 and 1412 respectively; and the brasses of Lady Marney, d.1549, and her two husbands. There are two modern stained glass windows by Hugh Powell.

HORNCHURCH (B4) *St Andrew*

This fine hilltop church with its noble tower and copper spire is a stirring sight as we approach from Upminster. It even used to serve as a

112

Hornchurch, St Andrew.

navigational aid for Thames pilots. It has a fascinating history, going back to 1158 when Henry II gave land in Havering to the priory at Montjoux in Savoy, eastern France. The monks there established a small daughter priory here, pastorally serving the whole Havering neighbourhood. It was they who built the oldest part of the present St Andrew's, viz. the nave with its twin four bay arcades of cylindrical piers, in the thirteenth century; the sedilia, piscina and squint in the chancel are also of that time. It was then too that the church and parish came to be known as Hornchurch; it is not certain why. The famous bull's head and horns on the east end of the chancel, a unique feature, are known to have been there in 1610 and were probably there for long before that.

Then in 1391, following a dispute, king Richard II confiscated this priory and its possessions, only to have it immediately bought in by William of Wykeham, bishop of Winchester to form part of the endowment of his new foundation, New College, Oxford. The close link with that college, patrons of the living, a link shared by Hornchurch's daughter parish, St Edward's, Romford, continues happily to this day. From that time their large parish, with its (then) chapels of ease at Romford and Havering atte Bower, was served by chaplains (later called vicars) appointed by the college. The church building was extended to much of its present plan in the fifteenth century. The statue of a bishop high up on the west face of the tower is believed to represent Wykeham. To commemorate the 600th

113

anniversary of his purchase of 1391, a splendid stained glass window by Goddard and Gibbs was inserted in the north nave wall. It depicts Christ blessing Hornchurch past and present and encapsulates the whole story in glass – even including a computer. There is an earlier window in the tower illustrating Montjoux and the earlier history. Both are well worth studying in detail.

Another recent work of art is the elegant pulpit with sounding board, or tester, installed in 1962 to replace an unsuitable Victorian one. It, and the statue of St Andrew on its front, were made by Gwynneth Holt. There are several outstanding monuments. They include a tomb chest of William Ayloff (d.1517) near the altar, and notable seventeenth-century mural monuments to Francis and Helen Rame (in the tower); Richard Blackstone and his wife (north aisle), Sir Francis Prujean, physician (south east corner) and Thomas Withering, postmaster to Charles I, and founder of the Royal Mail (tower). One final note: the north wall contains 'a great many bottles, placed both neck and base outwards', and there is a fine extension, 1970, to the south.

HORNDON ON THE HILL (B5) *St Peter and St Paul*

A lovely thirteenth-century church set in the midst of a most attractive hilltop village between the two hectic London-Southend roads, A.13 and A.127. On entering the church we are confronted by the massive interlacing beams of the timber framed belfry, strongly reminiscent of that at nearby Laindon in Basildon, another hilltop church. (Were the same carpenters involved in both?) Here, with cantilevers projecting into the nave, it supports a typically Essex glistening white painted weather-boarded belfry with shingled broach spire. There are aisles north and south with alternating cylindrical and octagonal piers in the four bay arcades. The roofs are largely original but incorporate two fifteenth-century king post trusses. In lieu of an earlier clerestory two dormers were added both north and south. The fine four-light east window has some late medieval stained glass. There is a good fifteenth-century font, and handsome Royal Arms of 1715 and a splendid Arts and Crafts lectern on eight ball feet made in 1899 to the design of C. R. Ashbee, who did a careful restoration of the church about that time. It has enamel inlays and some copper. An inscription on the monument of Daniel Caldwell (d.1634) and his wife concludes: 'And from rude hands preserve us both, until We rise to Syon Mount from Horndon Hill.' Before you leave the pleasant churchyard with its avenue of limes from porch to lychgate, look out for the Horndon Beauty (on the north east corner of the east window).

HORNDON, EAST (B4) *All Saints*

This unforgettable Tudor brick church is seen crouching on its grassy eminence, seemingly inaccessible, as you drive from Tilbury. It stands alone and aloof above the traffic's ceaseless roar at the junction of the London-Southend (A.127) and Tilbury-Brentwood (A.128) roads, a quiet oasis commanding a tremendous panorama over Bulphan Fen to the Thames estuary. Having located the key, kept nearby, you approach the church from its north side. To understand its complex story you need to study its unusual plan. Almost the entire church was rebuilt in brick in the late fifteenth century by the aristocratic Tyrells of nearby Heron Hall. With a low squat west tower it is basically cruciform with north and south transepts each of two storeys, but the original symmetry was destroyed by the large south chapel added a little later, c.1512. In the 1960s this church suffered a spate of appalling vandalism and theft, in the course of which all four bells and all the Tyrell brasses were stolen and the pulpit and communion table destroyed but in 1970 through the valiant efforts of Christopher Starr (who wrote the excellent guide) and others, forming themselves into the All Saints Society, it was rescued and repaired and is now in the care jointly of the Society and the Churches Conservation Trust. Services and recitals are held at regular intervals.

Of particular interest are the exquisite memorial slab to Lady Alice Tyrell (d.1422), described as the finest of its kind in England; the upper rooms in both transepts, that on the south with a Tudor fireplace, believed to have been designed as the residence of the priest; and the chancel ceiling with its fine bosses.

HUTTON (B4) *All Saints*
Well away from the village, the church with its shingled spire has its own charm. Originally fourteenth century, the exterior was extensively restored by G. E. Street in 1873; the work included the complete rebuilding and lengthening of the chancel. Amongst medieval features are the north porch, the crown post roof and arcades of the nave and the impressive slightly later belfry. There is a small brass of a man in armour with wife and groups of children, c.1525. Some of the Victorian additions are attractive: the delicate metalwork of the pulpit and lectern; the font of polished marble containing ammonites with an ornate wooden cover commemorating a woman lost at sea (1892); remains of the former painted reredos (1898).

ILFORD (A5) Hospital Chapel *St Mary and St Thomas of Canterbury* (A.118 Ilford Hill, near Ilford Station)
'Hidden behind a forbidding red brick wall and surrounded by the incessant noise and fumes of the continuous modern traffic, is one of Ilford's best kept secrets.' The hospital was founded c.1145 by Adelicia, abbess of Barking, as a hospice and refuge for sick and needy men – in effect an almshouse. Its work and status were not affected by the dissolution of Barking Abbey in 1539 and the chapel has been in continuous use for Christian worship, as it still is today. It seems to have

been rebuilt early in the fourteenth century as a simple nave and chancel, and was very thoroughly but sensitively 'restored', and partly rebuilt, and also enlarged by the addition of the north porch, organ chamber, south aisle, Lady Chapel and vestry towards the end of the nineteenth century. The result is that what we now see is partly fourteenth and fifteenth centuries but mostly late Victorian work of a high standard, and considerable charm.

The monument in the south chancel wall is said to be that of John Smythe, d.1475, master of the hospital. The effigy is original but the monument itself is an effective Victorian imitation of early Renaissance work. The north chancel wall contains interesting stained glass with arms and badges of the Greshams and other powerful merchant families. The reredos in the Lady Chapel is by Comper and there are two Morris and Co. windows at the west end, depicting St Clement and St Valentine, by Sir Edward Burne-Jones.

Great Ilford was originally in the extensive parish of Barking and many vicars of Barking, including the then youthful Hensley Henson, served as chaplains of Ilford Hospital.

ILFORD, LITTLE (A5) *St Mary the Virgin* (Church Road, Manor Park, London E12)

An unexpected survival in the drab surroundings of Manor Park is this unpretentious little old church (aptly described by Pevsner as 'not impressive but loveable') in its quiet leafy churchyard next door to the rectory. Its tiny nave and probably the lower part of the chancel walls are

Thomas Heron, 1517, St Mary the Virgin, Little Ilford

116

Norman, 'probably early twelfth century' (RCHM); the evidence, the small north window now looking into the vestry/Lethieullier chapel. The upper part of the equally diminutive chancel was rebuilt in dark red brick in 1724, when the south porch and Lethieullier chapel to the north of the nave were added. There is a simple timber belfry and early eighteenth-century west gallery, on the front of which is the Hanoverian Royal Arms (1714) nicely carved in wood. There are two brasses. One shows Thomas Heron d.1517 as a Tudor schoolboy with inkhorn and pencase (reproduced on page 116), the other the two children of Barnard Hyde, early seventeenth century. There are several good monuments: notably (i) William Waldegrave d.1610 and his wife (kneeling figures) and (ii) the Huguenot Lethieulliers, large urn and sarcophagus under an architectural surround, eighteenth century. There is an attractive sixteenth-century stained glass roundel with royal armorials etc. in the vestry chapel.

ILFORD, LITTLE (A5) *St Michael* (Romford Road, Manor Park, London E12)

In total contrast to the above, but in double harness with it, is its ultra-modern (1990s) daughter, St Michael's, about ½ mile (or less) from it, on the busy Romford Road. Simply but pleasingly furnished, with an inviting interior and an impressive bronze figure of Michael the Archangel outside above the pavement, it is always open and welcoming to people of all faiths and none as a place of prayer and quiet meditation, as well as Christian worship. Next door, and run in close conjunction with it, is the Froud Centre, named after a fine Anglican priest, still living (1995). The sacristan of both churches, Joan Klint, worked many years with Schweitzer at his hospital in Lambaréné, West Africa. Just one example, of many, of ongoing Christian work and witness in present day East London. The architect of church and centre is the partnership APEC.

INGATESTONE (B4) *St Edmund and St Mary*

The first sight of the massive brick tower is very impressive, whether seen from the High Street or across the fields. The dedication to St Edmund suggests that a Saxon church may have preceded the small Norman church revealed by the undisturbed coursing of the north wall; the south aisle was added c.1300 and the tower c.1470-1510. The Petre family of Ingatestone Hall added the south chapel (1556) and the early seventeenth-century chapel, both in brick. Apart from the tower, the Petre tombs are the main glory of the church: Sir William Petre (1572) and his wife under the brick arch between the chancel and the south chapel; Robert Petre (1593); the large monument, showing three generations, erected c.1625 by the 2nd Lord to his parents. The bust of Captain John Troughton, 1621, may be by Epiphanius Evesham.

INGRAVE (B4) *St Nicholas*

Of its period this church is unique in Essex. Built in 1734/5 by the eighth Lord Petre of Thorndon Hall for the newly united parishes of Ingrave and West Horndon to replace their two ruinous churches, it is a plain structure entirely of red brick, Flemish bond. Fronted as seen from the road by a massive west tower, square in plan but with octagonal turrets projecting north and south and rising above the main parapet, beneath which are three arched corbels and a large inscribed stone plaque above the (main) west entrance, it comprises an oblong, symmetrical nave with additional north and south doors, each with a circular window above, flanked by round-headed windows, and a narrower short chancel with two vestries. Nave and chancel have flat plaster ceilings. There is a plain Georgian pulpit and a fifteenth-century font from one of the earlier churches. In the sanctuary are two fine brasses from West Horndon, Margaret Wake in butterfly head-dress, 1466, and Richard Fitzlewis and his four wives, two each side of him, 1528. The organ, in pleasing case, 1856, came from Thorndon Hall's private chapel. There are six bells. Who the architect was is not known, but he seems to have been influenced by Vanbrugh and Hawksmoor, in his rural Baroque. *See also plate 38.*

INWORTH (C3) *All Saints*

It stands among trees on top of a slope next to the large old rectory. It was embellished with a handsome, well designed red brick Tudor-type tower and south porch in 1876, ascribed to Joseph Clarke, London architect, but surmised by Scarfe to have been designed by the then rector, A. H. Bridges. (A water colour of 1827 shows the church with an unassuming timber belfry.) The walls of nave and chancel have a rich texture due to the use of chunks of dark brown puddingstone mixed with flint and Roman brick. Two deep-set early Norman windows (one of which on the south side contains interesting bits of medieval glass) are particularly memorable. Inside, the low, narrow early Norman chancel arch has on both sides of it, and above, wall paintings revealed by amateurs, which may need expert conservation.

KELVEDON (C3) *St Mary the Virgin*

A large flint-built church in an almost isolated position at the south-western edge of the town, St Mary's is in some ways best appreciated from passing trains on the adjacent London to Colchester main line. This view is now partially hidden by a substantial extension built in 1993.

The nave dates from the twelfth century but in the thirteenth century first the north and then the south aisle were added. The chancel and tower were built in the fourteenth century, the top stage of the tower being completed in the fifteenth century when the clerestory was constructed. The little brick chapel on the north side was a sixteenth-century addition.

118

The south chapel was built in 1843 and a major restoration was carried out in 1877 by Blomfield, whose work included the east and west windows.

The church has many charming features. Outside there are carved beasts and grotesques. The sturdy simplicity of the cylindrical piers with their stiff leaf capitals cannot fail to impress. In contrast is the elegant column at the east end of the north arcade with four attached shafts and a foliated capital, now unfortunately mutilated where a three-decker pulpit was formerly built up against it. There are squints either side of the chancel arch. Looking up, the fifteenth-century wooden roof is very fine, with its elegantly carved spandrels to the tie-beams. Along each side, the imitation hammerbeams at the half bay intervals bear carved and painted figures holding a shield, a crown, a pipe and a book. In the south chapel there is a delicate pre-Raphaelite window by Louis David with a portrayal of the Annunciation. In the other window in the chapel, which dates from 1938, can be seen a pet tortoise, still remembered in Kelvedon.

KIRBY LE SOKEN (E2) *St Michael*
(For the meaning of Soken see under THORPE)
Here, centrally in the village, we have a tall stately East Anglian type west tower, faced with knapped flint, with a quatrefoil frieze at the base, great diagonal buttresses and battlements with flint and stone chequer design, all very imposing. It holds eight bells. The church itself was rebuilt, for a second time, in 1870 by Henry Stone, the vicar's architect son-in-law. (He also rebuilt Walton church.) Features include a parish chest with three locks and two compartments and some interesting stained glass, both Victorian and twentieth century. There are three good windows, two in the nave and one in the chancel, by Rupert Moore, all done in the 1970s. His RM is near the bottom right hand corner. One in the nave celebrates St Cecilia, patron saint of music, and depicts Bach and Palestrina as well.

LAINDON *St Nicholas* See under BASILDON

LAMARSH (C2) *Holy Innocents*
There are only five old churches in England with this dedication. The Norman round tower has three slit windows (for defence?). Like the rest of the church it has been plastered, and this combines with the quaint tiled conical roof put on it in 1869 and the mellow Tudor red brick porch, to give the little church a most agreeable appearance. The windows of nave and (not structurally separate) chancel are of different periods: the three lancets in the east wall are Victorian, not Early English! The feature of the rather dark interior is the fifteenth-century screen of ten bays with good tracery. *See also plate 7.*

119

LAMBOURNE (A4) *St Mary and All Saints*

Hidden in deep green-belt country between Romford and Loughton, this is a little church of 'quite exceptional charm and historical range' (Pevsner). A twelfth-century nave and chancel with a fifteenth-century timber belfry crowned with a lead spire, it was boldly and skilfully transformed in the early eighteenth century into what it is now.

You enter by a domestic style door under a flat canopy on carved brackets dated 1726, itself beneath a lunette and rustic weather-boarded gable, and pass under a west gallery provided by a London ironmonger in 1704, to behold what appears (so well have the Georgian plasterers disguised medieval king-post and tie beams) to be a completely eighteenth-century interior. This is full of good things – low broad chancel arch on brackets, candelabrum, eighteenth-century font, Hanoverian Royal Arms, monuments and hatchments galore, mostly to Lockwoods of Lambourne Hall, and (for good measure) a fine fourteenth-century wall painting of St Christopher in the nave and Swiss seventeenth-century glass in the chancel (south window). In 1963 five remarkably good modern sculptured figures (in fibreglass) by T. B. Huxley-Jones replaced the classical reredos. *See also plate 42.*

LANGFORD (C3) *St Giles*

Norman Scarfe in his *Shell Guide* describes this church as 'a great oddity'. It is unique because the Norman apse is at the wrong end. It is hard to date the original building. Roman tile and brick were discovered in the fabric in the 1930s, but most experts agree that St Giles' is of early Norman construction. The nave and chancel were constructed in the late eleventh century or early twelfth century with apses at *both* ends. In the fourteenth century the eastern apse was torn down and a square extension added to the chancel. Clear evidence of the apse can be seen in the floor tile arrangement which shows the line of the original wall. In 1881 the church was 'restored' by Edward Browning and its character greatly altered. The chancel was entirely rebuilt and the north aisle, south porch and north-east bell turret added. The wooden shingled spire was demolished.

LANGHAM (D2) *St Mary*

Langham is amongst those Essex churches of early foundation which stands close to the manor house, in this case two miles from the village. The distant roar of the A.12, which replaced Gun Hill as the original London road, fails to destroy the peace of this beautiful location amidst mature parkland trees, approached by a stately avenue of beeches. The Hall, now of *c.*1740, may not be seen through the trees, but the churchyard is closely overlooked by the charming Church Farmhouse, a good piece of Suffolk vernacular, painted by Constable. In the corner of the churchyard is the gault brick Hurlock schoolroom of 1832, 'designed for the daily instruction of poor girls of the parish into the principles of the Church of England; and for the reception of the poor and infirm between the services of the Sabbath'.

Pebble-rubble with limestone dressings is the basic construction and would undoubtedly have been originally lime-rendered to resemble stone. Romanesque fabric, with a fragment of re-used Roman brick quoin, can be detected in the nave north wall and chancel, both of which were remodelled and extended during the fourteenth century, with a south aisle of six bays to the nave with octagonal piers. A number of good fourteenth-century windows survive, several with carved head and grotesque stops. There is an intriguing recess in the south wall. The tall narrow tower is essentially thirteenth century with crude seventeenth-century brick pinnacles, with the scar of the more steeply pitched earlier nave roof visible on its east wall.

The south porch contains a cast iron plaque with an inscription suggesting an original site on Gun Hill nearby: 'The Dumb Animals Humble Petition. Rest Drivers rest on this steep hill, Dumb beasts pray use with all good will. Goad not, scourge not, with thonged whips, Let not one curse escape your lips. God sees and hears.'

Restoration took place in the 1860s and after a fire in 1879. Some bench-ends with poppy heads, an oaken dug-out chest and a fine thirteenth-century chest survive. The organ is of 1897 by William Hill, and above the north door are the Royal Arms of Charles II.

LAVER, HIGH (B3) *All Saints*
Not in itself a particularly distinguished church, though it has a Norman nave and a dignified, uncluttered Early English (thirteenth-century) chancel. What lends it peculiar interest is its historical connection with the Masham family in the seventeenth and eighteenth centuries (their altar tombs abound in the churchyard) and above all with the influential philosopher and polymath John Locke (1632-1704). He spent the last phase of his life as the guest of the Mashams at their seat, Otes (long since demolished) and was buried in the churchyard. His tombstone with the Latin inscription composed by himself (translation available), is now in the church. During his residence at Otes it became one of the chief intellectual centres of Europe, comparable to Voltaire's Ferney a generation later. His friend and hostess, Lady Masham, was a daughter of the Cambridge platonist, Ralph Cudworth, and Mrs Abigail Masham famously supplanted her cousin Sarah, duchess of Marlborough, as Queen Anne's favourite.

LAVER, MAGDALEN (B3) *St Mary Magdalen*
In its delightfully remote, secluded location, the first sight of the rustic weather-boarded, timber framed tower, so typically Essex, brings heightened pleasure. It is probably early Elizabethan. Outside on the south

Magdalen Laver

wall between tower and porch is the elegant tomb of Wm. Cole, 1729, sometime treasurer of St Thomas' Hospital. The nave is early twelfth century, the chancel a century later. Both were heavily restored, 1875. But the beautifully painted and lettered eighteenth-century board with the Decalogue, Lord's Prayer and Creed remains, though sadly, not in its proper place as reredos, and there is a much restored early fourteenth-century screen, with its ogee arches reminiscent of that at Bardfield Saling. A nineteenth-century rector here was William Webb Ellis who as a boy at Rugby picked up the ball and ran with it, thus pioneering rugby football. He founded the village school here, 1862.

LAWFORD (D2) *St Mary*
This exciting fourteenth-century church has much to offer the visitor, who is recommended to take binoculars. To begin with, there is its setting at the end of a narrow country lane, over against the mellow Elizabethan / Georgian Lawford Hall in its park. The churchyard commands a memorable view of the upper Stour estuary. The west tower has 'the richest patchwork of building materials in Essex: ginger septaria, coffee

coloured puddingstone, dark grey almost black flint, silver grey freestone, and at least three different shades of red brick' (Scarfe: *Shell Guide*).

Before entering through the charming timber porch, walk past the unpretentious nave to admire the dazzling external display of the very grand (Decorated) chancel (illustrated above), perhaps built by Sir John de Cokefield, lord of the manor, shortly before his death in 1341. On each side, north and south, it has two pairs of large three-light windows, each with different and highly original tracery patterns. (Also observe the nineteenth-century patterns on the tiled roof and the flint and brick in the walls below the windows and in the buttresses, with their niches.)

Now go inside. Pausing to notice the elegant eighteenth-century pedestal font, go to the chancel. The richness of the detail is over-whelming. Pevsner rightly says it is 'one of the most splendid monuments of its date in the county'. Note especially that on each side the four windows are under an internal wall arcade (itself a rare feature). Its arch moulds are carved with naturalistic owls, squirrels and foliage (cf. the contemporary 'Leaves' of Southwell Minster Chapter House) and, in the north-east bay, with delightful chains of athletic little men of Chaucer's time holding each other by one leg, while two play musical instruments. (These can only be seen, best on a dull day, by using binoculars.) There is equally spirited carving above the priest's door, sedilia and piscina on the south side, though this has suffered iconoclastic damage through being at eye level. Unfortunately insensitive Victorians tried to match this medieval work with an elaborate alabaster reredos. The Germans helped remove a

123

particularly garish east window in the 1939-45 War. It was replaced by something fairly innocuous but less aggressive. Notice the Elizabethan monument with effigies to Edward Waldegrave and wife.

Two other points: the church's seating capacity was enlarged 1826 by the addition of a north aisle to nave; and *c.*1990 a handsome and commodious north extension was added, one of the best in Essex (architect: Tim Venn). *See further illustration on page 207.*

LAYER DE LA HAYE (D3) *St John the Baptist*

Apart from the village, it overlooks Abberton Reservoir. There is evidence of Norman origins in the south east angle of the nave. Apart from the Victorian south aisle, almost everything, north porch (Pevsner wrong here) nave, chancel, and embattled west tower of Kentish rag is fourteenth century. Furnishing practically all Victorian or later. The feature of the church is the early sixteenth-century Purbeck marble tomb chest with canopy over to Thomas Tey and his wife 1543, in the north-east corner of the chancel by the altar. Pevsner is in error in dating this fifteenth century; his suggestion that it was used as an Easter sepulchre is plausible, but if so, only for a year or two before the Reformation swept such 'popish' ceremonies away. The large eighteenth-century obelisk in the churchyard commemorates a General Brown who as a cornet of horse served under Marlborough.

LAYER MARNEY (D3) *St Mary the Virgin*

A little south-west of the magnificent Tudor gatehouse of Layer Marney Tower stands the contemporary and equally grand church. Like the Tower, it was built by Henry, 1st Lord Marney (d.1523), courtier and Henry VIII's Keeper of the Privy Seal, and his son John (d.1525). Built on the site of an earlier church and entirely of Tudor red brick with blue diapering, it consists of west tower, nave, north aisle, chancel, north (chantry) chapel and *two* south porches. (The easternmost, chancel, porch is a great rarity.) Inside, it is light and airy due to the lack of stained glass (apart from a charming memorial window by William de Morgan, 1870, and sixteenth-century armorials in the north chapel). There is a large wall painting of St Christopher in the nave but the showpiece is the three fine Marney tombs; that of Sir William, d.1414, in alabaster was in the earlier church. The magnificent tomb of Henry, the first lord, with its lifelike effigy in black (Cornish?) marble, has an elaborate terracotta canopy and base in which the court influence of the Renaissance is apparent. There is a similar one to John, the second lord, but without canopy – he left £250 (then a very large sum) for the completion of the church. There is much else of interest, including two Tudor fireplaces (one retaining its chimney), two screens, a Jacobean pulpit, a very large chest – and a plough! *See also plate 43.*

124

1 (above). Bradwell on Sea: St Peter's-on-the-Wall, St Cedd's 'cathedral', c.653, facing east.

2 (right). Hadstock: late Saxon doorway and door.

5. Corringham St Mary: early Norman tower.

4. Great Tey: Norman tower.

3. Waltham Abbey: early Norman interior.

8. Margaretting:
timber belfry.

7. Lamarsh:
Norman round tower
and Tudor porch

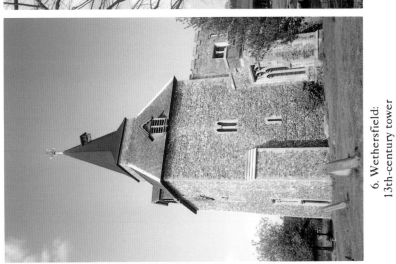

6. Wethersfield:
13th.-century tower

9 (above). Pentlow: Norman round tower and apse, the rest later.

10 (left). Mundon: typically Essex belfy.

11 (below). High Easter: 15th-century tower and Tudor porch and clerestory disguise Norman nave and chancel.

12. Thaxted: space and light
in the nave.

13. Saffron Walden: a detail of the nave
arcade and clerestory.

14. Wanstead St Mary:
classical interior, 1790.

15. Debden: from 18th-century Gothick
to medieval nave.

16. Castle Hedingham: Transitional Norman interior.

17. Rainham: Norman interior.

18. South Shoebury: Norman chancel arch.

19. Navestock: south aisle arcade partly of timber.

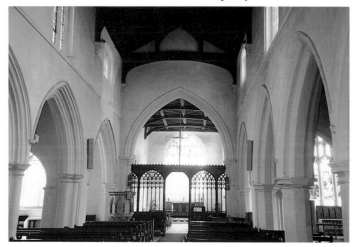

20. Newport: nave with aisles and transepts looking to chancel.

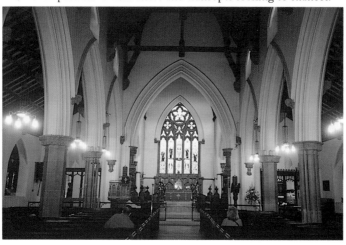

21. Romford, St Edward: Gothic Revival, 1849-50.

22. Chelmsford Cathedral: nave with ceiling of 1800 and organ of 1994 at west end.

23. Dedham: late 15th-century nave with contemporary roof.

24. Ardleigh: Butterfield's nave and chancel, 1882, showing decoration cleaned in 1996.

25. Barking, St Margaret: chancel looking west.

26. Black Chapel, near Ford End: medieval chapel with 18th-century furnishings.

27. Clavering: 15th-century screen and nave roof.

28. Great Bromley: detail of the 15th-century double hammerbeam roof.
Bellringers' hats inside tower arch just visible.

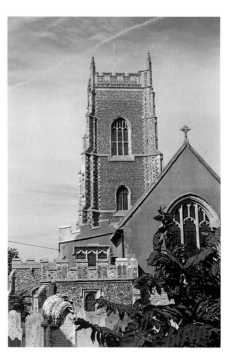

29. Great Bromley: 15th-century
puddingstone tower and
flushwork porch.

30. Brightlingsea, All Saints:
15th-century flint tower.

31. Dedham: 131-foot
flint tower of *c.*1500.

32. Castle Hedingham: Tudor
brick tower.

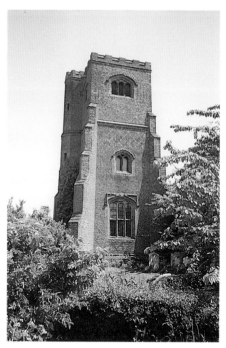

33. Bardfield Saling:
14th-century round tower.

34. Tolleshunt Major:
red brick tower of *c.*1545

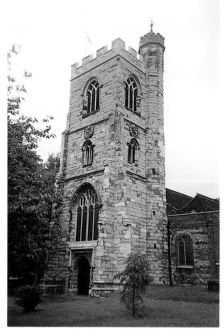

35. Prittlewell, Annunciation of Blessed
Virgin Mary: Kentish rag tower, *c.*1470.

36. West Ham, All Saints:
15th-century tower of Kentish rag.

37. Toppesfield:
brick tower built 1699.

38. Ingrave:
brick tower built 1734.

39. Dagenham, St Peter & St Paul:
tower of c.1800.

40. Stansted Mountfitchet, St John:
tower of 1895. W. D. Caroe, architect.

41. Toppesfield: interior from west gallery.

42. Lambourne: 18th-century remodelling of Norman church.

43. Layer Marney: tomb of Henry Lord Marney, d.1523.

44. Stansted Mountfitchet, St Mary: tomb of Hester Salusbury, d.1614.

45. Blackmore: effigy of Mrs Smyth, *c*.1600.

46. Arkesden: Cutte monument (1593).

47. Walthamstow, St Mary: tomb of Lady Lucy Stanley, c.1630.

48. Waltham Abbey. Tomb of Sir Edward and Lady Denny. and family. He died 1600.

49. Leyton, St Mary: part of monument to two Sir William Hickes, father and son.

50 (above). Copford: wallpainting in chancel and apse, much 'restored'.

51 (left). Great Canfield: East wall, centre, Madonna and Child, 13th century.

52 (below). Black Chapel: Commandments, Creed and Lord's Prayer, 18th century.

53. Great Warley: an Art Nouveau church of 1904, the Sanctuary.

54. Harlow: Potter Street Baptist Chapel, 1756.

55. Saffron Walden: Abbey Lane United Reformed Chapel, 1811, interior.

56. Saffron Walden: Abbey Lane United Reformed Chapel, 1811, exterior.

57. Manningtree: Wesleyan Methodist Chapel, built 1807.

58. Castle Hedingham: United Reformed Chapel, built 1842.

59. Coggeshall: Christ Church (formerly United Reformed), Stoneham Street, 1865.

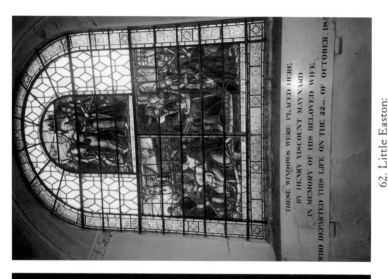

62. Little Easton:
one of two windows with
glass by Baptist Sutton, c.1621.

61. Messing.
East window, glass by van Linge, c.1630.

60. Rivenhall:
12th-century French glass
in the east window.

66. Harlow, St Paul:
mosaic by John Piper, 1959.

64. (top) Clacton on Sea, St Paul:
East window by Rosemary Rutherford, 1966.
65 (below). Harlow, Our Lady of Fatima:
glass by Dom Charles Norris, 1960.

63. Clacton on Sea, St James:
1913, Temple Moore, architect.

67. Brentwood: Roman Catholic Cathedral.
Built 1989-91. Quinlan Terry, architect.

Layer Marney, St Mary the Virgin.

LEIGH ON SEA (C5) *St Clement*

The church stands on top of Leigh Hill high above the old fishing town and the Thames estuary. Steps adjoining the churchyard lead down to the shore past a memorial to the Leigh fishermen who went to Dunkirk 1940 in their little ships, not all returning. The dedication to St Clement is appropriate to a maritime parish since he was allegedly martyred by being bound to a heavy anchor and cast into the sea, thereby becoming a patron saint of mariners.

The present church was built in the fifteenth and early sixteenth centuries to replace an earlier one on the same site. It is dominated by its 80 foot embattled west tower of Kentish rag with its stair turret rising high above it, a beacon for those afloat in the estuary. Entrance is through a Tudor red brick south porch, largely hidden by a nineteenth-century projecting south aisle. The nave and north aisle are fifteenth century but the chancel was extended in the nineteenth century. Its feature is the striking three-light east window, eighteenth century or early nineteenth century, hand painted in enamel to represent the Crucifixion with dramatic cloud effects and strong colours. Of similar date is the south-east chancel window. There is a series of brasses of the fifteenth, sixteenth and seventeenth centuries, notably of the Haddock, Chester and Price families. That of Richard Chester and his wife and family 1632 may have been engraved by Edward Marshall. Also a mural monument in the north aisle of Robert Salmon d.1641, Master of Trinity House, with which Leigh has historic links. He is shown frontally, black bearded and beruffed, his left hand on a golden ball. The fine East-Anglian-type font came from St Swithin's, Norwich (now redundant). As you leave the church notice the flat topped 'cutlass' tomb of Mary Ellis who died in 1609 at the age, it was said, of 119.

LEIGHS, GREAT (C3) *St Mary*

The church (illustrated below) is nicely situated on a minor road in the middle of the parish but a long way from most of the population. The round tower, with a spire (1882), and nave are Norman. The chancel of *c.*1330 has a fine large tomb recess, sedilia and piscina. The brass of a rector (1414) has a head taken from that of a priest, *c.*1370. The octagonal font

and traceried bench-ends are fifteenth century; there is a west gallery of 1720. The antiquary Andrew Clark, rector 1894-1922, kept diaries of Great Leighs' life in wartime (published in 1985).

LEIGHS, LITTLE (C3) *St John the Evangelist*

Down a narrow country lane off the A.131 Braintree-Chelmsford road stands this pleasant little church. It is built mainly of flint rubble with some Roman tiles. The early Norman nave with its flints laid in courses and the uncoursed thirteenth-century chancel are both under one continuous pegtiled roof. The south porch is of *c.*1890 and the bellcote and broach spire possibly also Victorian but entirely appropriate. The south doorway is thirteenth century and the door itself with scrolly hinges probably original. There are two Norman windows in the nave. There is a fourteenth-century font, a set of plain late medieval benches and a composite pulpit incorporating bits of various ages. There is a good wall monument to Herman Olmius (d.1726) in the nave, but the church's main exhibit is the richly detailed and much cusped fourteenth-century canopied recess in the north wall of the chancel, containing an oak effigy of a medieval priest *c.*1300 in eucharistic vestments, hands clasped in prayer. Norman Scarfe (*Shell Guide*) found it 'absolutely beautiful'.

LEXDEN (D2) *St Leonard*
In 1821 the posh suburban end of Colchester decided to pull down its unpretentious old church and build bigger and better on a slightly different site in its large, verdant, steeply sloping churchyard abutting the (old) London road as it winds through the village. The replacement was accurately described by Pevsner as 'cemented, a neo-Early English building with neo-Perpendicular window tracery. A west tower with a funny spire.' This funny spire looks for all the world as if it has been screwed on. The shallow chancel, deemed inadequate a century ago, was replaced in 1892 by a much longer, supposedly more dignified, flint faced extension with a five-light east window by Heaton, Butler and Bayne commemorating a squarson, John Papillon, rector and lord of the manor for nearly fifty years. Other memorial windows, though mostly good of their kind, shut out the light and make the interior solemnly gloomy. There is a west gallery, like much else, painted blue.

LEYTON (London E10) (A4) *St Mary the Virgin*
Incredible as it must now seem, until *c.*1840 this, the old parish church of Leyton, built on the site of its much smaller medieval predecessor, served a large sprawling country parish, then including Leytonstone. As London expanded, the area was increasingly favoured by prosperous City merchants for their rural retreats: they bought or built large houses now long since gone. This accounts both for the frequent, successive alterations and enlargements to the building over the years from 1822 onwards and for the exceptionally large number of monuments, several of them of top quality.

Regarding the fabric, no part of it is earlier than the seventeenth century. The substantial red brick west tower of three stages is basically of 1658, as is most of the north aisle wall. The attractive clock turret is late eighteenth century, the south aisle of 1822. The chancel has been rebuilt and enlarged more than once and a major reconstruction and reordering of

Sir William Hicks (d. 1680), at
Leyton St Mary.

the whole church occurred in 1932. The unusual octagonal piers of the nave arcades date from this time.

As to furnishings, the west gallery, on which stands the organ (badly damaged by arsonists, 1995), is of 1711. There is an interesting alms box of 1626, a fifteenth-century font on a later pedestal, a four-in-one hourglass from Bavaria (for timing sermons), and what is believed to have been a houseling bench for communicants in the chancel.

The most notable monuments are those of the Hicks family now in the base of the tower. Sir Michael Hicks (d.1612), secretary to Wm. Cecil, Lord Burghley, is portrayed in armour, which he never wore, and his son and grandson, both Sir Williams, are shown as standing figures, with one wife, in perukes and Roman costume; this monument is ascribed to Adye. There are also two early nineteenth-century monuments by Flaxman. John Strype, the ecclesiastical historian and biographer, was vicar of Leyton for the astonishingly long period of 68 years, from 1669 to his death in 1737 aged well over 90. *See also plate 49.*

LINDSELL (B2) *St Mary the Virgin*

A most endearing little church in its unspoilt rustic setting next to Lindsell Hall, approached between barns and other farm buildings. Outside it has a homely, warm texture of pebble rubble with red brick dressings but what strikes you immediately is the unusual position and appearance of the (low) tower at the south-west corner. It is believed to be Elizabethan, late sixteenth century. Before you enter, go round to the back of the church to see the remains of an anchorite's cell with a small window hatch into the sanctuary. Inside, what most impresses is the plain Norman chancel arch with a large squinch arch to the south of it to enable worshippers in the south aisle to see the action at the altar. The three-light east window has various fragments of ancient glass, attractively arranged. They include saints, armorials and two sixteenth-century Fytches of Brasonhead and their wives, at prayer. There is also a good fifteenth-century font and a brass of Thomas Fytche, d.1514, his wife and eleven children.

LISTON (C1) dedication unknown

This little church, only a mile across the Stour water meadows from Long Melford, is full of interest and character. Its humble exterior, dated Norman by a blocked north doorway, is dignified by (i) a handsome early Tudor west tower of diapered red brick with stepped battlements on a corbel frieze and (ii) a tiny south chapel added 1867, faced with knapped flint, Suffolk fashion.

Inside it is dark with much stained glass, some of it (e.g. a north window with roundels and the three-light west window showing St Patrick preaching at Tara (Kempe School 1923)) of high quality. There is a curious plaster tympanum dated 1701 with faint pargetting over the chancel arch, a good fifteenth-century chancel ceiling, a pretty chamber organ, a stately Baroque marble to Dr Poley Clopton d.1730, who founded the equally stately Clopton Asylum (almshouses) now housing the Cathedral Provost in Bury St Edmunds' Great Churchyard, and, finally, a deeply affecting little monument in the form of a piscina in the nave with an inscription commemorating the brutal murders of two Thornhill brothers, their wives, infant children and nursemaids at Cawnpore and Seetapore in the Indian Mutiny, 1857.

LITTLEBURY (B1) *Holy Trinity*

The large church of this pretty village is almost hidden from sight by trees and shrubs. It has two spacious sixteenth-century porches both with traces of fan vaulting. The Norman south doorway is unusual in its two roll mouldings and water leaf capitals. The north doorway is thirteenth or fourteenth century and the door itself has two shears carved on the horizontal batten over the wicket door – a reference to the wool trade. The north and south aisles embrace the fourteenth-century west tower on either side. A notable feature is the font, completely encased in early Tudor (?) linenfold panelling with an extremely elaborate crocketted and finialled corona. It, like much else in the church, has been much 'restored'. Indeed the chancel and all the east parts of the church were rebuilt 1870-75 by Edward Barr, architect, in an elaborate Early English style, and the impressive stencilled or painted Rood figures on the east wall above the chancel arch were presumably done at the same time.

MALDON (C3) *All Saints*

This sizeable town church has a complicated architectural history, a most unusual plan, and many points of interest. Chief of these is its thirteenth-century *triangular* west tower with shingled spire, three spirelets and a Sanctus bell. It is unique in England and owes its shape to having to fit between the end of the original nave (replaced in 1728 by the present one) and the old fish market in Silver Street. It holds eight bells. The church's south elevation as seen from High Street contains seven windows and runs unbroken the entire length of the building. In niches in the five western-most buttresses are early twentieth-century figures of notables connected with historic Maldon. Entering through the south door the eye is taken by the south aisle added in 1330, with its two tiers of elaborate decorative arcading on the south and west walls. An arcade of four bays with piers of Purbeck marble separates it from the nave. Beneath it is a crypt reached by a vaulted spiral staircase. East of it and south of the chancel is the D'Arcy chapel (fifteenth century) with the Washington window given in memory of Lawrence Washington, a seventeenth-century rector of Purleigh, ancestor of George. There are also D'Arcy and Wentworth monuments, and, near the organ, one commemorating Thomas Cammock, his two wives and twenty-two children. In the nave, on the north wall, are three hatchments and the Royal Arms of Charles II.

MALDON (C3) *Friends' Meeting House* Butt Lane

The first Quaker meeting house in Maldon was purpose built on land off High Street in 1707. After various ups and downs in the eighteenth century it eventually proved too small for the numbers attending, and in 1820 the present meeting house was built, and the old one sold for £200 – sadly it was destroyed by fire in 1962.

It is a modest oblong building, clearly urban, not rural, in character, of dark red brick with a slate roof. The plain late Georgian facade is diversified by three blind windows framed in pleasing rubbed brick, two large round arched windows flanking a smaller circular one over the central porch. Inside, as at Great Bardfield, it is partitioned by a wooden screen into two main meeting rooms, originally one for men and one for women. When the two sexes began to worship together in 1863, the former women's room was subdivided and used for various purposes. Apart from the judicious lowering of the ceiling to reduce the cold in winter, the meeting room is exactly as it was built and furnished, and, as such, conducive to the Quaker tradition of waiting quietly upon God in gathered fellowship for the utterance of His Holy Spirit through individual members. The three tiers of plain benches facing the entrance were originally provided for elders and 'recorded ministers', but are no longer needed for that purpose. The high windows flood this room with light. There is a small graveyard in front of the meeting house, shaded by trees.

MALDON (C3) *St Mary*

This picturesque old church down by the Hythe serves the rapidly expanding eastern end of the town and features prominently in views of the shipping on the Blackwater. Its massive, squat, heavily buttressed west tower has a Tudor brick top with stepped battlements and above that a little eighteenth-century spire on an octagonal weather-boarded base. It has a wide Norman nave with characteristic thick walls: the original chancel arch responds clearly show that it was wider than the present one. The south aisle added in 1886 has two features of very recent date (early 1990s) – a striking window by Mark Angus commemorating the millennium of the famous Battle of Maldon 991, fought nearby, and the entrance to a well designed red brick extension, polygonal with central lantern, projecting south into the churchyard. The nice altar rails and font are of *c*.1700.

MALDON (C3) *United Reformed Church* Market Hill

The earliest meeting house for Maldon's Dissenters was built in 1696 at his own expense by their founder minister, Joseph Billio, whose energetic Puritan preaching is thought to have given rise to the (now dated) expression 'like Billio'. He stares at us with stern disapproval from his contemporary portrait in oils in the vestry of the present chapel.

The chapel Billio built was replaced by the beginnings of the present structure in 1801. This newer building was enlarged by stages and owes its present impressive appearance (illustrated above) to its refronting *c*.1860 'but still with classical reminiscences' (Pevsner). Its stone facade has a ground floor loggia with four Ionic columns and a pediment above the first floor (gallery). With its four sided galleries it is said to have a total seating capacity of 900 or more. The fine pulpit could go back to the earlier chapel. There are some large Victorian tombstones in the adjoining graveyard, indicative of the chapel's prosperity in its heyday.

MANNINGTREE (D2) *Methodist Church* South Hill
John Wesley visited Manningtree and Mistley in 1785, when he was over eighty. He wrote in his journal: 'I found a lively society and one of the most elegant congregations I had seen for many years.' Manningtree has been a lively stronghold of Methodism ever since. Replacing an earlier, probably much smaller, building, the present church (or Wesleyan Chapel as it used to be called) was built at the top of South Hill in 1807 and cost £1,200. Of white brick, the broad facade is a handsome Georgian composition, in keeping with the elegance of the original congregation. It consists of a projecting portico of five bays with two Tuscan columns at the centre; above it an upper storey with three round-headed windows between four brick pilasters, supporting a pediment, topped by a pretty cupola visible from quite a distance – all very decent and gentlemanlike. Inside, facing the rostrum/pulpit and organ, is a substantial three sided gallery supported on cast iron piers. It is said to be the oldest Methodist church in Essex. Next door is a useful hall built *c.*1932 and extended 1981. *See also plate 57.*

MAPLESTEAD, GREAT (C2) *St Giles*
In the midst of its village, this church is chiefly notable for two things; its Norman west tower and apse, and the two fine seventeenth-century monuments in the south transept. The tower is unbuttressed and its parapet and battlements are probably fifteenth century. It was extensively repaired in brick on its east and south faces after a seventeenth-century lightning strike. Between the tower and the apse the church has undergone many alterations over the centuries, resulting in a complex ground plan and a dark, gloomy interior. The south transept added in the fourteenth century was extended later by the Deane family of Dynes Hall to accommodate their monuments. On the east side is that of Sir John Deane, d.1625; he is shown in plate armour semi-reclining, leaning on his elbow; on a shelf above are his widow, two sons and four daughters, all kneeling. Opposite is one to Lady Deane, d.1633. It is by William Wright of Charing Cross, sculptor. It shows her standing upright in her shroud with her son Dru reclining at her feet, in armour, arms folded.

MAPLESTEAD, LITTLE (C2) *St John the Baptist*
Unique in Essex and one of only five round churches in England (the other four, including the Temple Church in London, being older), St John's was built by the Knights Hospitallers, *c.*1335. It was drastically 'restored' in the 1850s, so that its external appearance and its windows and furnishings (apart from its font) are Victorian or later.

Little Maplestead, looking west.

The quasi-monastic military Order of the Knights Hospitaller of St John of Jerusalem was founded in 1092 at the time of the First Crusade. Its object was to assist and protect Christian pilgrims to the Holy Land and to offer them hospitality there. It came to England *c*.1144 and, with its head-quarters at Clerkenwell, began to acquire land and influence. Thus in *c*.1185 Little Maplestead and its existing parish church were given to the Order by Juliana fitzAudelin and a 'Commandery' and 'Hospital' established. A century and a half later the church was built, or rebuilt, by the Knights, supposedly modelled on that of the Holy Sepulchre in Jerusalem, and therefore basically circular with a rotunda on six pillars and arches and an apsidal chancel, to serve both the parish and the 'Hospital'. When the Order was dissolved in 1540, the building was left as the parish church. The font is older than the church, possibly Saxon, and must have come from an earlier church.

The tiny building has everything in proportion: the chancel pews seat two people each and even the organ is of an appropriate size. The rotunda is topped by a wooden belfry, with one bell. The vicar of the Maplesteads is appointed by the Knights of the Order of St John, who organise the First Aid and Ambulance service, and their device of the Maltese Cross is evident in the church.

MARGARETTING (B4) *St Margaret*

This typical Essex church stands at the end of Church Lane on the far side of the level crossing from the Hall. Its twelfth-century origins are visible in the lower part of the north wall of the nave, but the building is mainly fifteenth century. The chancel, with its early sixteenth-century windows, was probably rebuilt and widened then; the east wall was rebuilt in F. Chancellor's restoration of 1869-70. The church is uncommonly rich in medieval woodwork; the north porch and belfry are also fifteenth century. The belfry, designed as an extension to the nave, has ten massive posts; the lower stage of the exterior is vertically weather-boarded with a shingled upper storey and broach spire. Inside, the tower arch is brick. The nave roof rests on stone corbels carved with the signs of the evangelists. The late fifteenth-century octagonal font also has interesting carvings, including a square and compasses, and a seventeenth-century domed cover. During the restoration of the chancel, the only remaining Jesse window in Essex was transferred to the east window. The alabaster reredos depicting the Feeding of the Multitude, carved by Thomas Earp, was erected in 1878; the plasterwork in low relief on the east wall dates from 1918. There are brasses to James and Mary Gedge (1556) and a fine recently restored alabaster monument to John and Catherine Tanfield (1625). A good series of hatchments commemorates the Benyon and Vachell families. *See also plate 8.*

MATCHING (B3) *St Mary the Virgin*
In deep, lush, wooded country, far from Matching Green and Matching Tye, the church's setting could not be more idyllic. It has Matching Hall, its barn and dovecot and a huge pond with its fishing lodge for neighbours, while adjoining the churchyard is the fifteenth-century timber framed and plastered Marriage Feast Room, still regularly used for its designated purpose. Unique?

After all this, the church itself is something of an anticlimax. Apart from its fifteenth-century arcades of the north and south aisles, with their cylindrical piers, it was all rather unexcitingly rebuilt in 1875 by Sir Arthur Blomfield, largely at the expense of Lord Rookwood of Down Hall. Still, it retains a rather battered late medieval font, a good Jacobean pulpit given in 1624 and some plain old benches. And there are interesting brasses of John Ballett (d.1638), his wife Rosa and their two sons and six daughters, all shown in their contemporary costume, and one good Baroque mural monument.

MERSEA, EAST (D3) *St Edmund King and Martyr*
A little-restored church now mainly of fifteenth-century Perpendicular character, East Mersea is of ancient origin and occupies an isolated location next to the Hall, on a formerly moated site.

Septaria, presumably dredged from the nearby foreshore, and now heavily weathered, provides most of the walling mixed with a little flint, knapped to form flushwork panels at the base of the tower. The plan is of west tower with polygonal stair turret, nave with four-bay north aisle and south porch and a two-bay chancel.

The chancel now appears to be the earliest part, with fourteenth-century features of Decorated two-light windows. Otherwise the windows are mainly Perpendicular. In the nave three timber intersecting tracery windows of eighteenth-century date survived nineteenth-century restoration, when such things were generally considered undignified. The south door is covered by a seventeenth-century porch of red brick and timber with painted balusters and arched heads.

Inside, the limewashed austerity of the post-Reformation atmosphere may still be felt and is enhanced by the survival of the seventeenth-century pulpit with its iron hourglass holder and tester with pendants, albeit now marooned on a high base with no stairs. The box pews have gone, leaving behind expanses of nice gault brick paviours. Little is Victorian, save the charming intricate lamp and candle holders.

Fragments and small panels of Flemish glass are dotted around. Other features to note are the fifteenth-century font, the painted Royal Arms of George III and a little framed hatchment to Edward Bellamie, d.1656, adorned with skulls and crossed bones. There is a curious little brass in the chancel floor to Mawdlyn Outred of 1572 with a verse in English by her husband, the then rector.

MERSEA, WEST (D3) *St Peter and St Paul*
A smaller church than its neighbour at East Mersea, it serves a much larger population. The stumpy west tower is Norman with a later top, the rest of the building late medieval with a brick chancel and north porch and a south aisle with fourteenth-century arcade. The nave was heightened in brick 1833 and the round cartouches with biblical texts evidently date from that time. The font is thirteenth-century Purbeck marble. An odd feature is the (incongruous but charming) terracotta lunette over the south door in the style of the della Robbias of Renaissance Florence. Is it genuine and if so how did it get here? There are good carved Royal Arms and a well designed modern extension to the south.

MESSING (C3) *All Saints*
An unprepossessing approach through a dull red brick tower of 1840 and a nondescript nave in no way prepares the unsuspecting visitor for the excitement of the small but exquisite chancel, furnished in the Laudian High Church fashion of the 1630s before the Civil War, which it miraculously managed to survive, unscathed, here in Puritan Essex. Under a handsome plaster ceiling richly moulded and picked out in pale blue, cream and gold, the pulpit, chancel stalls (for communicants) and walls are panelled in dark oak and carved with Jacobean motifs, leading us up, over the black and white chequered marble floor, to the altar and its reredos with Lord's Prayer, Creed and Commandments finely inscribed in gold lettering on black. Above and contemporary with it is an even greater rarity,

a three-light east window of lovely seventeenth-century stained glass depicting the Six Works of Mercy (St Matthew 25 verses 35 and 36). This is attributed to one of the van Linges, whose distinguished work is mainly seen in Oxford. The carved Royal Arms of Charles I dated 1634, with the Prince of Wales' feathers on the reverse, hangs in the south transept. *See also plate 61.*

MIDDLETON (C1) *All Saints*

Dwarfed by the imposing old rectory next door and nestling between a wooded slope and a large pond, this modest, secluded little church makes an unforgettable picture, inviting comparison on several points with another similarly situated Stour valley church, six miles downstream on the *Suffolk* bank at Wissington. Both are Norman with distinguished architectural features, both have unsophisticated but delightful timber bellcotes, and both were severely 'restored' by the Victorians.

Under a vestigial Tudor south porch, the handsome Norman doorway of two orders and its medieval panelled door prepare us for the impressive, elaborate Norman chancel arch with its concentric half circles of zigzags, its double columns, the inner one with chains of triangles, and its decorated abaci extending to both nave walls. There are also two fourteenth-century recesses and one thirteenth-century one. A fine feature is the large incised Purbeck marble slab in the fourteenth-century chancel commemorating James Samson, rector (d.1349, Black Death victim?). He is shown in Eucharistic vestments. Beside the pseudo-Norman organ case is an intriguing Tudor Royal Arms (*c*.1500). The 'hot' Victorian glass in the chancel makes it rather gloomy.

MISTLEY with MANNINGTREE (E2) *St Mary and St Michael*

Both Mistley and its former chapel of ease in Manningtree have had bad luck with their churches and now have only one between them, the rather prim mid-Victorian Gothic church designed by Wadmore and Baker and erected in New Road, Mistley, 1870. Built of Kentish rag, it has a south-west tower and broach spire with six bells, a nave with north and south aisles and a chancel terminating in an apse, all in the, then fashionable, Decorated style.

It replaced a Georgian church of great originality at Mistley Thorn, of which the elegant twin towers, designed by Robert Adam in 1776, remain, well cared for by the Georgian Group. Manningtree church, for the most part dating from 1616, a building of immense period charm, was scandalously allowed to fall into disrepair and demolished *c*.1960.

MOUNT BURES (C2) *St John*

It stands high on the Essex bank looking across the Stour to Bures in Suffolk. The cruciform church is hard by the grassy mound on which a Norman castle once stood and it too is of Norman foundation, although the crossing tower and spire and the transepts were (re?)built in 1875. The chancel, nave and fifteenth-century south porch (with Sackville arms in the spandrels of its entrance arch) all exhibit Roman brick quoins.

MOUNTNESSING (B4) *St Giles*

The church stands out well on a south facing slope by the handsome Hall, with a pond full of bulrushes in front. It is well away from the village in rolling wheat fields.

The weather-boarded belfry and spire in the west bay of the nave rise above the brick west wall, dated 1653 in an attractive pedimented false window; heavy S-cramps secure the belfry timbers. The nave walls were rebuilt in Bodley and Garner's restoration of 1888-1891, reusing old materials (puddingstone, flint, limestone and brick) to make a pleasing mosaic. The brick chancel, with simple Gothic tracery, dates from 1805.

The interior is dominated by the massive timbers of the belfry with unusual cruck shores at the west end of the aisles. The mid thirteenth-century north arcade has capitals with good stiff-leaf and a head, which appears to be bridled rather than a 'green man'. The nave has a crown-post roof. There is a thirteenth-century dug-out chest. The carvings on the fifteenth-century font, brought from Hutton in 1873, include three fishes in a circle and a compass, square and mallet. The reredos of 1726, with paintings of Moses and Aaron, and the contemporary altar rails, with twisted balusters, came from Little Waltham. A small stained glass window in the north aisle, depicting St Giles, is from the Kempe studios.

MUNDON (C4) *St Mary*

In a remote rural setting close to Mundon Hall in the Dengie peninsula, this attractive little church became pastorally redundant years ago. Fortunately it was 'adopted' by the admirable Friends of Friendless Churches. They began by putting its picturesque timber tower, scarcely higher than the nave roof, into good repair, and later the church itself, as funds permitted. The tower has a square centre base, like its prototypes, Navestock and Margaretting, with north, south and west 'aisles'. The 'aisle' roofs are tiled and are only eight feet from the ground. The upper part is boarded, with a tiled pyramidal roof. There is a timber north porch. The interior has a large eighteenth-century clear glass east window, box pews and a pulpit with sounding board. Although the parish is now united with St Mary's, Maldon, a service is held here once a year. This is a good example of a rescue by the Friends, who welcome new members. For details write to St Ann's Vestry Hall, 2 Church Entry, London EC4V 5HB. *See also plate 10.*

NAVESTOCK (B4) *St Thomas the Apostle*

The church is approached along winding lanes and lies close to the Hall. It has the earliest and one of the finest Essex bell towers, with a large belfry and a tall shingled spire; the structure has been carbon-dated to *c.*1193 and was originally free-standing; the four main posts are braced with long slender timbers. The main body of the church is plastered. The Norman origins of the nave are visible on the north wall with its blocked doorway with fine original ironwork. A fourteenth-century window has been inserted into a thirteenth-century arch in the north wall; nearby is a small attached column with a battered but still beautiful 'stiff-leaf' capital. The south aisle was added against the belfry, *c.*1250. The arcade between the nave and aisle has four wooden piers plastered to resemble stone. The chancel is fourteenth century with an original tie beam.

The wooden pulpit (1967) was designed by Gwynneth Holt, who also carved the hands. There is a wide range of distinguished monuments mainly to the Greene and Waldegrave families, notably John Greene in judge's robes, 1653, and Edward Waldegrave, 1809, by John Bacon, jun. A tablet commemorates James Ford, vicar 1830-50, founder of the Ford Lectureship at Oxford; his successor was the historian William Stubbs. Maurice Greene, composer and organist (d.1755), was a member of the Greene family of Bois Hall. In 1940 a land-mine fell near the tower and did extensive damage, but the main structure stood up well. The crater in the churchyard is now a small garden. *See also plate 19.*

NAZEING (A3) *All Saints*

A picturesque little church in its retired position out in the country, far from the populated parish nucleus on the Hertfordshire border. Approached through a pretty churchyard, its focal point is the rich dark red texture of its nicely proportioned Tudor brick tower with higher stair turret. The timber south porch is roughly of the same period and has a floor of tiles on edge. The nave is basically Norman but there is a later north aisle with arcade piers typical of fifteenth-century Perpendicular, i.e. four shaft four hollow with capitals only for the shafts. The font too is of that same period and there is an ancient church chest. All the other fittings are Victorian.

NEWPORT (B2) *St Mary the Virgin*

The large parish church of this attractive main road village and former market town lies pleasantly secluded off the road to Clavering. Like Good Easter, it once belonged to the London collegiate church of St Martin le Grand. It has a stately west tower, Perpendicular in style with four embattled polygonal turrets and big transomed three-light belfry windows; it comes as a surprise to discover that it is a convincing rebuild of 1858. There is a handsome fifteenth-century south porch of two storeys, embattled and pinnacled with a three-light window between two niches

Newport, St Mary the Virgin.

above the entrance. This leads in to a clerestoried, embattled nave with north and south aisles, a crossing between north and south transepts, and a wide chancel. Outside, the church looks all of the fifteenth and sixteenth centuries but its building history is complicated and extends from the thirteenth century to the Reformation. It includes an embattled brick clerestory added to the chancel in the early sixteenth century. The roofs of the nave and chancel are original. The font is thirteenth century and has heavy gabled trefoil arches.

Now for the fittings. The unusual fifteenth-century screen has wide six-light openings with intricate fretted tracery and there is a fifteenth-century wooden lectern. But the church's greatest treasure is the unique dual purpose chest/portable altar in the south transept. Dating from *c*.1300, it has three bands of decoration on its front, shields, lozenges and circles. Inside the lid, which when open acts as a reredos, are five panels of painting on wood: said to be the earliest such paintings in England, predating the Thornham Parva retable in Suffolk. They depict, left to right, St Peter, Our Lady, Christ Crucified, St John and St Paul. This is still in use as a communion table. Nor is this all. There are two fine brasses, Thomas Brond 1515 and Nightingale 1608. In two north transept lancets is fourteenth-century stained glass, acquired by this church *c*.1900. One shows St Catherine holding the wheel on which she was martyred, the other Michael the Archangel slaying the dragon.

As you leave the church, look up at the sundial high on the porch; it says 'Many a man is well paid for abusing time.' *See also plate 20.*

NOTLEY, BLACK (C2) *St Peter and St Paul*

In its secluded location in the lane leading down to the Hall, this little two-cell church has undergone much drastic 'restoration', partly as a result of war damage. Its Norman origin is indicated by the (renewed) stonework of the north and south doorways and by the slit windows. The framework of the belfry rests on eight massive posts with 'trellis' strutting north and south as well as east and west.

The church's claim to inclusion in this gazetteer is that the father of natural sciences, John Ray (1627-1705), son of the village blacksmith, was vicar here and is buried just outside the south wall. A translation of the long Latin epitaph on the obelisk which marks his grave is to be found in the chancel. His many books on plants, birds and insects laid the foundation for their scientific classification. He was a devout and thinking Christian, the author of *The Wisdom of God in the Works of Creation* (1692). Essex as well as Black Notley has every reason to be proud of one of its most distinguished sons.

NOTLEY, WHITE (C3) *St Etheldreda*

The original dedication of this church is unknown; it was dedicated to St Etheldreda quite recently on the basis of a fragment of thirteenth-century stained glass now in a small window in the vestry, thought by some to represent her. The church, on the edge of the village, is one of those frequently met with in mid Essex, with timber belfry and shingled spire on four tall posts; in this case the weather-boarding has lately been renewed – the original structure dates from the turn of the fifteenth/sixteenth century. But the church itself is at least Norman if not pre-Conquest in origin, and a bequest in a will of one Leofwine, 998, of 'half a hide of land on the east side of the street to Notley, to God's servants' could possibly refer to it. It is known from nineteenth-century excavations that the chancel ended in an apse, but the most striking evidence is the chancel arch, which is a plain round-headed opening roughly dressed with Roman bricks or tiles without any dressed stone. On either side of it facing the nave are large plain round-headed niches. There are traces of medieval wall paintings above the chancel arch and some were uncovered in 1991 on the south wall of the nave above the south arcade of circular piers. The piers of the north arcade are octagonal. The nave and north and south aisles are under one big roof. The wooden south porch is fourteenth century.

OAKLEY, GREAT (E2) *All Saints*

The church stands some way from the village in a shady, sloping churchyard. The square, stumpy west tower was built of septaria, but

THE GAZETTEER

repaired in 1766 with red brick and capped with a weather-boarded belfry and a pyramidal tiled roof. The long plain nave is twelfth century (see the tell-tale north window) and has an equally Norman Purbeck marble font. The chancel has a large four-light Perpendicular east window and a small blocked north doorway whose jambs are carved with (damaged) angels etc.

OCKENDON, NORTH (B5) *St Mary Magdalene*

A church hard to find but well worth the effort. Entered through a Norman south doorway with unusual stilted round arch and plain tympanum above a pointed arch, it consists basically of Norman nave and chancel, north aisle added in the thirteenth century, north (or Poyntz) chapel *c.*1300, and square embattled west tower *c.*1450. The fifteenth-century roofs remain in nave and north aisle. Of interest are the Jacobean pulpit and the fifteenth-century tower ladder, but the two outstanding features are (i) the stained glass, chiefly medieval, and (ii) the remarkable series of brasses and monuments, mainly of the Poyntz family, in the north aisle and chapel.

(i) The glass, expertly repaired, is in the east windows of the chancel and north chapel and includes a thirteenth-century St Helena holding the True Cross and a fifteenth-century St Mary Magdalene as well as some early armorials. There is also an Arts and Crafts window, 'Emmaus' by Heywood Sumner.

(ii) Of the many interesting Poyntz monuments the *pièce de résistance* is that of Sir Gabriel, d.1607, and his wife Audrey. Their recumbent effigies lie on a marble altar tomb backing against the north wall with heraldic achievements and six shields of arms and above it a large, handsome oak canopy or tester with cornice and five pendants, its soffit painted with clouds, sun, moon and stars. Of equal interest because so rare, if not unique, are the eight little monuments commissioned by the same Sir Gabriel in 1606 to commemorate his ancestors, all shown kneeling in period costume.

North Ockendon was apparently known in the middle ages as Ockendon Seven Fountains. A spring that rises near the south-east corner of the churchyard is said to have been used by St Cedd to baptise converts.

OCKENDON, SOUTH (B5) *St Nicholas*

This church was brutally 'restored' in 1866. Even so, much remains of interest. Nevertheless the Norman north doorway, described as 'splendid' by Pevsner and 'tremendously rich' by Scarfe, has in fact been so roughly handled that it is hard to tell how much, if any, of the original survives. There is a round tower, one of the six in Essex, but the whole of the top stage has been rebuilt in typically unconvincing Victorian Norman. (The lower part is genuinely thirteenth century.) The whole church has been recladded East Anglian style in black knapped flint which gives it an impressively gaunt and stern look. Inside it is more rewarding and when it

141

has had the major repairs at present (1995) needed and proposed, it should look good. An unusual survival is the seventeenth-century hourglass stand fixed to the (Victorian) pulpit. There is a mutilated brass. But the showpiece is the fine monument in the north chapel to Sir Richard Saltonstall (d.1601), former Lord Mayor of London, his wife Susanna (née Poyntz from North Ockendon) and their six sons and nine daughters – all of them depicted (illustrated left).

ONGAR, CHIPPING (B4) *St Martin*

'Chipping' was Saxon for market. The early Norman parish church of this little market town lies modestly tucked away behind the shops and houses lining the east side of the High Street. Beyond it is the moated earth mound of the Norman castle. Built *c.*1100 of coursed flint rubble (see especially the south chancel wall) with some reused Roman brick, St Martin's consisted originally simply of nave and chancel. When, in 1884, it was extended by the addition of a south aisle and chapel, this entailed the loss of the Norman south (main) doorway. A small west porch was built and the present entrance made at the same time. The north doorway was blocked: there is a recess for a holy water stoup nearby. Some narrow Norman round-headed windows remain and in the east wall is evidence of two tiers of lancet windows, later replaced by the present three-light east window with excellent stained glass by Leonard Walker, 1929. The church has a typically Essex weather-boarded belfry and shingled broach spire, probably fifteenth century. There are eighteenth-century dormers in the roof. The nave roof, probably fourteenth century, is of tie beams and king posts; the prominent arch braced chancel roof was strengthened by extra braces in the seventeenth century. They have pendants. The chancel arch was rebuilt in the fourteenth century and the massive square font is of the same, Decorated, period. The shuttered aperture in the north chancel wall was from an anchorite's cell; through it he or she could see and hear Mass at the High Altar. There is a good seventeenth-century pulpit, Georgian communion rails, and a nice Georgian west gallery on Tuscan columns, behind which is the timber framing of the belfry. Few monuments, but one by Nollekens to a Mrs Mitford, 1776 with mourning cherubs.

ONGAR, CHIPPING (B4) *United Reformed Church*

This chapel, modestly hidden behind a row of cottages and approached through an archway beneath them, was built in neo-classical style in 1833, when it cost under £900. But, like most of its kind, its origins go back to 1662 when Puritan sympathisers withdrew from the parish church and set up separate congregations of Independents, later Congregationalist, finally merging in the United Reformed Church, *c.*1955. Its most notable minister, from 1811 to 1829, was Isaac Taylor, father of Jane and Ann who wrote *Twinkle, Twinkle Little Star.* Shortly after his time, the youthful David Livingstone from Blantyre, Scotland, came here to begin his training as a missionary. When detailed to preach at a local chapel, on seeing the congregation he lost his nerve and fled. The then minister formed the opinion that Livingstone would never make a missionary!

ONGAR, HIGH (B3) *St Mary*

The church has what Chipping Ongar lacks, a Norman south doorway, 'one of the most ornate in Essex' (Pevsner). It has one order of columns, a curved lintel with zigzag, echoing that of the arch, and, between them a tympanum, also curved, with rosettes. After this everything else is anti-climax, but the chancel is Early English, there are a seventeenth-century pulpit and communion rails and a brass to a civilian. The Victorian tower is a visual disaster.

ORSETT (B5) *St Giles and All Saints*

A large church (by Essex standards) with a complex building history, devoid of charm but with much of individual interest. At first sight it seems divided down the middle by an arcade into two naves and chancels of equal size, but in fact the nave and chancel are on the south side, the nave, originally Norman, entered by a Norman south doorway and the chancel fourteenth century. The north aisle was added in the thirteenth century and the north or Whitmore chapel, now overcrowded with monuments, hatchments and militaria, in the fourteenth century. The tower is at the west end of this north aisle. It has a large projecting north-west staircase; the upper stages were rebuilt in dark red brick in the seventeenth century and there is a pretty little white painted weather-boarded spire.

Below the nave west window is a stone frieze of Italian eighteenth-century sculpture in five panels of low relief, scenes from the Gospel story. There are some good brasses though mostly incomplete, some palimpsest (i.e. re-used). Three monuments are by Westmacott, a competent early nineteenth-century practitioner; the standard of the rest is not high. The four-light chancel east window by Wailes of Newcastle *c.*1845 is painfully glaring. There are others by him too.

OVINGTON (C1) *St Mary*

This totally unassuming little church down a quiet narrow lane next to the Hall serves one of Essex's tiniest parishes. It has a well attended service once a month, and is obviously much loved and well cared for. Nave and chancel are under one roof. There is a plain Norman font and the church itself seems to be of Norman origin. A curiosity is that, like its neighbour Tilbury juxta Clare, with which it used to share a parson, it has odd bits of Victorian masonry stuck on outside by an Anglo-Catholic parson's wife.

PEBMARSH (C2) *St John the Baptist*

The church presides over the parish from its elevated position above the village street. Apart from its earlier (thirteenth-century?) tower, it is mostly fourteenth century; clerest-oried nave, north and south aisles, and chancel. Externally it gets much of its distinctive character from the warm Tudor red brick of its handsome south porch, with two tiers of crowstepped gables, and from the equally mellow parapets and battlements with which the tower, clerestory and aisles were crowned, probably when the porch was built, *c.*1500. Sadly the spacious interior lost most of its character when the Victorians scraped the plaster off the walls to reveal its flint rubble bone structure. The pride of Pebmarsh is its fine, large military brass, the earliest in Essex. It commemorates Sir William Fitz-Ralph (d.1323), showing him hooded in chain mail, with legs crossed (reproduced left).

PELDON (D3) *St Mary the Virgin*
It has a big west tower, battlemented, with a higher stair turret and a stone nave with brick clerestory and hammerbeam roof. The short, abrupt chancel, with east window of three lancets, is a rebuilding of 1859. There is a plain octagonal thirteenth-century font on nine stone cylinders. The decor is markedly Low Church.

PENTLOW (C1) *St Gregory and St George*
How pleasing it is, this unpretentious country church so distant from its tiny village, half hidden from the road as it stands near the Stour across from its Suffolk neighbour, Cavendish. The lower part of the unbuttressed round tower (one of Essex's six) may well be Norman but is in any case later than the nave and chancel (with its tell-tale Norman apse still intact). The evidence is the fine Norman west doorway into the tower ground floor. This should be seen from inside the tower, the upper part of which, its top window and battlements, is fourteenth century: it houses five bells. The church itself was 'modernised' in the later middle ages, but it retains its square Norman font with elaborately carved interlacing and foliage, crowned by an octagonal fifteenth-century cover, much restored in the nineteenth century. The eighteenth-century communion rails have good twisted balusters. North of the chancel is a chapel dating from *c.*1600 when it was built or more probably rebuilt, with a nice coved ceiling and some pretty glass in its (reused) fifteenth-century window, to contain the grand tomb of a judge, George Kempe, d.1606, his son John, d.1609, and daughter-in-law, who all repose recumbent in effigy on top with John's fourteen children (four boys and ten girls) kneeling below. *See also plate 9.*

PITSEA *St Gabriel* See under BASILDON

PLESHEY (B3) *Holy Trinity*
Generations of retreatants spiritually and morally refreshed and renewed by a stay at the Diocesan House of Retreat in this peaceful village will have been intrigued and, possibly, mildly disconcerted by the forbiddingly gaunt, cruciform Victorian Gothic church next door, in its churchyard innocent of tombstones. If they ventured inside, they would find that Fred Chancellor, who built it in 1868 to replace a medieval predecessor, did not totally destroy the old church but incorporated part of its bone structure, viz. the crossing arches north, south and west, dating from *c.*1400. Everything else is Victorian or later – with one important exception. Two superb eighteenth-century classical monuments from the old church were salvaged and rebuilt in its successor. They are (1) that to Samuel Tufnell of Langleys, Great Waltham d.1758, by Sir Henry Cheere, sculptor. It is 'a standing wall monument with excellent portrait on top of a straight sided sarcophagus and in front of a grey obelisk' (Pevsner); (2) also attributed to

Cheere, one to Tufnell's uncle, Sir William Jolliffe, d.1749, entirely rococo in feeling. Much has been done in recent years to soften the asperities of this building and make it more suitable for the less formal, more intimate worship of today.

PRITTLEWELL (C5) *(Annunciation of) St Mary the Virgin*
Essex's biggest town got its name early in the nineteenth century from being the South End of the ancient parish of Prittlewell. This large church, prominent at the north end of Victoria Avenue is, therefore, the mother church of Southend. It stands in an ample tree lined churchyard, until *c.*1930 surrounded by picturesque old buildings now swept away.

The antiquity of the site is proved by the existence in the, otherwise Norman, north wall of the chancel, of part of an early Saxon doorway, dated by experts seventh century. The church's piecemeal development can be described broadly as follows. First, presumably in the seventh century, a Saxon church. This was replaced some four centuries later by the Norman nave and chancel, of which the full extent of the north wall and the three west bays of the nave remain as the core of the present building. In the thirteenth century three arches were pierced through the Norman south wall; they have plain octagonal piers. The fourth and final stage of the building's growth in the fifteenth and early sixteenth centuries gave the church its present appearance, as seen from the west and south. The grand Perpendicular west tower of Kentish rag in four stages, with diagonal buttresses, its top stage with three-light bell openings, battlements chequered in flint and stone, and tall pinnacles, rising to a total height from the ground to the top of the pinnacles of 110 feet, was built *c.*1470. The handsome two storey south porch, and the south aisle and Jesus Chapel, again with fine chequered battlements and typical three-light Perpendicular windows, followed. Inside, the five remaining bays of the nave and chancel have tall slender octagonal piers and higher arches. The east window of the Jesus Chapel has some notably fine continental (German?) sixteenth-century glass in the style of Dürer, brought here *c.*1800. From a purist point of view it is said that in the fifteenth century they apparently could not afford a north aisle to balance the south aisle, and a full length clerestory. (There *is* a very short one.) This would have avoided the lopsided appearance of the interior commented on by many visitors and would have given Southend an even finer mother church. It is also regrettable that Prittlewell is one of the very few Essex churches to have had its plaster (and wall paintings) ruthlessly scraped off by the Victorians. It would be splendid, but expensive, to have it replastered and then limewashed, but how much lighter it would then be! *See also plate 35.*

PURLEIGH (C4) *All Saints*

A hilltop church commanding tremendous views over the mostly flat Dengie Peninsula. Its sturdy fourteenth-century embattled west tower with powerful angle buttresses, chequer flushwork and alternate horizontal bands of flint and stone is impressive, seen from near or far. The church, apart from its Tudor brick gabled south porch, seems all of the fourteenth century too, nave, chancel and aisles. The windows which indicate this date were restored with American money in memory of Lawrence Washington, rector 1632-43. Good Georgian furnishings include the excellent pulpit and staircase with twisted baluster rails, the altar rails and the brass chandelier, 1758. The fine eighteenth-century altarpiece with large paintings of Moses and Aaron signed by I. Fairchild is sadly no longer *in situ* but preserved at the west end. The Royal Arms of George III above the tower arch are unusual in that they incorporate a medallion profile portrait of the king.

QUENDON (B2) dedication unknown

A small church up a quiet lane off the busy A.11, it comprises nave with three bay north and south aisles, a little sixteenth-century chancel, and a weather-boarded belfry of 1963. The cylindrical piers of both arcades are thirteenth century but the fabric underwent a severe nineteenth-century restoration. The organ at the west end is in a fine eighteenth-century organ case, said (like the more famous one at Little Bardfield) to have come from the chapel of Jesus College, Cambridge. The church has been greatly enriched through the residence in the parish of the distinguished church architect Stephen Dykes Bower, d. 1995. His taste and colour sense is manifest wherever one looks, notably in the waxed oak chancel screen, reredos and armorials.

RADWINTER (B1) *St Mary the Virgin*

As suggested in the Introduction (p. 18), this church, along with a handful of others (Little Braxted, Foxearth, Littlebury and Rainham), occupies a special place among Essex churches, as illustrating and exemplifying the virtues and positive achievements rather than the defects and excesses of Victorian church 'restoration'. In *this* case we are particularly fortunate in that the events of the two decades 1867 to 1888 during which this restoration took place have been minutely documented in a totally fascinating book *A Deuce Of An Uproar* (Friends of Radwinter Church, 1988). This chronicles, in forty racy letters from the architect, Eden Nesfield, partner of the more famous Norman Shaw, to his client and friend Fred Bullock, the generous and well-to-do rector 1865-1916, the progress of their joint enterprise and the ideals and practical thinking underlying it.

That achievement is considerable and still there to be enjoyed. Had it not been undertaken the tower would almost certainly have collapsed and Radwinter and posterity would be the poorer. As it is, the basically fourteenth-century church was very largely rebuilt and refurnished (but retaining the original arcades and nave roof) by a gifted, practical and sensitive architect and parson, working in close harmony and both influenced, like Geldart at Little Braxted, by the Oxford Movement and the consequent Anglo-Catholic Revival. Nesfield's health failed *c.*1885 and his place was taken by the young Temple Moore, who was later to build St James, Clacton on Sea (1913), q.v.

To summarise their achievement, the old nave and north and south aisles were extended by one bay and the chancel rebuilt. Both were externally faced with flint with some layers of red tiles. Among the new furnishings designed by Nesfield were a high altar, backed by an early sixteenth-century Flemish reredos, bought by Bullock, and carved with reliefs depicting the life and death of Our Lady; a three-manual Miller organ in a richly decorated case; a new pulpit; a spectacular chancel screen of wrought iron with 'very pretty' scroll work (Pevsner); above it a candle beam with seven candles each side of the Rood, and a new font completely encased, like those at Littlebury and Thaxted, in and under a tall Gothic canopy. Nesfield's individual genius is perhaps best displayed in the oversailing, pargetted upper storey of the original fourteenth-century timber porch. Following the fire of 1874 which devastated Radwinter, Nesfield, again working with the paternalistic parson, practically redesigned the whole village centre. The tower was rebuilt on the original lines by Temple Moore, 1887-8.

RAINHAM (B5) *St Helen and St Giles*

This, because it is so astonishingly complete and unspoilt, is one of Essex's best smaller Norman churches. It is late Norman, *c.*1170, and was probably built by Henry II's Justiciar and son-in-law, Richard de Lacy. Of septaria and some clunch, it consists, as it has done from its beginning, of nave with north and south aisles of three bays, chancel and low, square west tower. Later alterations and additions were minimal, and the main restoration, carried out between 1897 and 1910, under the experienced architect-parson Ernest Geldart, was done with exemplary care and sensitivity.

Don't miss (i) outside, the handsome priest's door in the chancel with its round arch of two orders with chevron (zigzag) ornament; (ii) the massive square piers of the north and south nave arcades, with attached corner shafts; (iii) the unusual shape of the small clerestory windows (possibly due to an eighteenth-century alteration); (iv) the grand chancel arch with its zigzag ornament; (v) the two Early English wall arches north of the chancel arch, behind the pulpit – the only major later alteration; (vi) the very remarkable arrangement of windows in the chancel east wall: three stepped round-headed lancets above the altar, and, high above them, a large round window flanked by two narrow slits; (vii) the fifteenth-century chancel roof – tie beams and king posts; (viii) a graffito in the rood loft staircase near the bottom, of a cog, or two-masted sailing boat in use on the Thames in the late middle ages. There are two interesting brasses, mounted on wood, in the north aisle. *See also plate 17.*

RAMSDEN BELLHOUSE (C4) *St Mary*
The suffix Bellhouse, to distinguish the parish from Ramsden Crays, refers *not,* apparently, to the timber belfry, which with the south porch is the only surviving ancient feature of the church, but to a family of local medieval magnates called Belhus (cf. Belhus Park, Aveley).

The glistening white painted belfry built on four posts, with its shingled spire and internal aisles, north, west and south, is an excellent example of the typical Essex construction, as seen at neighbouring Stock and West Hanningfield. The church itself, stone nave and brick chancel, was rebuilt in 1880.

RAMSEY (E2) *St Michael*
There is something very moving about the sight of Ramsey church tower on its hilltop as the main road approaches Dovercourt and Harwich. Its stability has often given cause for alarm. People have responded to various appeals and it is still there, a bit like Lawford tower, compact of a wonderful jumble of building materials, a cause for rejoicing! Just look at those corner buttresses, especially that on the south-east. After the tower the church may, but should not, come as an anti-climax. Simply nave and chancel, there is a Norman window and doorway on the north side as evidence of its antiquity, while the chancel's east window, a rectangle of three lights with two transoms, is that rare thing, Elizabethan. The main south door and doorway is indeed 'a handsome piece' (Pevsner), fifteenth century. There is a thirteenth-century sedile in the otherwise Elizabethan chancel and a pulpit of the same period. Finally, at the back near the organ is a rarity, the (much faded) Commonwealth coat of arms *c.*1652.

RAWRETH (C4) *St Nicholas*
This church is included as an example of the 'restoration'/part rebuilding of a medieval church by the ubiquitous parson-architect, Ernest Geldart of Little Braxted. It makes an interesting comparison with his work there and at Rainham (q.v.) and Stanford le Hope (q.v.).

At Rawreth the fifteenth-century tower, the north arcade and the west wall of the north aisle are all that survive of the old church following the 'restoration' he carried out in 1882. 'His' chancel is higher than the nave. He used flint flushwork and, in the north porch, flint, stone and red tiles. Pevsner thought it 'a rather gaudy design' and Scarfe a *'tour de force'.* What do you think? There is a good Elizabethan brass of Edmund Tyrell (d.1576) and his wife. After a long period of neglect, Rawreth church is now well equipped and in excellent repair and decoration.

RAYLEIGH (C4) *Holy Trinity*

The church stands at the north end of the market place on a fine hilltop site, shared with the remains of an eleventh-century motte and bailey castle and a tower windmill. Built largely of ragstone, the church is big, with its best face on the south side facing the town. The origins of the chancel lie in the early twelfth century. The massive square tower, rising some 70 feet, is diagonally buttressed with an embattled parapet and stair turret; it was erected after 1394 using stone from the former castle by permission of Richard II. The nave was rebuilt in the fifteenth century. The south chapel, with flint chequerwork below the windows, was built as a chantry chapel after the death of William Alen (1517); the fine Gothic tomb is said to be that of his son Richard (1517). The south porch, also early sixteenth century, demonstrates the virtuosity of the Tudor bricklayers with stepped battlements on a corbel frieze and a fine vaulted roof. The interior of the church is spacious and well lit by the aisle windows. The rood staircase in the north aisle has a cusped upper doorway; the fifteenth-century screen nearby came from the Lady Chapel of Runwell church. Other features of interest are a medieval dug-out chest, the consecration cross on the tower arch, the remains of a Jacobean ringing gallery and Barrington family brasses (1416, 1420). The old north doorway of the church has been reopened to lead into a substantial new construction of hall and church offices. The total complex will provide a Christian campus for the twenty-first century.

RETTENDON (C4) *All Saints*

The splendid Kentish rag tower is one of the most conspicuous landmarks in South Essex, crowning the horizon as seen from the Southend-Chelmsford road – a fine sight. It is embattled, and has diagonal buttresses, a projecting stair turret and a low pyramid roof. The church itself has a late Norman south doorway and a thirteenth-century chancel with stalls with poppy heads decorated with animal carvings, a dog, lion, bear and monkey. There is a north aisle with a three-bay arcade of short octagonal piers with concave sides.

But the surprise is the prodigious monument to Edmund Humfrey, d.1727, which takes up the entire east wall of the north aisle. It is signed by the otherwise almost unknown sculptor, Samuel Chandler of Wanstead, d.1769. It is described by Ruper Gunnis (*Dictionary of British Sculptors 1660-1851*) as 'a towering mass of marble ... it has a reclining figure of the dead man, while above him in niches stand life-size figures of his parents and grandparents; it is overpowering for a village church, but is nevertheless one of the most important early eighteenth-century monuments in England'. There is also a brass of *c.*1535 with a civilian, two wives and children.

RICKLING (B2) *All Saints*

Yet another isolated church, a mile and a half from the large village green where most of the people live. There is here much to admire.

The oldest part is the thirteenth-century nave, to which was added *c.*1340 a south aisle with a two-bay arcade with one quatrefoil pier. The tower, except for its, later, top stage, also dates from this time as can be seen from its windows – it has low diagonal buttresses – as does the chancel. So the main accent is fourteenth century, Decorated, as exemplified in the ogee canopied recess and tomb chest in the chancel north wall and in the screen, still with its original doors, an excellent, unspoilt, example of the woodwork of its period. A century later is the equally good, equally unspoilt, pulpit, and the tomb recess in the south chancel wall. The font too is fifteenth century. Notice also the good seventeenth-century church chest in the chancel.

Two nineteenth-century features deserve notice. They are the elaborately carved oak reredos with its canopied carving in low relief of the Adoration of the Lamb – it is Belgian and dates from 1879 – and the striking three-light east window above it with glass depicting our Lord stilling the storm on the Sea of Galilee. It is in memory of General William Inglis, Lord of the Manor. The Victorian restoration seems to have been conservative.

RIDGEWELL (C1) *St Lawrence*

At the end of a lane in the middle of this attractive village, the church is aptly described by Scarfe (*Shell Guide*) as 'prosperous Perp., unusual in Essex'. It is late fourteenth century or early fifteenth century of a type more often found across the nearby border in Suffolk, built at a time when Ridgewell certainly prospered. The embattled west tower in four stages with angle buttresses and a stair turret is flint rubble and houses five bells, two of them fourteenth century. The church itself consists of south porch, clerestoried nave with north aisle and chancel with north chapel (occupied by the organ) and vestry. It has a fine nave roof of four bays with collar beams on arched braces, every other one resting on shafts standing on corbels. The small canopied niches retain (defaced) figures. The dado of the screen remains with some original colour on the tracery: but no painted panels. The font is fifteenth century. What is said to be the oldest funeral bier in Essex, with octagonal legs and telescopic handles (seventeenth century?), is in the north aisle. There are some medieval graffiti.

RIVENHALL (C3) *St Mary and All Saints*

Seldom are appearances quite so deceptive. At first sight the gaunt gray Gothic exterior of 1838 holds no promise of glory within. Before entering, walk round outside, noting that considerable sections of the unattractive rendering have been carefully removed, to reveal early walling and round-headed lancets, especially on the north side of the chancel. In fact the underlying structure is basically late Saxon, c.980, built on the site of a Roman villa. Excavation by archaeologist Warwick Rodwell 1971-78 clearly established the earlier history. Inside, note (i) the handsomely rebuilt and re-cased organ on its excellent loft at the west end. It was in St George's Chapel, Windsor and was rebuilt by Alan McKirdy, who also designed the loft; (ii) the (rare) Royal Arms of James II over south door; (iii) numerous hatchments and monuments, notably that of Ralph and Elisabeth Wyseman 1602, with three sons and three daughters in its predella, and the unusual cast iron ledger of Thomas Western 1706, also the priests' stone coffin lids. But most of all admire the church's greatest treasure, the jumble of very early French stained glass in the three-light east window. This was bought in 1840 with brilliant serendipity by the then curate, D. B. Hawkins, from the curé of Chenu near Tours; it is some of the earliest glass in England, comparable with Canterbury and Chartres. In the centre light are four roundels including a Christ in Majesty, Annunciation and Entombment – all late twelfth century. Left and right are two archbishops wearing palliums and bottom right Robert Lemaire, knight, on caparisoned horse. Outside, north, is an admirable octagonal extension designed by Laurence King c.1975. There is, too, an attractive modern church of St Francis at Silver End in the parish; thatched, it was a barn. *See also plate 60.*

ROCHFORD (C4) *St Andrew*

The church is some distance from the town, from which it is cut off by the railway. It adjoins Rochford Hall, said to be the birthplace of Anne Boleyn and now a golf clubhouse; as a result, the church has retained a rural setting, with the greens to the south and the Hall across a lawn to the west. The church, dedicated to the patron saint of mariners and fishermen, stands near the headstream of the Roach, although this is no longer obvious. The earliest part of the present building is the early fourteenth-century north aisle. In the late fifteenth century the chancel and the south aisle were rebuilt, the south porch added and the tower stair turret begun. The fine embattled tower, constructed of diapered brick, was completed before the death of Thomas Butler, earl of Ormonde (1515). The brick north chapel, of the same date, has two slightly later timber framed gables, imparting a domestic character. In 1862 the walls of the nave were raised and circular clerestory windows inserted by William Slater. The whole interior has a cared-for feel. The tall brick tower arch is especially fine. The north aisle contains a small brass to Maria Dilcock (1514); the Youth Chapel at the east end has a modern marquetry cross fashioned on the organ case. The south aisle has a fifteenth-century piscina. The chancel has a brick squint and communion rails, c.1700, with twisted balusters. The large well-ordered churchyard contains the grave of James Banyard (d.1863), the founder of the Peculiar People, a religious sect which had its beginnings at Rochford.

RODINGS, THE (B3)

Of the eight churches in this group between Dunmow and Ongar, all are interesting but none outstanding. ABBESS RODING, heavily restored and with a very dark interior, has a Georgian pulpit with sounding board and two excellent Jacobean wall monuments. BEAUCHAMP RODING stands in splendid, remote isolation, is semi-derelict and has several fierce Victorian windows. LEADEN RODING has a charming sixteenth-century pulpit and good communion rails. MARGARET RODING boasts a fine, elaborate Norman doorway and door. WHITE RODING is probably the finest church with a Norman nave and contemporary font, an Early English chancel and an embattled west tower of *c*.1500. The chancel arch is Norman and there is a good Georgian wall monument.

ROMFORD (B4) *St Edward the Confessor*

When this church was built, 1849-50 (architect John Johnson), replacing an earlier one on the same prominent site in the market place, Romford was a typical small Essex market town. Even forty years later the population was under 10,000. Now it is an outer London shopping centre and residential town and the population of the borough of Havering, of which Romford is the largest part, is over 250,000; and yet this church with its 162 foot spire still dominates the scene.

Constructed of Kentish rag with Bath stone dressings, it was designed strictly in the Decorated style of the early fourteenth century much in vogue with High Victorian architects such as G. G. Scott. Indeed St Edward's might almost have been by him. A large tall building with a wide nave and north and south aisles and a spacious, dignified chancel terminating in a five-light east window with typically elaborate tracery, it is conservative for its time in being provided with a west gallery on which the original organ was sited, as is its fine present-day successor also by J. W. Walker and Sons, now of Brandon, Suffolk. St Edward's is justly proud of its renowned musical tradition and its choir of forty-five choristers, men and boys, who have sung in many cathedrals.

When in 1849 the old, late medieval St Edward's was demolished to make way for its successor, three of its historic monuments were transferred hither. Two are in the porch, presently needing repair. The third is the splendid Elizabethan monument to Sir Anthony Cooke, d.1576, Tudor courtier and statesman of Gidea Hall, Romford, and his wife, two sons and four daughters, all shown in effigy, kneeling. This large monument is now on the north wall at the west end of the nave. There are, too, many more recent memorials. When the chancel was re-ordered in 1976, with a raised extension for a portable nave altar, the opportunity was taken to record the town's links with an historic past. New communion rails in wrought iron and oak were erected, bearing twelve coats of arms of families which served Romford down the centuries.

Next door to the church is the fifteenth/sixteenth-century Church House, formerly the Cock and Bull pub. It has belonged to the parish since 1908 and currently houses the parish office and acts as a venue for social, pastoral and counselling purposes. *See also plate 21.*

ROWHEDGE/EAST DONYLAND (D2) *St Laurence*

The old church of East Donyland was demolished in 1838 and a new church built in its stead down in Rowhedge, the riverside hamlet where most of the people lived. The architect chosen was William Mason of Ipswich, who about the same time designed the neo-Norman St Botolph's in neighbouring Colchester (q.v.). Here 'Early English' was the style chosen and the new church was built, like St Botolph's, in the then fashionable white brick, in conscious imitation of the Chapter House of York Minster! It is, says Pevsner, 'quite remarkably original'. It has groups of five stepped lancet windows on three of its eight sides, two entrances, and a pyramidal slate roof, visible from Wivenhoe across the Colne. Inside, there is an east gallery, the good fourteenth-century font from East Donyland and (also from there) a quaint monument to Elizabeth Marshall, d.1613, with a most curious inscription in the style of John Donne, but not by him. At the time of writing there is a handsome early eighteenth-century altarpiece, said to have been designed by Hawksmoor, from Minster in Sheppey, but its fate is currently under discussion.

RUNWELL (C4) *St Mary the Virgin*

Surrounded by suburbia, this little medieval church is one of very few really old buildings in the joint parishes of Runwell and its entirely twentieth-century urban neighbour, Wickford. It has a well proportioned west tower of Kentish rag with a round stair turret and a short shingled spire and there are two handsome timber porches, north and south, both fifteenth century like the tower.

Inside, the visitor is left in no doubt as to the dedication and the churchmanship. There is plenty of colour – a rector *c.*1930 was handy with his paint pot and specially addicted to reds and blues – and there are several statues of the Virgin. The oldest feature is the thirteenth-century four bay arcade separating the south aisle/chapel from the nave; high up in its east wall above the altar is a little window with fragments of medieval glass. Apart from this arcade, St Mary's is basically late fourteenth century. The chancel was extended in 1907 and the rood screen erected two years later.

THE GAZETTEER

In a recess in the chancel north wall is a medieval tomb slab with a raised cross with a long shaft. Nearby is a small tablet with two brass kneeling figures to Eustace Sulyard (d.1547) and his wife Margaret.

SAFFRON WALDEN (B1) *Our Lady of Compassion* Roman Catholic, Castle Street

Here is an unusual church. In a quiet little street backing on to the churchyard wall of the mighty (Anglican) parish church, it is a converted wooden tithe barn, probably predating the Reformation. It attained its present status when the Spanish Vincentians who had been serving the neighbourhood, and who built the adjoining presbytery *c*.1920, returned to Spain after the end of the Civil War in 1939. Simply, even austerely, furnished, it is the least assertive of buildings, perfectly adapted to the needs of present day Catholic worship.

SAFFRON WALDEN (B1) *St Mary the Virgin*

Riding high above the roofs of the historic town, this stately church, the largest in the county, has undergone many transformations in the course of its history, two of them at the hands of architects of high renown. The present building is very likely the fourth on the site, and incorporates, in the chancel arcades and the arches leading from the chancel chapels into the north and south aisles of the nave, elements from its predecessor dating back to *c*.1250. At the west end the tower and spire, soaring to a total height of 193 feet (and thus just topping Thaxted) was designed and built in 1831/2 by Thomas Rickman, the Quaker architect whose classification of the successive phases of Gothic into Early English, Decorated and Perpendicular has proved its usefulness for a century and a half; some of his other work may be admired in the New Court and Bridge of Sighs at St John's College, Cambridge.

But Saffron Walden's greatest glory is its noble seven bay nave and immensely wide aisles. Here too there is a strong link with Cambridge (only fourteen miles away). For a building contract of 1485 exists with Simon Clark and John Wastell, master masons at King's College Chapel. Wastell also designed the nave of Great St Mary's, the university church, with its many points of close resemblance to Saffron Walden church. Walden's nave is not the least of his great achievements. Mostly built between 1475 and 1525, it is fifty-four feet high with tall slender piers and a particularly splendid clerestory consisting of three-light windows coupled together in pairs in each bay with blank panelling below. Beneath that is a string course with fleurons and below *that*, the spandrels of the arches are finely carved with quatrefoils and various motifs including the saffron crocus. The piers are identical with those of Great St Mary's. The low pitched roofs of nave and aisles are original (as is that of the chancel). Eleven of the nave bosses are variations on the Tudor rose and the

155

pomegranates of Catherine of Aragon. The doors to the north and south porches (both now vestries) are also original and impressive. At the west end hangs the Garter banner of Lord ('Rab') Butler of Saffron Walden (d.1982) with its rebus of three cups, giving a pleasing splash of colour. The handsome Royal Arms above the tower arch are those of Charles II.

In the north chapel, with its seven-light east window, is the plain tomb of John Leche, vicar from 1489-1521, and his sister Dame Joane Bradbury, both generous benefactors of the church when the nave was being built. The chancel screen designed by Sir Charles Nicholson was given in 1924 and the rood figures above it in 1951. The two banners in front of it are recent and in keeping with the richness of the nave.

It must be confessed that the chancel, with its poor east window and drab Victorian reredos, comes as a sad anti-climax after the splendour of the nave. The organ, originally built in 1824 and rebuilt 1971/2, has exceptional musical quality and range, but, apart from its splendid Royal Trumpet pipes, seen above the south chapel screen pointing down the nave, its housing is nothing special. Nor are the other furnishings and monuments with the sole exception of that to Thomas, Lord Audley (d.1544), the despoiler of Walden Abbey. It is of black marble, finely carved with armorials. *See also plate 13.*

SAFFRON WALDEN (B1) *United Reformed Church* Abbey Lane

The original Independent chapel or meeting house on this site was built following the Toleration Act 1690; a picture of it is in the vestry. But a congregation was gathered here *c.*1664 by Jonathan Paine, deprived of his Bishops Stortford living in 1662, and it is claimed that dissent hereabouts began even earlier with the energetic preaching of the Protestant martyr John Bradford, burnt in 1555.

A new and larger Congregational chapel was built in 1811, and later enlarged. It is of red brick, cemented in front to give a pleasing late classical facade of two storeys with a broken pediment. The impressive portico supported on four Ionic columns and the fanlights over the south doors are certainly original Georgian features, but the fenestration looks Victorian, certainly later than 1811.

Inside there is a three sided gallery supported on the usual thin cast iron Gothic piers, with an organ in an unusually handsome case at the back, and a long, dignified pulpit forming the rostrum. *See also plates 55 & 56.*

ST OSYTH (E3) *St Peter and St Paul*

The parish church lies just outside the precinct of St Osyth Priory, an Augustinian foundation of the early twelfth century with a magnificent late fifteenth-century gatehouse which is perhaps the finest example of East Anglian flushwork. Parts of the monastic structures were incorporated after the Dissolution into a splendid mansion by Lord Darcy.

It is a remarkable church with its grand early sixteenth-century nave with red brick arcades like a north German hall church, with huge aisles that completely conceal the body of the nave from the outside (illustrated above). An extraordinary combination of materials in the aisles makes a richly decorative show, of chequerwork knapped flint and septaria to the north and red brick with black diapering to the south. Enormous Perpendicular windows have decorative ferramenta supporting expanses of glass.

The earlier church, which survives to the east and west, was itself an unusual structure with an eastern transept which was partially incorporated in the new aisles. Faced in septaria, the chancel and transept remains are of thirteenth-century date; their triple-chamfered arcades are handled remarkably awkwardly, with a peculiar eight-shafted pier to the south side.

The tower, rendered stumpy by the proportions of the new nave, is fourteenth century, heavily buttressed and linked to the south aisle by a smart sixteenth-century red brick stair tower. Evidence of a twelfth-century nave, in the form of a single square respond, can be found inside on the west wall south of the tower arch.

Inside, the nave is revealed to be disconcertingly off-centre to the earlier tower and chancel, and the truncated brick responds show that a new chancel was intended, but never completed. The wide main vessel is spanned by an attenuated hammerbeam roof; the more satisfying aisle roofs are luxuriantly foliated to the north and richly moulded to the south.

Darcy family monuments distinguish the chancel: a pair of grandiose wall monuments to the first and second Lords Darcy and their wives of c.1580 with recumbent alabaster effigies. Lucy, countess of Rochford, d.1773, has a grey and white marble wall monument with sarcophagus and draped urns. In the south chapel John Darcy, d.1638, rests uncomfortably on one elbow, in the stylish manner of the day. Most of the chancel floor is taken up by a 'sheepfold' communion rail (1888) which replaced a previous seventeenth-century wooden rail of similar design.

SALCOTT cum VIRLEY (D3) *St Mary*

A plain but pleasing church in the village street, it has a handsome embattled fifteenth-century tower of the East Anglian type with knapped flint flushwork in the parapet. The nave and chancel are of the same period, much renewed after the 1884 earthquake. Especially notable is the handsome eighteenth-century pulpit with nice marquetry in its panelling. The modern organ in a well designed case is under the tower. The ivy covered ruins of Virley church are in the garden of the old rectory.

SAMPFORD, GREAT (B2) *St Michael the Archangel*

This large church 'stands pleasantly on a small eminence by the roadside' wrote Essex historian Peter Muilman in 1769. Indeed it does, and visitors enjoy its handsome Early English and Decorated architecture as well as the views across the cornfields bordering the river Pant. The deanery status that seems to explain the scale of this church in such a small village is an historical problem, for no one knows its origin. The series of seats under deep pointed canopies on both sides of the broad early fourteenth-century chancel may well have been for the clergy of the twenty-one neighbouring parishes comprising the deanery.

The present church's building history begins with the big south chapel adjoining the chancel. This is late thirteenth century (*c.*1275) and survives as the south transept of a previous church, incorporated a little clumsily into the new fourteenth-century building which is all the rest of St Michael's. This chapel has a curious east window formed of two coupled two-light windows with a sexfoil circular window above and between. The large south window is bricked up. Beneath it, inside, is a fourteenth-century empty gabled tomb recess with deep gabled niches either side. They are partly obscured by clutter as this chapel now serves as a vestry. The capitals of the piers forming the arch into this chapel from the south aisle have some lively stone carving in which can be made out oak leaf foliage and an owl, a snail, a pig and a 'green man'. Be sure not to miss it. The rest of the church, embattled west tower, nave with north and south aisles with arcades of four bays and the chancel with its great east window, was all built in the first half of the fourteenth century in the then prevailing Decorated style. The unusual absence of monuments and lack of stained glass enable us to appreciate the quality of the architecture the better. The surviving wall paintings, though faded and damaged, include a representation of the seven deadly sins in the form of a tree. There is a graffito of a nine-men's morris. The roofs are mostly original.

Visitors and congregation enter and leave the church by what some consider the finest fourteenth-century saltire braced door in Essex. It still retains its original wrought iron strapwork and studding.

Detail of a drawing of Little Sampford
by Edward Bawden.

SAMPFORD, LITTLE (B2)
St Mary the Virgin
This church is one of the most delightfully situated in Essex. It nestles below high trees in the arable environment of classic Essex 'corn and copse' country. Historically it belongs to the traditional association of church and manor. Documentary evidence shows that there was an earlier church on the site before the present building was erected in the fourteenth century.

Built of flint and pebble rubble with limestone dressings on sloping ground, it is a long, low structure with a very individual tall thin west tower of four stages, heavily buttressed and crowned with four big pinnacles and a low leaded spike. (In 1687 a visitation report noted 'There wants a weather cock upon the steeple.') The nave has a north aisle with an arcade of five bays and a clerestory of quatrefoils set in circles. The main entrance is through the north porch but there is another, of brick, on the south with a (sixteenth-century?) brick framed window to the west of it. The chancel, rebuilt in the fifteenth century, has a broad five-light east window. There is a dug-out chest, a screen and good communion rails. In the chancel there are sixteenth- and seventeenth-century monuments to Grenes and Tweedys and in the north aisle to eighteenth-century Peaks. Outside, before you leave this attractive church, notice the enigmatic head of a boy in a hat. The interesting story is in the church guide and the hat, a medieval one, in Saffron Walden museum.

159

SANDON (C3) *St Andrew*

The church, set in its beautifully kept churchyard, is next to the village green with its magnificent Spanish oak. The nave was built in the twelfth century as was the chancel, although the latter was extended in the fifteenth century. At some stage the exterior was plastered, but this was removed in 1906 to reveal the original construction with Roman brick quoins. The north aisle was added *c.*1350. The tower, diapered with St Andrew's and primatial crosses, and the attractive south porch, both brick, were added during Cardinal Wolsey's ownership of the manor of Sandon Hall. Care was taken, when in 1993 a meeting room was added, to design and build it in keeping with the church. The hammerbeam roof of the nave was replaced in 1878, only the eastern truss remaining, but the wagon roof of the chancel is original. The church's chief treasure is the late fifteenth-century carved oak pulpit on a slender 'wine-glass' pedestal. A twelfth-century pillar-piscina has been preserved. There is a seventeenth-century communion table. Monuments include a small brass to Patrick Fearne, parson 1588, and an inscription to the wife of Brian Walton, rector and editor of the Polyglot Bible. The Royal Arms are dated 1730.

SHALFORD (C2) *St Andrew*

In its lush, leafy churchyard on the fringe of the village near the upper reaches of the Blackwater, this attractive church is something of a rarity. Unlike most, it seems to have been built, all of it, in one century, the fourteenth, though not all at one time. The nave with its north and south aisles was apparently built first, *c.*1330 and the chancel a little later. Later still, probably after the Black Death (1349), the clerestory was added, the south aisle widened, and the south porch and west tower, now housing five bells, built. The clues to this architectural history are the shape of the windows and style of their tracery and the design of the nave arcades. St Andrew's retains its medieval screen, font, sedilia and piscina and some of its fourteenth-century glass in the tracery of some windows, as well as good altar rails of *c.*1700. But the two unusual features are (i) the three canopied tomb recesses, one in the chancel and one in each aisle (whose tombs were they?) and (ii) examples of nineteenth-century straw plaiting – a frontal of 1872 and the (probably contemporary) text over the chancel arch.

SHEERING (B3) *St Mary the Virgin*

This church stands on rising ground a little apart from the village. It was drastically altered internally in Victorian and Edwardian times.

The south door by which we enter is late fourteenth century and still has its original lock. The nave, to judge from the north-west quoin incorporating Roman brick, appears to be originally Norman but has been altered out of all recognition, first by the erection of the highly unusual triple chancel arch *c.*1875 and later by the addition of a north aisle in 1902.

Surprisingly in view of all this disturbance, the medieval roofs of nave and chancel remain intact. The chancel dates from c.1400 and the unbuttressed west tower is basically thirteenth century but its top stage, brick parapet and battlements c.1500. The original Norman font, badly damaged, is in the tower but the one in use is a replica. The main treasure of the church is its glass, ancient and modern. The tracery of the five-light east window frames late medieval glass depicting the Coronation of the Virgin. The west window in the tower is by the distinguished modern artist John Hayward. It depicts St Nicholas in eucharistic vestments.

SHENFIELD (B4) *St Mary*

The immediate surroundings of this church have retained their rural character, especially if approached from the north. The exterior view is dominated by the tower, with a weather-boarded belfry and shingled spire, and the south porch, both fifteenth century. The early sixteenth-century brick north porch is set in a short length of brick wall. Only the thickness of the walls of the nave reveals the thirteenth-century origins of the building. The church was thoroughly restored by W. G. Bartleet in 1863 and 1868, the chancel being extended on each occasion. When the north aisle was added in the fifteenth century, the fine and unusual timber arcade was erected and the massive timber framework carrying the bell turret was constructed; the rood beam and the tie beam at the west end of the nave are of the same date. The carvings on the late fourteenth-century font include a green man. There is a fifteenth-century stone credence table built into the east wall of the chancel. Under the tower, there are early seventeenth-century pews with panelled ends in front of the alabaster reclining monument to Elizabeth Robinson, who died in childbirth, aged 15, in 1652. There is a Royal Arms of Charles II. Glass includes work by Kempe, a window depicting Archbishop Samuel Harsnett, whose livings included Shenfield, and an armorial window (1911) with the arms of George V, Queen Mary and the diocese of St Albans.

SHOEBURY, NORTH (D5) *St Mary the Virgin*

Until very recently (1994) this church stood solitary but new housing has grown up round it, bringing new pastoral and evangelistic opportunities. It is basically all thirteenth century. Of the nave the south aisle was demolished leaving its walled-in octagonal piers and arches visible and exposed to the elements. The chancel is broad and spacious but low. The east window is a triple lancet, mostly clear glass, flanked by commandment boards and with a dignified free-standing altar with Laudian frontal. The west tower is also thirteenth century in its lower parts. The pyramidal roof in two steps was added later. There is a comical rustic south porch. The square font on five supports has *fleur de lys* in the four corners on top; an unusual motif.

SHOEBURY, SOUTH (D5) *St Andrew*

St Andrew's, a country church for most of its long life, now sits in its vast churchyard, still (1996) used for burials but soon to be closed. It is not far from the beach, but surrounded by late nineteenth- and twentieth-century housing and now approached from Church Road to its north. It retains its basically Norman nave and chancel, evident not only in its north and (more elaborate) south doorways and its impressive chancel arch with one order of columns. Later centuries have all made their mark. Both north and south of the chancel arch are pointed recesses, with another at right angles to it in the south nave wall. Were they for side altars? The nave roof is probably fourteenth century, of octagonal king posts and cambered tie beams on braces. The rather stumpy west tower is fourteenth century with eighteenth-century red brick parapets and battlements. The nave, chancel and tower are of flint rubble, ragstone and septaria. A striking feature of the interior is the modern wooden candelabra down the middle of the building. *See also plate 18.*

SOUTHEND, SOUTHCHURCH (C5) *Holy Trinity*

When the old parish of Southchurch was engulfed by expanding Southend, instead of pulling down the original little Norman church and replacing it with a new much larger one, it was decided to retain it, reduced in status to become the south aisle of a large new nave to the north designed by J. N. Comper and built in 1906, with the old Norman north doorway moved to the west end of the new nave. The new church was eventually completed with the addition of a spacious, light and dignified new chancel, vaguely Gothic in style and designed this time by F. C. Eden, in 1932. A new east window, the Works of the Lord, was added in 1956. The result of all this, at least as seen from the A.13 to the north, is not entirely satisfactory. It looks what it is, a hotch-potch, but in this way historical continuity was secured at the cost of architectural consistency. Three features of the old church survive *in situ*, the plain Norman south doorway, the fifteenth-century timber belfry on its eight posts, and, perhaps the most interesting, a tomb recess and Easter sepulchre in the (original) north chancel wall.

SOUTHMINSTER (D4) *St Leonard*

The big, ungainly parish church of this large village or small town is, by any reckoning, a strange building with a tangled history, and to write about it freshly and intelligibly is a challenge! Others, notably Pevsner and Scarfe (both of whom should be read), have rather unkindly made merry with it: '... largish, odd and aesthetically unsatisfactory; its nave has the shape of an early C19 Methodist chapel' ... 'covered by plaster rib vaults of an entirely unconvincing weight, a regrettable mistake...' Thus Pevsner. Scarfe writes: 'interior a great let-down or rather blow-up'.

In order to comprehend what has happened here, it would be as well to resist the temptation to dive in through the great north porch (its finest feature) and first to go round the tower to contemplate the *south* side of the nave. First notice the Norman south doorway with its consecration crosses (?) on the left hand jamb. Observe, too, that there are three 'layers' of building here, all with different, contrasting, materials. The original building has twice been heightened, first in flint with four clerestory windows (notice the eighteenth-century blue sundial in their midst). Then, above that, in red brick. Now return to the north side to see the same three levels there, except that there the brick has been cemented. Then spend a little time to admire the stately fifteenth-century two-storey porch with its three richly canopied niches over the entrance, its powerful diagonal buttresses, and its beautiful star shaped tierceron vault with carved bosses, all a great rarity in Essex (cf. Chelmsford Cathedral and Thaxted). There are steps leading up to the upper room with an original door at the bottom, inside.

Now see what a wide, tall nave you are in and glance up to the plaster vault decried by Pevsner. The fifteenth-century font is rather the worse for wear. Then walk east to note the two large transepts, north and south. They were added in 1818/19 when the church was much extended eastwards. The energetic vicar who achieved this was Alexander Scott, vicar 1803-1840, who had been chaplain to Lord Nelson at Trafalgar when the great admiral died in his arms. The church possesses the so-called Nelson Relics (see the guide leaflet for details) thought to have been collected and left by Scott. The chancel and three-sided sanctuary date from this time, though their furnishings are Victorian, and constitute a major anticlimax.

To return westwards, the tower with its massive south-west buttress propping it up is in its upper stages fourteenth century but looks, and is, unstable and unfinished.

When the church was visited in May 1996, all its eastern parts were in scaffolding up to the ceiling and two valiant lay *volunteers* were engaged on redecorating the interior, a mammoth task which had already taken them three months of cold weather. Heroic. May their efforts be richly rewarded. But something should be done about the east end.

SPRINGFIELD (C3) *All Saints*

The church stands in an attractive rural setting near the green. The nave is Norman with Roman brick reused for quoins and coursing. The early fourteenth-century chancel has two of the windows carried down below a transom to form 'low-side' windows; the north doorway has an early sixteenth-century wooden door. The west part of the tower was rebuilt in brick in 1586; the present brick stair turret, arrangement of the buttresses and lower windows date from the restoration by Chancellor in 1881. The church's chief treasure is the beautiful mid thirteenth-century font, richly carved with stiff-leaf foliage and flowers, and perhaps the best in Essex. The chancel, which is approached through a restored fifteenth-century screen, has a contemporary piscina and some re-set sixteenth- and seventeenth-century glass. There are seventeenth-century paintings of Moses and Aaron and an attractive Royal Arms of 1791. A replica of the brass of Thomas Coggeshall, in armour, 1421, is housed in a recent extension.

STAMBOURNE (C1) *St Peter and St Thomas*
The massive, unbuttressed Norman west tower dominates as the church is approached from the road. It is of rubble with some freestone on the west elevation near the top, and incorporates Roman brick in windows (as in similar Great Tey), and, also like that tower, was given an embattled parapet in the fifteenth/sixteenth century. The tower arch has some decoration on north abacus. The church itself, nave, three bay north aisle, chancel and north chancel chapel, is fifteenth century and early sixteenth century (porch). This rebuilding is largely, if not all, due to the munificence of the MacWilliam family, whose arms are finely carved in stone in the arch of the north chancel chapel, and blazoned in the five-light east window, which, in opposite corners, depicts a MacWilliam husband and wife kneeling, *c*.1530. There are handsome double canopied niches in the splays of two other windows. On the north side dado of the good but restored chancel screen are four well preserved painted figures – left to right, a decapitated saint (Denys?) holding his mitred head in his hands, St George, St Edmund and a king, probably Edward the Confessor, with orb and sceptre. A fifteenth-century font, large chest and good Royal Arms (George III) are also to be noted.

STAMBRIDGE, GREAT (C4) *St Mary and All Saints*
The church stands away from the village above the river Roach. There is pre-Conquest work in the north wall of the nave and chancel, between the north-west corner of the nave and the clergy vestry. The south aisle was added *c*.1300 and the chancel rebuilt and extended in the fourteenth century. The tower and the north porch were added in the fifteenth century. The porch has a late fifteenth-century crown post roof. The brick parapet of the tower was added during the Napoleonic war. The interior was extensively restored in 1881, but contains a fourteenth-century piscina with a corbelled-out basin resting on a man's head and a late fifteenth-century font with an octagonal bowl with quatrefoils containing flowers and shields. There are a number of interesting windows: the Rankin window by Henry Holiday; one commemorating the founders of the Ratcliff Settlement in East London; a small window from Little Stambridge church (demolished 1891); the Winthrop window, made at Whitefriars and dedicated in 1971. John Winthrop (1588-1649), governor of Massachusetts

and founder of Boston, was married at Great Stambridge in 1605 by the Puritan rector, Ezekiel Culverwell, whose teaching had a lasting influence on him.

STANFORD LE HOPE (B5) *St Margaret*

At first sight this sizeable church is a confusing jumble of assorted periods and styles, beginning with the most prominent, both Victorian. The north-east tower, designed by architect-parson Ernest Geldart, of Little Braxted (whose work is often met with in Essex), and modelled on that of St Mary's, Prittlewell, was built in 1883. Likewise the vestries which mask the former west front of an originally Norman nave. The north nave arcade of alternate circular and octagonal piers is thirteenth-century Early English, and the corresponding south arcade a century later. The chancel too, in which are fine sedilia and, facing them, a typically fourteenth-century ogee arched recess containing a fifteenth-century tomb chest, Decorated. The screen into the south chapel is of *c.*1400 as is the chapel itself. The font is of Purbeck marble, dating from *c.*1250. There are notable Fetherstone and other mural tablets. In the churchyard is the gruesome tomb of Thomas Adams, who in 1765 'obeyed the awful summons with true Christian temper'.

STANFORD RIVERS (B4) *St Margaret*

A pleasant avenue of limes leads up to the west door of this attractive church set in unspoilt green-belt country. The nave is twelfth century, with small round-headed slit windows north, west and south. The timber belfry with leaded spire is built on the usual four posts with intersecting braces. There is an early thirteenth-century octagonal font of Barnack stone supported by colonettes, and with shallow pointed arches on each face. Behind it is a pleasing twentieth-century mural of a nativity scene in front of this church. The chancel is fourteenth century (Decorated) with later clerestory windows. There are some brasses under the altar and some medieval oak benches.

STANSTEAD MOUNTFITCHET (B2) *St John the Evangelist*

Because the old church, St Mary's (see below), was dilapidated and so far from this little town, St John's was built centrally as a chapel of ease in 1889. It became the parish church later, when St Mary's was declared redundant and taken over by the Redundant Churches Fund, now the Churches Conservation Trust. St John's is interesting as an early, conservative work by W. D. Caroe, a pupil of J. L. Pearson, an enthusiast for Arts and Crafts and the founder of an architectural dynasty. It is essentially an essay in Perpendicular in (very) red brick from nearby Birchanger, with limestone dressings and much competent stone carving – all of it by Nathaniel Hitch. It consists of nave with south aisle and short south transept, and chancel; and there is a stone balcony at the back, with four centred arches much in evidence. The showpiece is the slightly later (1895) south tower through which the church is entered. At the top, though not high, it is a coruscation of turrets, battlements and pinnacles, very effective. It is a pity it is not more prominent on the Stanstead skyline. *See also plate 40.*

STANSTEAD MOUNTFITCHET (B2) *St Mary* Old Church
If you enjoy Norman ebullience and seventeenth-century monuments, St Mary's is for you: not recommended otherwise. It is a long way to fetch, and return, the key. And in any case don't be put off by its unattractive nineteenth-century flinty exterior as approached from the road. Two savage nineteenth-century 'restorations' have left it practically rebuilt. Apart from the 1692 brick tower (and that was Gothicised) only the strong Norman features were retained intact: the fine south doorway with its two orders, tympanum and zigzag ornamentation and an impressive chancel area. There is also a large font, said by Pevsner to be *c.*1300: it looks earlier. There are two outstanding Jacobean monuments. That to Hester Salusbury, d.1614, is by the great Epiphanius Evesham (cf. his Lord Rich at Felsted). Hester is shown recumbent 'dressed and ready for heaven' (Scarfe) in high hat, ruff and farthingale. Her father, Sir Thomas Middleton, d.1631, Lord Mayor of London, reclines grandly in a high canopied tomb in the sanctuary. If you do go, do notice the lovely bishop's chair with (later?) mitre, of *c.*1730 in the chancel, also the nice communion rails. *See also plate 44.*

STEBBING (B2) *St Mary the Virgin*
This splendid church stands proud and high amid a cluster of old houses at the south end of the village. Apart from its fifteenth-century (Perpendicular) nave roof and clerestory it is all of one period, the apogee of the Decorated style *c.*1350 or a little earlier. The characteristics of this rich and lively style can be studied and enjoyed here and at Lawford better than anywhere else in Essex, especially the sheer quality of the stonework in the five-bay arcades, the screen, sedilia and graceful window tracery. The west tower, heavily buttressed, is surmounted by a short, recessed, leaded spire. The south porch, picturesquely topped with Tudor brick, has unusual quatrefoil side windows. Once inside, we are struck by the light spaciousness of the wide nave and its north and south aisles. Stop to admire the clustered piers and observe the vigorous carving of the very individual headstops. The north aisle has the remains of its medieval reredos. Then pause to take in the chief glory of this fine church, its stone rood screen, its three arches with their intricate tracery, spanning the wide chancel arch. There is a slightly later one at nearby Great Bardfield (obviously an attempt to go one better) as well as plainer examples of this extremely rare

Stebbing's screen photographed by Edwin Smith.

feature at Bramford, Suffolk (earlier) and Bottisham, Cambs. (later). This screen, dismantled at the Reformation, was cleverly reconstructed from its original, surviving, components in 1884, apart, of course, from its central figures – the empty cross looks, and is, Victorian. Study the details from both sides. Then go into the large, wide, light chancel, noting especially the big east window, the contemporary sedilia and piscina and the excellent Georgian communion rails. There is a large brass of a lady and a particularly fine oak chest.

STIFFORD (B5) *St Mary*
Uncomfortably close to the A.13 but in a village street with a surprising number of thatched cottages stands this church with its rather squat west tower surmounted by a shingled broach spire. The church is built mainly of flint, though a distinctive dark rusty sandstone is used for quoins in the south wall. The round-arched north doorway reveals the nave at least to be Norman. The decorative ironwork on the door is thirteenth century. South of the chancel was added a chapel which for Essex is an unusually well preserved example of the Early English style. The elegant arcade between nave and aisle has moulded responds which terminate in carved heads, that to the east preserving colouring which may be original. The chancel was rebuilt and probably extended eastwards in the fourteenth century. There is much of interest in the church. The font, supported on slender columns, is of *c.*1300. The nave roof has a short stubby crown post with very thick braces. There is a good collection of fourteenth-century brasses on the east wall of the chapel. The pulpit is dated 1611, and the church chest 1713. An old stair with solid oak treads rises to the upper stages of the tower. In the aisle there are two notable examples of stained glass: the so-called 'Healing Window' by Henry Holliday, restored after war damage; and the west window (1929) by Leonard Walker in his very distinctive style.

STISTED (C2) *All Saints*
(Pronounced with a long i – Sty-sted.) Quite a large church, much altered in early Victorian times, with a south east tower and shingled broach spire built in 1844. It turns out to be surprisingly rewarding. It was an archbishop's peculiar directly subordinate to Canterbury under the jurisdiction of the dean of neighbouring Bocking. It stands by itself, a little aloof, at one end of its picturesque village, set in lovely country. Its rector for much of the nineteenth century was E. M. Forster's grandfather, Charles (rector 1838-71).

The nave with its wide aisles and arcades of five bays (or in fact of three with narrow arches each end), is basically Norman, late twelfth century. The capitals of the easternmost piers on both sides deserve careful scrutiny with their lively carving of grotesque heads etc: the rest are plain.

The chancel is a little later, Early English, with, in the east wall, *five* (renewed) stepped lancets. It is here that the excitement of Stisted begins. For these five lancets, and three more in the north and south chancel walls, are filled with most brilliant and wonderful Flemish glass of the sixteenth and seventeenth centuries, some twenty-five individual panels in all. They were brought from a monastery at Steinfeld in the Rhineland near Aachen by the enlightened Victorian squire Onley Savill-Onley of Stisted Hall. There is more of this valuable collection in the Victoria and Albert Museum. It is a great treasure. There are some interesting monuments and a handsome early Georgian pulpit.

STOCK (B4) *All Saints*

The church stands behind a small green at one end of the village; the large churchyard seems strangely bare, having been cleared of most of its headstones in the 1960s. The Garden of Remembrance (1953) is sited where a landmine fell in 1940, causing severe damage to the nave roof and walls. The Norman origin of the building is suggested by the thickness of the south and west walls. The tower, with its dark vertical weather-boarding, pierced by tracery, and contrasting white horizontal boarding above, topped by a spire, makes a striking first impression. Try to view the interior with its impressive four vertical posts, which may be late fourteenth century, and central green man boss. The north aisle has an interesting crown post roof, *c.*1400. The south porch, although considerably restored, also has a crown post roof. The chancel was rebuilt in 1848; the reordering by Laurence King was completed in 1981. The north chapel, built in 1904, was originally the organ chamber. The brass to Richard Twedye (1574), in armour, is set in a former altar stone with consecration crosses; he founded the almshouses across the road. The altar rails (1774; gates 1949) were the gift of the Revd William Unwin (rector, 1769-87), the friend of William Cowper and William Wilberforce. The glass in the chancel was designed by Reginald Bell (1948-50); the windows in the nave by Farrer Bell (1959) have jewel bright colours. The figures of Christ, the Virgin Mary and St John, formerly on the rood, carved in limewood by Gwynneth Holt (1955), have been moved to the north aisle (1995). Despite all these changes, this church retains a sense of serenity and devotion.

STOCK (B4) *Our Lady of Mount Carmel* Roman Catholic

This church near the residence of the bishop of Brentwood was created out of a Victorian school. It presents a clever and imaginative re-use of a redundant building. The conversion was done with flair and taste. This was, incidentally, the first Roman Catholic church to receive a grant from the Friends of Essex Churches.

STONDON MASSEY (B4) *St Peter and St Paul*

The Saxons had a clearing in the forest about one mile south-east of the ford across the river Roding on a hill with gravel subsoil which they called Stondon 'stone hill'. The name Massey comes from Serlo de Marci, the first Norman lord of the manor whose house would have been at the site of Stondon Hall near the church. It was probably he who built the church about 1100. The building is still a good example of a small Norman church. The nave walls stand three feet thick, with high slit windows and a tall south doorway made of squared tufa stone and no keystone; in the wall adjoining the doorway there is a slot six feet deep for a beam to bar the door. The original masonry can be seen outside in the west wall; it is made of flints laid to courses, some laid herringbone-wise, with occasional courses of Roman tiles, some of which have been used to form a zigzag pattern in the gable. Originally the chancel terminated in an apse, the foundations of which were seen in the nineteenth century. The point at which the apse began corresponds with a crack in the south wall of the chancel which is visible outside. The square-ended chancel was built in the fifteenth century.

The timber belfry with curved bracing supporting a shingled spire has been tree-ring dated to 1408. The nave has a crown post roof which is probably of much the same date. The simple chancel screen dates from the end of the fifteenth century. There are two good brasses of 1570 and 1573, and an excellent Jacobean pulpit and reading desk with the date 1630 carved on the desk. A monument to William Byrd, one of the greatest of English composers, was erected in 1923. He lived in Stondon Place for thirty-one years until his death in 1623. He asked to be buried in Stondon, but no memorial was raised then, perhaps because he was a Roman Catholic and feelings ran high at that time. A north chapel was built in 1873 as a memorial to Philip Herman Meyer, a local benefactor.

STRATFORD (A5) *St John the Evangelist*

With the population of West Ham (which then included the hamlet of Stratford) rising dramatically in the early nineteenth century, the local church authorities found it essential to build a new church right in the centre of Stratford. By 1833 the necessary £18,000 had been raised, and without great difficulty; a prime site was chosen on the unfenced village green, and Edward Blore, a fashionable architect who had worked on Westminster Abbey and Buckingham Palace, was commissioned to design St John's. He chose the Early English style and the use of yellow brick to build a church with a broad nave and aisles, and a shallow chancel, with seating for 900. There was to be an extensive graveyard and roomy vaults beneath the church: the fee for an individual burial in a vault was fixed at £105 and there was no shortage of takers! There were plenty of well-to-do city magnates in the parish. The crowning glory was the south-west tower and spire with stone pinnacles. The interior with its arcades of clustered columns is impressively spacious but a little colourless and bleak.

Gerard Manley Hopkins, the Jesuit poet and mystic, was baptised here, in 1844. The tall Gothic Martyrs' Memorial was later erected on the spot outside the west door where in 1556 eighteen Protestants were burnt at the stake. The chancel was lengthened and provided with a five-light east window in 1884. During the 1940-41 blitz when the East End was heavily bombed night after night, the crypt was used as an air-raid shelter. The only serious damage to the church was the destruction of the east window, which was replaced in 1955 with a fine depiction of the Crucifixion with the Risen Christ above, by Gerald Smith. After the war, with so many homes destroyed, the population, and with it the congregations, dropped as dramatically as they had risen a century earlier. But St John's remains a focal point in Stratford and congregations, often multi-racial, are on the increase.

STRETHALL (A1) *St Mary the Virgin*
On the extreme north-west tip of Essex in open, windswept, undulating country near an old Roman military road, lies this little Saxon church, almost in a farmyard. At least the nave is Saxon as we can see from the typical long and short quoins (corner stones) at the south-west corner, and from the chancel arch with its crudely moulded three strips running round the arch and down both sides to the floor. Both these features are paralleled in the Saxon tower of St Benet's, Cambridge, not so far away. The chancel probably dates from *c*.1050, i.e. just a few years before the Conquest. The square unbuttressed west tower is in three stages and is said to be of the fourteenth century though the lowest stage looks much earlier. Inside it forms the baptistery with a Norman twelfth-century font in it. The chancel is mostly fifteenth century and contains the handsome canopied tomb of John Gardyner, d.1515. There are two medieval bells in the tower, one, the treble, cast by William Revel about 1350, an early date. The roof of the nave is probably fifteenth century; and there are some attractively carved old corbels. Finally a well preserved brass of a priest in academical dress, Thomas Abbott, rector, d.1539.

STURMER (B1) *St Mary*
Up a semi-private drive to Sturmer Hall, well out of sight of the village, this little church has a Norman nave and chancel, though with later windows, fifteenth-century tower and Tudor brick south porch. From the blocked north doorway the nave is dated by Pevsner eleventh century, possibly pre-1066, but the remarkable Norman south doorway with its crudely carved tympanum (sun and moon?) and its two weird heads projecting at the top on either side of the door is, he says, slightly later, i.e.

The two heads on the Norman south doorway at Sturmer.

twelfth century. Presumably the original main entrance was on the north and a century later it was decided to make a new one on the south. Another feature is that the nave has an unusual double hammerbeam roof, the spandrels with pierced, fretwork-like, tracery. The organ is on a twentieth-century west gallery. Finally, Leofsunu, the Sturmer warrior who fought in the Battle of Maldon, 991, is commemorated in the nave a thousand years after his valiant death.

SUTTON with SHOPLAND (C4) *All Saints*
Sutton is still a country parish on the outskirts of Rochford. Its church is an unpretentious building of ragstone rubble, basically Norman and consisting of nave and chancel with a typically Essex timber belfry on eight posts and a south porch bearing the date 1633. The main entrance is through a particularly fine doorway of three orders of columns, partly restored in 1869 but evidently thirteenth century, Early English. The glory of the church, however, is the equally fine Norman chancel arch. There are Norman windows high up on both sides of the nave, and others, later, of different periods. On the chancel north wall is a handsome monument to Chester Moor Hall, Bencher of the Inner Temple, d.1771, of Sutton Hall, the inventor of the achromatic lens telescope. The epitaph describes him as a 'judicious Lawyer, an able Mathematician, a polite Scholar, a sincere Friend and a Magistrate of the strictest Integrity'.

From Shopland church, demolished 1958 when the parish was merged with Sutton, is a damaged military brass of Thomas Stapel, king's armourer, d.1371.

The Norman chancel arch at Sutton.

TAKELEY (B2) *Holy Trinity*

This church shyly hides itself away far from the straggly village, down a lane off the A.120. It is quite large. The chancel is the oldest part, thirteenth century, the nave and south aisle with its arcade of octagonal piers seems fourteenth century while the low embattled west tower and flint faced south porch are fifteenth century. There has been much restoration and the fittings are mostly, if not all, Victorian or later – with one famous exception. It is what most visitors go to admire, the tall, elegant, much crocketted fifteenth-century font cover. It has been much, but well, restored and compares with those at Fingringhoe and Thaxted in Essex and the still more magnificent Suffolk examples at Ufford, Worlingworth and Sudbury St Gregory, all of the same period.

TENDRING (E2) *St Edmund*

The nave and chancel are basically thirteenth century and the impressive timber north porch, by which we enter, fourteenth (illustrated overleaf). The rest, including the west tower and spire, erected 1876, is mostly Victorian *with one major exception* – 'the extremely unusual hammerbeam roof truss close to the west end' (Pevsner). Let him, the expert, describe it and explain its significance: 'It stands just above the north and south doorways, and so the ingenious carpenter framed these by posts, then connected them by a gable, and from these gables started his braces for the hammerbeam. The tracery detail of the gables is clearly of the fourteenth century, and not too late in the century either, and thus this truss, as far as one can say, is earlier than the hammerbeam roof of Westminster Hall, in

173

The wooden porch at Tendring.

the text books still called the earliest in existence ...' (Pevsner, *Essex*, 2nd edn, p. 378).

TERLING (C3) *All Saints*

In the centre of its attractive village, overlooking the large sloping green with, beyond and out of sight, Terling Place, seat of the Strutts, Lords Rayleigh, whose monuments are in the chancel and graves in the far south-east corner of the churchyard. The chancel is thirteenth century. The nave has been much rebuilt and enlarged with north and south aisles with four bay arcades. The thirteenth-century font is of Purbeck marble. There are three sixteenth-century Rochester family brasses, two Elizabethan now fixed to the east wall of the south aisle, the third a large sixteenth-century knight and wife. A replica of Thorvaldsen's 'Come unto Me' statue of Christ is the centrepiece of the modern reredos. But the church's most striking feature is the elegant classical west tower of diapered red brick and Portland stone quoins, dressings and string courses. An inscription dates it 1732. The mason was Anthony Goud, who was living in Springfield at the time. His handsome tower, 'strongly reminiscent of New England' (Scarfe, *Shell Guide*), is crowned with a somewhat incongruous rustic shingled spire.

TERLING (C3) *United Reformed Church*

Facing the parish church across the green this agreeable two storeyed building of red brick with blue diapering is said by Pevsner and Scarfe to be late seventeenth century and certainly looks it. Christopher Stell, however, the leading authority on chapels, maintains that it was built in 1752, in which case, if he is right, it was distinctly old-fashioned! The gabled brick porch, added 1895, is aesthetically regrettable. The interior was drastically re-arranged at the same time, but still includes a handsome chandelier from its early days.

TEY, GREAT (C2) *St Barnabas*

The visitor may well wonder why in the twelfth century such a grand church was built for what must have been, and still is, a small village. Be that as it may, in 1829 the parish was faced with a dilapidated over-large church and decided to reduce it to more suitable dimensions instead of attempting to repair the whole structure. A false economy as it turned out, since the demolition of the Norman nave and its replacement by a truncated appendage west of the crossing tower cost double the estimated cost of repairs. The central tower, built *c.*1160, with its much later embattled parapet, is of four stages – the second with two groups of three arches on each face, the third with two large windows and the top stage with three bell openings, the middle one with a colonette, most of them with Roman brick dressings, like the quoins. The combination of these with flint rubble and ironstone gives it a pleasing warm texture. It holds a peal of

The tower at Terling.

eight bells. Inside, plain Norman arches support the tower east and west, complemented by fourteenth-century arches north and south, for the fine light chancel and two small transepts were rebuilt in the fourteenth century and exhibit typical delicate Decorated window tracery, piscina and sedilia. In 1829 a west gallery was inserted in the rump; on its front the arms of the reigning monarch, George IV. A handsome lately restored escutcheon of Charles II is in the south vestibule. The church is beautifully kept. *See also plate 4.*

TEY, LITTLE (C2) *St James the Less*

This unassuming little Norman church, a single cell building ending in an apse and with a simple white painted bellcote with slated pyramid roof, stands at the end of a quiet country lane as it has done for nine centuries. It has several Norman windows and a south doorway with a tympanum carved with Norman lozenge shaped diapering. The most noticeable feature of the exterior is that the gable roof over the apse overhangs clumsily. It has been pointed out to the writer that the cause of this is that the building was originally thatched. The furnishing of the interior is plain, Victorian. As this goes to press, the church is full of scaffolding to enable expert conservators to uncover exciting medieval wall paintings. Those beginning to emerge are a Last Supper, the Three Living and the Three Dead and (probably) a St Christopher, all on the north wall.

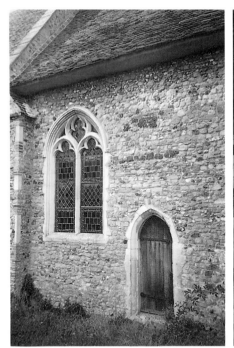

Marks Tey: the texture of the puddingstone wall and the wooden font.

TEY, MARKS (C2) *St Andrew*

At the end of a quiet lane away from the noisy and traffic-infested main road village. Unforgettable at first sight are the two top stages of the west tower. Destroyed in the Civil War siege of Colchester, 1648, the upper part of the tower was replaced in oak with *vertical* weather-boarding including the battlements. It is capped by a short shingled spire. The base of the tower and the rest of the fabric, Norman nave and fourteenth-century chancel, displays 'a rich mixture of Roman brick and iron-bound, rust-coloured conglomerate' (Scarfe). There is a sixteenth-century timber porch and, a great surprise: a fifteenth-century font, beautifully carved in *oak*.

THAXTED (B2) *St John the Baptist, Our Lady and St Laurence*

Thaxted church is surely the best known and most memorable in Essex. Approached from the south, the 181 feet high Northamptonshire style spire can be seen across the fields from miles away, dominating the little town huddling beneath it, and, as one draws nearer, presiding unforgettably over the graceful Guildhall of the Cutlers, whose medieval prosperity helped to build it. From the north it comes as a complete surprise as one rounds the bend at the top of what Alec Clifton-Taylor described as one of the prettiest streets in England.

The impact of the interior is even more stunning, particularly as most visitors have to stoop to enter the small wicket door in the richly handsome north porch (illustrated, right). Immediately apparent are those qualities for which Thaxted church is most famous: the dramatic sense of space and light. These are due to the whiteness of all available walls and columns, the vast size of the windows (largely free from stained glass although what there is is good and well worth studying, especially the fifteenth-century glass in the north chancel aisle and south transept and Kempe's deeply satisfying early twentieth-century east window), the absence of heavy woodwork (no pews!) and above all the immense

width of the aisles, both of which are several feet wider than the great central nave, with its wonderful clerestory.

Thaxted church was begun in the mid fourteenth century with the nave arcades and finished 170 years later c.1510. The chancel arcades with their unusual pierced spandrels are particularly noteworthy. The great high pulpit with its sounding board is of c.1680. The Georgians added a few good fittings and carried out essential repairs after severe storm damage to the tower, spire and both transepts. The Victorians fortunately left Thaxted well alone and much of what little harm they did has been unpicked. The great renewal of the church occurred under Conrad Noel, a Christian socialist and much loved but controversial priest appointed vicar by Lady Warwick in 1910, who reigned here until 1942. He and his followers filled the church with beautiful things, most famous of which is the glorious iron 'stella' (candelabrum) designed by the Arts and Crafts architect Randall Wells. It hangs in the central crossing, focal point of the entire church.

Observant visitors will find much to repay their attention: the carving of St Catherine at her wheel high up on a pier near the chapel which bore her name; the hammer and sickle on a twentieth-century oak chest; the stone reredos in the north transept; the famous Lincoln organ in that transept, on which Gustav Holst played (and is said to have composed the hymn tune 'Thaxted'); and the equally impressive choir organ at the west end under the tower, with its beautiful late eighteenth-century case and pipework by G. P. England.

The font is late fifteenth century and has a magnificently carved cover with folding doors so that it is permanently fixed in position and not hoisted aloft for baptisms. The roofs are all original. That of the south aisle is rich with bosses, carved with symbols and heraldic emblems which tell of the patronage and manorial history of Thaxted in the fifteenth century when it was a kind of medieval Sheffield, famous for its cutlery.

Because Thaxted in later centuries was never a rich and flourishing place, apart from monumental brasses and beautifully engraved ledger slabs in the chancel, the church is largely devoid of monuments; of those that are in the church, the one to seek out is the bronze head of Conrad Noel. It is by Gertrude Hermes. *See also plate 12 and illustration on page 8.*

THEYDON GARNON (A4) *All Saints*

This delightful church stands on a hill overlooking the noisy intersection of the M.11 and the M.25. If ever there was a contrast this is it. The best approach is south from Epping through Theydon Bois over the M.11 and take the lane about ½ mile on the left. Here you will find the church in a particularly well kept churchyard. The exterior has several noteworthy features. First the tower – a massive battlemented structure of red brick actually dated 1520. Secondly the north aisle of 1644, again in red brick. Thirdly the two dormer windows in the south roof of the nave and finally the tiny window high up in the east wall above the four-light east window. What was its purpose? On entering the church one is struck by the loving care lavished on its maintenance. Note the massive roof structures, no doubt oak from the nearby forest. The north aisle has a fine five bay *timber* arcade, of 1644, and a handsome panelled vaulted ceiling, five good hatchments and the Arms of George III. There is an eighteenth-century two-decker pulpit with sounding board, attached reading desk and elegant staircase, and good communion rails with twisted balusters, 1683. Brasses include one to Wm. Kirkeby, rector, d.1458 and there are several eighteenth-century mural monuments to members of the Archer family.

THEYDON MOUNT (B4) *St Michael the Archangel*

Rebuilt in whole or in part 1611/14 after a disastrous lightning strike, this charming little hillside church in unspoilt green-belt country so near London became almost a private chapel/mausoleum of the Smith/Smyth family of the great Elizabethan mansion of Hill Hall nearby, itself severely damaged by fire a few years ago. There is much to see. First, the exterior, all of warm red brick, nave, chancel, west tower with low spire, and Dutch

looking tower staircase and south porch. Inside, notice first the tiny font by
the church door, a black marble basin on a pillar with a carved face above it
– reputedly brought back from Italy in the seventeenth century by a Smith.
There are no fewer than nine Smith hatchments and many tombs of that
illustrious family, including four splendid ones with effigies in the chancel,
all of the sixteenth and seventeenth centuries, also a Smith helm and
surcoat high up on the south side. The truly great Sir Thomas Smith
1513-77, scholar, jurist, statesman, diplomat and author, lies to the north of
the pleasant (1957) altar and reredos and opposite his nephew Sir William
(d.1626) who rebuilt the church and completed the Hall, with his wife
Bridget and their three sons and four daughters. Part of the seventeenth-
century reredos flanks the striking east window of 1918 by de Gleyn,
depicting the Archangel Michael between St George and Joan of Arc. The
west window has some good sixteenth- and seventeenth-century armorial
glass. Finally, a great rarity, up in the nave roof is a maiden's garland,
coronal or crant. It was an old custom thus to commemorate a girl betrothed
to be married who had died before the wedding.

THORPE LE SOKEN (E2) *St Michael*
Thorpe, with its neighbours Kirby and Walton, constituted the ancient
soken or independent jurisdiction of the Dean and Chapter of St Paul's,
who owned extensive lands hereabouts from very early times.

In its large arboreal churchyard off the High Street, the church is
overshadowed by its mighty Tudor red brick tower with blue diapering,
diagonal buttresses, and stepped battlements. The church below was
largely rebuilt, apart from the north aisle (which retains its original roof), by
W. White in 1876. The dominant note of the walls is buff coloured septaria
and for dressings he used red sandstone. The three-light windows of the
north aisle have most unusual tracery.

The not unsatisfactory Victorian Gothic interior, with its five-bay
arcades north and south, has real dignity. White incorporated two features
of the medieval church. The fine fifteenth-century octagonal font with
heraldic shields on each face stands on a Norman plinth which looks like
the base of a cylindrical pier. And there is a battered stone recumbent
effigy of a knight, traditionally associated with Landermere, the ancient
wharf on Hamford Water, in Thorpe parish. He lies under a (rebuilt) early
fourteenth-century canopy on the south side of the chancel.

The modern feature of the church is the extremely handsome west
gallery under the tower with its elegant access staircase. Designed by
Jeffrey Couzens, it was built in limed oak by Nick Mills of St Osyth and
dedicated in 1991. It houses a well displayed permanent exhibition of
absorbing interest, illustrating every aspect, personal, social, civil and
ecclesiastical, of Thorpe's history. In 1991 it deservedly won an award from

the Augustine Courtauld Trust under the auspices of Essex's Rural Community Council.

On the opposite side of the street from the church, modestly hiding behind a house, is an eighteenth-century weather-boarded Baptist chapel.

THORRINGTON (D3) *St Mary Magdalen*

Standing in a farmyard well away from the village, this isolated church is chiefly notable for its fine embattled west tower of knapped flint, less ambitious but otherwise akin to that of nearby Brightlingsea, and totally East Anglian. It can actually be dated. A brass on its floor tells us that it is the benefaction of John and Margery Deth *c.*1480. The south porch is fourteenth century; flint and septaria with old red tiles most unusually serving as dressings to quoins and openings.

THURROCK, GRAYS (B5) *St Peter and St Paul*

Grays is no beauty spot, and its principal church, while incorporating bits and pieces of the original structure, was practically rebuilt in 1846 – not a good period. Enlargement in 1867 involved the extension of the nave to its present length and the addition of a north aisle. The plain east and west crossing arches are basically twelfth century.

But what lends distinction to an otherwise, frankly, dull church is the series of four large stained glass windows by Philippa Heskett, inserted in the south and west walls of the nave between 1973 and 1980. While her great five-light west window, Christ in Glory, is outstanding, in all four, complex Biblical themes are handled with assurance and uncommon insight with the use of harmonious colour and good (perhaps in some cases overcrowded) design. Each one deserves unhurried attention. Together they afford a refreshing modern variant to hackneyed iconography.

THURROCK, WEST (B5) *St Clement*

This church with its striking black and white striped tower lies in the shadow of the huge Proctor and Gamble soap and detergent factory, near the north bank of the Thames. Redundant since 1977, its future has been secured through the generous intervention of its multi-national neighbour which in 1987 assumed responsibility for the church as part of its 150th anniversary celebrations. St Clement's, of course, has a very much longer history. Excavations have shown that the twelfth-century church had a circular nave, the foundations of which are visible at the base of the fifteenth-century tower. Round churches were built in imitation of the church of the Holy Sepulchre at Jerusalem and often belonged to the Templars or the Hospitallers, though there is no known connection with either at West Thurrock.

180

To the east of the round nave, there was a rectangular chancel. This eventually became the nave and a new chancel was built adjoining it, the old round nave probably being used as a baptistery. As it is today, the church is substantially thirteenth century in form, with modern repairs and restoration. Since 1987, the roof has been repaired, unsightly modern fixtures removed and the interior redecorated and re-equipped for occasional services with a dignified altar, and, behind it on a platform under the east window, an organ made by the celebrated organ builder Hugh Russell in 1806 for St Runwald's, Colchester. After that church's demolition in 1878, it went to Pattiswick church, now a house, ending up here, where it looks and sounds fine! The church is also used for community purposes as a meeting place and conference centre. It was, incidentally, the scene of the funeral in the successful film *Four Weddings and A Funeral* (1993). But redundancy and subsequent vandalism has cost the church most of its original fittings, including some good brasses, of which, however, replicas are in the north aisle. Fortunate survivals are the (damaged) alabaster effigies of Sir Christopher Holford (d.1608) and his wife in the north chapel, several medieval tiles, and a few fragments of medieval glass. The churchyard is managed to encourage and preserve its wildlife, and is home to the rare Lesser Calamint.

Arrangements to visit must be made with Proctor and Gamble. *See colour picture on the back cover.*

TILBURY JUXTA CLARE (C1) *St Margaret*

Exceedingly picturesque in its rustic setting in the fields, away from the tiny village, but near Tilbury Hall, this remote church is best seen just before harvest. Its sylvan churchyard is faithfully delineated in Francesca Greenoak and Clare Roberts' delightful *God's Acre: the Flowers and Animals of the Parish Churchyard* (Orbis, 1985). Its diapered Tudor brick tower was the gift of Elizabeth, countess of Oxford (of Castle Hedingham) in 1519. The church itself, nave, chancel and south porch, is earlier than seems to be suggested by its Perpendicular windows. Not only is there a strange plaster dragon (?) above the west window in the tower, and an Elizabethan pulpit, but there are also several faded wall paintings in the nave, the most interesting of which, on the north wall, shows 'a Tudor man with white horse in front of a house with contemporary brick nogging' (Scarfe). The stencilling round the chancel arch is Victorian as are the bits of carved stone stuck into the outside chancel walls.

TILBURY, EAST (B5) *St Catherine*

There is a strong, persistent, and in all likelihood well founded tradition that the embattled south-west tower and south aisle of this church, along with the nearby vicarage, were destroyed by gunfire from the Dutch fleet in the Thames on 23 July 1667. (The evidence was subjected to an exhaustive critical examination by the antiquary Miller Christy in the *Essex Review* October 1905, pp. 221-231. His conclusion that 'it seems most probable that the injury to the church ... was caused during the battle fought in Tilbury Hope within gunshot of the church' has been challenged again recently, but, at least in the writer's view, unsuccessfully.)

Before this catastrophe East Tilbury church must have been that rarity in Essex, a complete Early English thirteenth-century church, tower, nave with north and south aisles and chancel, prominent and alone on slightly higher ground near the foreshore, whereon Coal House Fort (built by General Gordon 1866-71) now stands adjacent to the churchyard. What remains is impressive enough – north arcade of four bays with alternating cylindrical and octagonal piers, and the noble chancel with its three stepped east lancets and others north and south. The tower arch and the evidence of the former south arcade in the botched up south wall of the church, together with the stump of the abortive rebuilding of the tower in 1917, show what might have been. There is a nice Elizabethan pulpit, a fish mosaic on the floor by the vicar's stall (1966) and the church is still lit by oil lamps, like nearby Fobbing. There is a graffito of a sailing ship on the west door jamb.

TILLINGHAM (D4) *St Nicholas*
In this most attractive and unspoilt, unselfconscious village of truly Essex, white painted, weather-boarded cottages and houses grouped round the village green, the parish church is an integral part of the picture. It has two Norman features, its north doorway and its font, a square bowl with some worn carving, on a probably later base, an excellent Early English (thirteenth century) chancel with three stepped lancets under a quatrefoil in the east wall and a contemporary piscina and sedilia, and, from the Victorian period, a rather good screen with rood figures and a south aisle added in 1866. The west tower was built in the fourteenth century, its battlements later.

In the village there is a chapel of the Peculiar People, still apparently in regular use. This sect originated in Rochford, Essex and flourished exceedingly for a time.

TILTY (B2) *St Mary the Virgin*
Seen in the distance across the fields and the quiet valley of the upper Chelmer, halfway between Dunmow and Thaxted, this exquisite little church with its tiny surrounding hamlet draws one like a magnet. It was built, the nave first *c.*1220, as 'the chapel outside the gates' of the Cistercian abbey of Tilty founded in 1153. Of this abbey practically nothing else survives, only a shapeless fragment in the meadow north of the church. All Cistercian monasteries were provided with these chapels,

The chancel at Tilty photographed by Edwin Smith.

primarily intended for use by the local workforce, visitors, and women (who were never allowed within the precincts). Rural Essex's other Cistercian abbey, founded a decade earlier at Little Coggeshall, also retains a *cappella extra portas*, also thirteenth century, with much in common with the Tilty nave. But such survivals are rare elsewhere in England.

183

Here there are deeply splayed lancets, three in the west wall and four each in the north and south walls, and two plain doorways. The piscina for the original altar *before* the chapel's extension remains in the south wall, under the (higher) easternmost lancet, together with an aumbry and a second piscina further west, all three now used as cupboards. The homely porch is seventeenth century (it contains a plan showing a reconstruction of the abbey) and the delightful belfry and cupola, eighteenth century.

But what lends such distinction to Tilty church is the 'taller, wider and much more ambitious chancel' (Pevsner) added *c.*1330. With its three glorious windows, the east of five lights with immensely intricate tracery recently reconstructed, the north of three and the south of two, and its sumptuous sedilia and piscina (notice the head stops), it is of national importance as a copybook example of Decorated architecture at its most exuberant, comparable in Essex, to Lawford chancel and Little Dunmow. There are other treasures too, medieval floor tiles, three fine brasses, two hatchments (one of the seventeenth century), an excellent modern Jacobean style pulpit, two thirteenth-century stone coffin lids recovered from the abbey, and a font made of a mortar and other bits and pieces. Notice also the roof. This chapel seems to have become the parish church for Tilty and Duton Hill early in the seventeenth century. It is beautifully maintained, and greatly loved.

TOLLESBURY (D3) *St Mary the Virgin*

This church, consisting simply of tower, nave and nineteenth-century chancel, is on the east side of the village square, and has a markedly welcoming atmosphere. Its massive squat tower, housing ten bells, is basically Norman, like the nave, but its upper stages, battlements, pinnacles and buttresses were completed in Tudor brick. Apart from this its main features are its glass and its font. The east window is a good one by Kempe, 1902, but particularly interesting is a handsome three-light window in the nave, called 'The Seafarer's Window'. Designed by Derek Wilson and dedicated in 1963, it shows the Risen Christ in the centre light with Peter and the miraculous catch of fish as described in St John 21. In the side lights are yachts and local coastal craft such as a 'stackie' and a Tollesbury oyster smack, all accurately depicted in lovely colour. The font, known as 'The Swearing Font', is inscribed 'Good people all I pray take care that in ye church you doe not sware As this man did'. Apparently in 1718 a man 'came drunk into ye church and cursed ... in the time of Divine Service'. Remorseful, he paid the churchwardens £5. The money was used to buy a new (and very plain!) font, suitably inscribed.

TOLLESHUNT D'ARCY (D3) *St Nicholas*

An attractive church, its nave and west tower, both embattled, and south porch of grey Kentish rag in contrast to the humbler chancel, but all

Embattled Kentish rag at
Tolleshunt D'Arcy.

evidently of the fifteenth-century Perpendicular period, including the fine double doors in the porch. In the porch too are two good modern (1967) windows, one depicting St Nicholas, 'patron saint of sailors and little children'. Inside, the west end is dominated by a modern organ loft in light oak with the case and pipework of a powerful three-manual organ given in 1958, the elaborate, carved, console of which is in the chancel. In the north or D'Arcy chapel are (i) the typically Elizabethan monument of Thomas D'Arcy, d.1593, his (Florentine) wife and their nine children, with kneeling figures, (ii) a window with fragments of old stained glass including one showing a lovely tulip, and (iii) perhaps most interesting of all, a collection, fixed to boards, of monumental brasses, mostly of the Boys and D'Arcy families. But they include three pieces of a Flemish brass of *c.*1375 showing extracts from the Apostles' Creed, held by SS Philip and Bartholomew, and a seated figure of the Madonna and Child. Two of the D'arcy brasses are palimpsests, i.e. reused pieces of an earlier brass on the reverse.

TOLLESHUNT KNIGHTS (D3) *All Saints*

This rural parish originally included what is now the large modern village of Tiptree, which began to grow from nothing in the 1850s, was given its own modest church of St Luke (architect: Ewan Christian) in 1855, and now has over 8,000 inhabitants. As Tiptree grew, its mother parish dwindled in relative importance, until *c.*1960 its remote, isolated little church became redundant. The former rectory had by that time become the centre of an Eastern Orthodox monastery, founded by a Russian émigré, Archimandrite Sophrony, who died in 1993 with a reputation for sanctity. A mutually satisfactory arrangement was reached with the diocese of Chelmsford, whereby the old church was leased to the Orthodox for maintenance and regular use by them. This little, towerless, fourteenth-century church, down a leafy lane far from its village, is therefore furnished, in accordance with the requirements of the Orthodox liturgy, with a simple ikonostasis (screen with painted ikons of Our Lord, his Mother with her Child, and saints) beneath the chancel arch. There is a battered stone effigy of a knight in armour, holding his heart in his hands, from which perhaps the parish got its distinctive name. Orthodox services are held daily except in winter. The monastery has its own, very beautiful church, but this is naturally not open to the public, save on very special request.

TOLLESHUNT MAJOR (D3) *St Nicholas*
Dwarfed by its massive tower this unpretentious little church overlooks the Blackwater estuary. Its nave and chancel, structurally undivided, were built in the fifteenth century of puddingstone and septaria, giving it a pleasing gingery texture. Its windows and doorways are square headed. A good timber porch designed by Ernest Geldart, the parson architect from Little Braxted, was added 1888. But the church is dominated by its large and splendid west tower, built *c.*1545 by Stephen Beckingham. It is in rich dark red brick with blue diapering. It has a big north-east stair turret and diagonal buttresses with no fewer than five set-offs. The west window is of three large lights, transomed. Inside, St Nicholas' is plain and simple, cheered by being painted a warm dairy cream. *See also plate 34.*

TOPPESFIELD (C1) *St Margaret*
The splendid red brick tower of 1699 is a landmark on the horizon, visible for miles. In memory of a generous rector, Robert Wilde, it is highly individual with its round arched windows, obelisk pinnacles and semi-circular troughs between 'battlements'. Daniel Hill the bricklayer (see tablet on west face) did a superb job. The church, with its south aisle, has a beautifully light, cheerful interior, colour washed pinky cream walls, white plaster ceiling, and with only one stained glass window, and that pleasing. Another excellent feature is the mellow Georgian west gallery with lower stage of tower staircase visible from nave. There is a plain eighteenth-century pulpit and one monument particularly worth noting. It is to Dorcas Smyth (d.1633) on the north chancel wall. By John Colt, son of the famous statuary Maximilian, it shows various emblems: a beehive for industry, a sheep on a book, a hand pointing up, and more books on their sides. A brass and a figure of a cross-legged knight of *c.*1260 are apparently hidden under the organ. *See also plates 37 & 41.*

TOTHAM, LITTLE (C3) *All Saints*
Modestly secluded in its tree lined churchyard next to the Hall but far from the village, this charming little church has a very odd looking tower. Its base is promisingly faced with squared knapped flints, but evidently disaster struck soon after it was begun in 1527 and it was later completed in homely Essex white painted weather-boarding with a pyramidal roof. But

the pride of the church is its flamboyant late Norman south doorway of two orders with the unusual feature of square blocks with rosettes a third of the way up the columns. Inside, first to meet the eye is the fifteenth-century octagonal font with a kind of pattern book of eight different tracery reliefs on its faces. There is a delightful early nineteenth-century Gothic organ case, recently repainted; and in the thirteenth-century chancel an excellent mid seventeenth-century Samms monument with three kneeling figures beautifully sculpted.

Norman arch at Little Totham.

TWINSTEAD (C2) *St John the Evangelist*

The third church on the site since the demolition of the medieval one in 1790, St John's was designed by Henry Woodyer (cf. Old Harlow) and consecrated in 1860. Pevsner's description cannot be bettered. 'Nave, chancel and bellcote. Red brick with a wild admixture of black and yellow brick decoration outside and with bands and trellis inside ... very much in the style of Butterfield. The large, low, pointed window in the chancel, almost like a triangle, is also an oddity.' Oddity or not, it is powerful stuff and as a rural exercise in Ruskinian/Butterfieldian polychrome takes some beating.

For good measure there is a triple 'Early English' chancel arch of stone with iron tracery, a richly coloured east window by Hardman of Birmingham, and good Stuart brasses of Isaac and Mary Wyncoll. By their valiant exertions the late Colonel John Clark, churchwarden, and his wife Ruth, stalwarts of the Friends of Essex Churches, saved this delightful church from impending redundancy, God be praised.

ULTING (C3) *All Saints*

This tiny church has much puddingstone with flint rubble in courses in its walls. It underwent a drastic 'restoration' in 1873 which gave it its belfry and its east and west windows, only leaving its original lancets in the chancel and nave to proclaim it Early English, thirteenth century. The

187

interior was totally Victorianised and even the octagonal font which Pevsner thought 'of Purbeck marble' looks distinctly suspicious. But its delightful situation right on the north bank of the Chelmer secured its place in this gazetteer. You can dive in from the churchyard.

UPMINSTER (B5) *St Laurence*

The church is in the centre of the old village, now a town of 12,000. The oldest part is the powerful west tower; the two lower stages, with clasping buttresses, were built *c*.1200, the rest a little later. It has a pyramidal lead roof, surmounted by a timber lantern and spire and bears a strong resemblance to those of Wethersfield and Fyfield. There are four bells.

Although the three bay north arcade is fourteenth century (Decorated), the rest of the church is nineteenth and twentieth century. Extensive additions and alterations were carried out 1928/9 from the designs of the ubiquitous Sir Charles Nicholson. They included the rebuilding and furnishing of the chancel, together with St George's Chapel on the south side and the Lady Chapel to the north. There is some lovely heraldic glass dated 1630 in a two-light window in the north aisle; all the other windows are twentieth century. There is a fine collection of brasses mounted on wood, depicting figures in contemporary costume and armour between 1455 and 1636, also some interesting memorials to local families. The living is in the gift of the Holden family; there were five successive Holden rectors between 1780 and 1970, and only one change of incumbent between 1799 and 1904.

The name Upminster (compare Southminster in the Dengie peninsula) suggests that this was the site of an early Saxon church or minster.

VANGE *St Chad* see BASILDON

WAKERING, GREAT (D5) *St Nicholas*

The church lies at the eastern end of the linear village in an immaculate churchyard, which escaped flooding in 1953, although only standing eighteen feet above sea level. The nave and chancel were built *c*.1100; the tower of ragstone, septaria and flint was added in two stages during the twelfth century. In the late fifteenth century a two storey west porch, with a projecting staircase wing, was erected in front of the early fifteenth-century tower doorway; the upper part of the porch, known as the priest's chamber, is now used as a Sunday school. The south porch was added in the early sixteenth century. The Lady chapel was built in 1843. The nave roof with octagonal crown posts rests on nicely carved stone corbels. The fifteenth-century rood stairs were discovered in 1870. There are fragments of fifteenth-century wall painting, possibly an Annunciation, and an eighteenth-century text. The late Georgian Creed and Commandments are at the back of the church. The font of *c*.1200, with a square bowl carved with ornamental crosses and interlaced arcading, was brought from East Horndon church in 1970.

WAKERING, LITTLE (D4) *St Mary*

The church stands halfway along the village on the east side. The nave and chancel were built early in the twelfth century. The fine west tower of coursed ragstone rubble, with a flint chequerwork parapet, was erected between 1416 and 1425 by John Wakering, bishop of Norwich, and Anne, countess of Stafford; the panels containing their arms are very worn. The tower has a stair turret and slender spire. In the nave, an early thirteenth-century recess has been used as a war memorial. The fifteenth-century rood stair has a section of the rood beam cut off at the sill level of the upper doorway. The chancel was restored in 1878 at the expense of St Bartholomew's Hospital, patrons from 1190 to 1960; it contains a fifteenth-century piscina. The Royal Arms are dated 1769; the village whipping post is on display. *See also note on Barling (p. 31).*

WALDEN, SAFFRON, see under SAFFRON WALDEN

WALTHAM ABBEY (A4) *Holy Cross and St Lawrence*

This vestige of the church of a once large and wealthy abbey dominates the old centre of the small market town. It is visible from as far away as the M.25. Close to, it is still imposing but rather melancholy, a scarred stump altered by later rebuilding and restoration. But the interior has suffered much less than the exterior. Basically it consists of seven bays of the nave of a grand collegiate church built, it appears, towards the end of the eleventh century and in the early years of the twelfth century. With its three storeys of arcade, gallery (triforium) and clerestory and alternating round and composite piers, it is an important example of Romanesque architecture, in line with the great Norman cathedrals and abbeys. Some of its features correspond closely to those in Durham and Norwich cathedrals, notably the spiral and zigzag grooving of four of the round piers, said by Tom Fuller (of the *Worthies*, vicar here in the 1650s) to have originally been filled with brass. A later medieval attempt to Gothicise the nave is seen at the west end. Its effect was to weaken the fabric and it was discontinued.

Excavation by the Waltham Abbey Historical Society in the 1980s indicates that this church was the successor to an early Saxon timber one, superseded in turn by a mid-Saxon stone church comparable to Brixworth, Northants. It was to this church early in the eleventh century that Tovi, standard bearer to king Canute, brought from Somerset a miracle-working stone cross, a relic that explains the future prosperity of the foundation, and its dedication. The church was rebuilt on a much grander scale by Harold, brother-in-law and successor of Edward the Confessor, c.1060. His body was interred by the high altar after his death in the Battle of Hastings, 1066.

Waltham Abbey.

Herringbone masonry in the exterior of the east wall of the south aisle may be the most conspicuous survival of the church he built, assuming, that is, that the existing building is slightly later. (This is the orthodox view, but it is by no means certain.)

The church was enormously enlarged with its refoundation as an Augustinian abbey by Henry II in 1177 – part of his expiation for the murder of Becket. The full extent of the enlarged church, at 400 feet long one of the biggest in England, can be seen from the foundations visible in the grass to the east. Fragments of the cloister exist to the north together with a fourteenth-century gateway and bridge, and a smithy uncovered by excavation. The ground plan in the official guidebook is helpful here.

At Henry VIII's Dissolution of the monasteries all the abbey buildings were demolished (1540 onwards) with the sole exception of the nave, which, as at Hatfield Broad Oak and St Botolph's, Colchester, had long served as the parish church and was preserved as such. A west tower was added in 1556, using materials from the demolished parts. This partly obscures the west front added in the fourteenth century, the best surviving feature of which is the great west doorway. The top storeys of the tower were rebuilt in their present form in 1905 – not an improvement!

The present appearance of the interior owes much to the restoration in 1859/60 by the noted Victorian architect William Burges. Two features are outstanding. First the handsome, colourful nave ceiling designed and painted by Sir Edward Poynter, its lozenge patterns strongly influenced by

190

those in Peterborough cathedral; and secondly, the more controversial east wall with its rose window and three lancets filled with surpassingly beautiful stained glass by the pre-Raphaelite Burne-Jones with, below them, the four reliefs framed in gold and depicting Nativity scenes, constituting the reredos, itself surmounted by a string course carved with two of Æsop's fables, separated by the Lamb of God!

In contrast with the grandeur of the nave is the delicacy of the fourteenth-century (Lady) chapel, with its lovely windows south and west. It has a well preserved Doom painting above the altar and a vaulted undercroft now used as a visitor centre.

Furnishings include a splendid seventeenth-century pulpit with tester and a completely plain octagonal font of Purbeck marble, possibly twelfth century. Of the many monuments two are outstanding, that of Sir Edward Denny (d.1600), his wife and ten children – it was his father to whom Henry VIII granted the abbey and who demolished it – and the charming table tomb to the sea captain Robert Smith, d.1697. It shows his ship the *Industria* in full sail through a sea full of dolphins. *See also plates 3 & 48.*

Walthamstow, tomb of Sir Thomas Merry.

WALTHAMSTOW (A4) *St Mary*
A little of old Walthamstow survives in the quiet neighbourhood of this, the original parish church, with its three acres of churchyard (maintained by the local district council), in which there are said to be nearly 1,250 tombstones. The great tomb chests crowded together in the immediate perimeter of the church are indicative of the social prestige of the parish before it was engulfed by London.

This impression is reinforced in the church itself, notable more for the number and quality of its monuments than for its architecture. The exterior with its uniform buff coloured render is pleasing, but deceptive, in that, apart from the west tower, built by Sir George Monoux *c.*1535, it looks, and is, early nineteenth century. But inside, the nave and

191

chancel arcades, also part of Monoux's rebuilding, are intact. There are galleries north and west and a charming little eighteenth-century font.

As well as mural monuments there is a fine collection of brasses, including that to Monoux. On the north side of the sanctuary is the only Essex monument by Nicholas Stone, the greatest, probably, of our English 'statuaries'. It was commissioned by the handsome cavalier Sir Thomas Merry to commemorate his wife Dame Mary, and depicts them both, with four of their children, in a composition of great classical beauty. *See also plate 47.*

WALTHAM, GREAT (B3) *St Mary and St Lawrence*
This large church with a fine west tower is situated on a bend in the main road going through the village. Built of flint and pebble-rubble, it is basically Norman with a fourteenth-century south aisle, but was restored by Chancellor from 1863. The north aisle was added in 1875. Internally, the nave roof is impressive with alternating tie and hammerbeam trusses. There are late fifteenth-century pews with traceried bench ends at the south end of the church and medieval armorial glass in the south aisle. Brasses to the Wiseman and Everard families, *c.*1580-1617. The most outstanding monument was erected in 1611 by Sir Anthony Everard (d.1614) after the death of his wife (1609); the reclining figures are in two tiers under a coffered arch with round headed windows containing original glass. A monument (1703) commemorates Hugh Everard, lost on the Goodwin Sands.

WALTHAM, LITTLE (C3) *St Martin*
The church is at Brook Hill, on the outskirts of the village. The nave is basically Norman; the chancel was rebuilt in the fourteenth or fifteenth centuries. The west tower, built in the first half of the fifteenth century, was much repaired in brick in the sixteenth or early seventeenth centuries. The church was extensively restored by F. Chancellor, *c.*1882-8, when the north aisle with good capitals was added. Interior features include a medieval dug-out chest and the brass of John Maltoun (1447) in armour. Among recent additions are the east window (1951), adapted from Raphael, but incorporating local scenes, and the glass tower screen (1982).

WALTON ON THE NAZE (E2/3) *All Saints*
For centuries Walton, the third of the Soken trio (see under THORPE), has suffered the depredations of the North Sea. A prebendal stall in St Paul's Cathedral named *Prebenda consumpta per mare* refers to its endowments lost through erosion at Walton.

The ruins of its medieval church finally disappeared in 1798. It was eventually replaced on a new site inland by a plain brick church of the 1830s and this in turn by the present sizeable building designed by Henry

Stone (who had earlier rebuilt Kirby church, q.v.) and built piecemeal, as funds allowed, from 1873 onwards, the tall west tower finally being completed in 1896. The church consists of a long nave with a south aisle of five bays and a chancel with a five-light east window in the Decorated Gothic style. Its Victorian stained glass commemorates P. S. Bruff, Walton's principal nineteenth-century developer, who brought the railway here.

WANSTEAD (A4) *St Mary*

Turn off the A.12 when driving into London and discover this oasis of eighteenth-century calm. Approached through tree lined roads of tidy early twentieth-century houses, this elegant church suddenly appears behind its railings. Built in 1790 (architect: Thomas Hardwick) in severely classical style away from the site of its sixteenth-century predecessor, it was designed not only to afford more accommodation, but also to complement the great Palladian mansion of Wanstead House nearby – though that was totally to be demolished in 1822. Fortunately St Mary's was new enough to escape 'modernisation' by unsympathetic Victorians and so remains in immaculate condition almost exactly as built. Also, as the population

continued to expand, another church, Christchurch, was built on a more central site in the 1860s in fashionable High Victorian Gothic and this, mercifully, came to absorb the energies and enthusiasm of the parishioners, so the older church was left in peace.

St Mary's tall west portico has two pairs of Tuscan columns supporting an entablature. Above the plain pediment, the dome crowning the lovely small bell turret is supported by four pairs of diagonally placed Ionic columns. There are two storeys of tall plain windows north and south corresponding to the three sided galleries within. The interior is lit principally by the top windows. The nave has five bays of tall Corinthian columns on high pedestals. A lofty pulpit, its handsome rayed tester upheld by two gilded palm trees, cheerfully presides over a sea of lockable box pews, which also fill the galleries. A splendid organ case in the west gallery faces the narrower chancel with its austerely beautiful sanctuary and

The pulpit at Wanstead St Mary.

The box pews in the north gallery at Wanstead St Mary.

altarpiece. Transplanted from the older church, a Baroque monument of overwhelming magnificence fills the south side of the chancel. Attributed to John van Nost or Ost, it commemorates Sir Josiah Child (d.1699), tycoon, governor of the East India Company, and his son. There is also a characteristic neo-Classical monument by Flaxman in the north gallery below a delightful Hanoverian Royal Arms in a glass roundel.

This coolly serene church stands in a vast overgrown graveyard which is a history lesson in itself of the development of Georgian, Victorian and Edwardian fashion in tombstones. *See also plate 14.*

WARLEY, GREAT (B4) *St Mary the Virgin*
Its medieval predecessor fell into ruin last century and was finally demolished in 1966. In the meantime red brick Christchurch was built in 1855 to serve the built-up part of the parish, which had become an overflow of Brentwood. In 1904 a local magnate, Evelyn Heseltine, built a new church in rural Great Warley in memory of his brother Arnold (d.1897). No expense was spared. His architect was Charles Harrison Townsend, but the furnishing and interior decoration was entrusted to Sir William Reynolds-Stephens, a leading exponent of the then still fashionable Art Nouveau. The exterior (rough cast walls, spire, apse) is pleasant, but unremarkable, and does nothing to prepare us for the inside. Here every inch of wall and roof is decorated with a wide variety of materials and all the furnishings

down to the minutest detail designed to convey symbolic meaning and produce an overwhelming aesthetic impression. In this it succeeds! The focal point is the chancel apse seen through the dominant screen with its six brass trees with gnarled roots 'growing' from an Irish marble base and bearing deep red glass pomegranates (or roses?) upheld by angels of oxidised silver. The chancel walls are covered with grey green marble and the ribbed vault with silver-like aluminium. The centrepiece of the reredos is a metal figure of Christ. The whole church is a prime example of Edwardian opulence and aestheticism – probably the best Art Nouveau church in England. *See also plate 53.*

WARLEY, LITTLE (B4) *St Peter*
What a pleasant surprise to find this unspoilt little church so close to the hectic London-Southend road (A.127). It has Tudor Little Warley Hall for a neighbour. The church is a brick and stone sandwich: the fifteenth-century ragstone nave between the chequered red and black brick tower, a rebuild of 1718 with one fifteenth-century bell, and the heavily buttressed Tudor brick chancel, its east wall with three lancets rebuilt in brick in the early nineteenth century. The nave, with king post roof and plaster ceiling, has a low rood loft staircase and – another surprise – in a niche a reclining alabaster figure of Father Time complete with scythe, from a vanished seventeenth-century tomb presumably. It has a good set of seventeenth- or early eighteenth-century box pews and pulpit and a seventeenth-century pedestal font. The tiny chancel retains its simple eighteenth-century (?) altarpiece of Commandments, Creed and Lord's Prayer, nicely lettered.

On the north side of the altar is a black and white marble and alabaster monument to Sir Denner Strutt, baronet, and his first wife Dorothy, d.1641. He lies on a shelf with his wife above under a canopy with fat cherubs drawing back the curtains. Opposite is the plainer tomb, also with effigy, of the third Lady Strutt, d.1658. There is also a tiny brass, Anne Tyrell, 1592.

WEALD, NORTH (A3) *St Andrew*
Weald is Saxon for forest and there is still a northern extremity of Epping Forest 1½ miles west of the church across the airfield. St Andrew's looks down over part of the former A.414 Chelmsford to Harlow road, now by-passed. It is a handsome building with tiled nave and chancel and a fine tall slender Tudor brick tower, its main feature, beautifully textured with small Tudor bricks in English bond.

The nave, south aisle and Lady Chapel were built *c.*1330 of flint rubble with larger dressed stone and some Roman tiles. The windows have reticulated (i.e. net-like) tracery, some with ogee arches and bits of medieval glass, those in the chapel and aisle being notable. The chancel was rebuilt in 1867 in fourteenth-century style. The large east window has excellent modern glass representing Christ in Majesty. The north door, seen from outside, is original with decorative ironwork hinges.

The interior is beautifully kept and furnished in the Anglo-Catholic tradition with a rood – a large Crucifix – suspended from the chancel arch.

WEALD, SOUTH (B4) *All Saints*

This, the large historic mother church of Brentwood, stands impressively on a hilltop in lovely undulating wooded country much of which forms Weald Country Park. The big embattled west tower of Kentish rag built about 1500, a fine Norman south doorway and the (rebuilt) Early English arcade between the south aisle and the nave are all that survived the major extension and reconstruction by the ruthless Victorian architect S. S. Tevlon in 1868. This reduced the former nave to a south aisle and provided a new wide nave and chancel. The vase-like font is of 1662, its cover Victorian. There is a Victorian reredos of alabaster carved in high relief to depict the entombment of Christ, and a lot of stained glass, much of it of good quality by Kempe and his disciples, and including two nice Flemish renaissance panels in the west (tower) window, but it all makes the church terribly dark.

There is also a collection of ten brasses *c*.1450-1634, some only fragmentary but all of interest. One of the brasses commemorates Sir Anthony Browne, d.1567, a leading judge and founder of Brentwood School. There is a similar collection of later monuments, all but one of them in the tower but one, very large, in the south (Tower family) chapel. One of those in the base of the tower is by the famous sculptor Sir Francis Chantrey. It commemorates F. J. H. Wollaston B.D., F.R.S., vicar of South Weald, rector of Cold Norton and archdeacon of Essex, shown in profile. The inscription begins 'He went to bed in perfect health October 11th 1823 and was found a corpse on Sunday morning. Reader reflect.'

WENDENS AMBO (B1) *St Mary the Virgin*

Pastoral reorganisation is nothing new. 'Ambo', Latin for 'both', tells us there were originally two Wendens, Great and Little. In 1662 the dilapidated redundant church of Little was demolished and everything concentrated here at Great. Wendens Ambo is wholly delectable. The unforgettable picture postcard setting at the top of a lane of ancient cottages should not make us forget to admire the church from the south-east corner of the churchyard to see how nicely it composes, in steps: the squat Norman tower with its Hertfordshire spike, short clerestoried nave with high pitched tiled roof, porch and south aisle, and lower tiled chancel with what looks like a miniature south transept but turns out to be a nineteenth-century organ chamber.

South Weald.

Wendens Ambo.

St Mary's started as a simple Norman tower, nave and chancel. The aisles were added and the chancel enlarged and rebuilt in subsequent centuries, the south aisle being prolonged west alongside the tower.

Inside, things to look out for include the domed font cover, the king post nave roof, the screen, the unusual, slender and attractive sixteenth-century pulpit, the charming early nineteenth-century organ case, a military brass, a rococo cartouche high up in the nave below the clerestory window, and remains of wall paintings.

WESTCLIFF ON SEA (C5) *St Alban* St John's Road

Probably the best of Southend's late nineteenth- and twentieth-century churches, it is an early work of Sir Charles Nicholson, 1898-1908, tucked away in a densely packed urban area, not easy to locate. Despite an unprepossessing exterior with a low south-east tower and the same flint and red brick texture as his much later church at Frinton, inside it is a gem of dignified Edwardian High Church architecture. It comprises a large nave with north and south aisles, in striking black and white, with a south-east Lady Chapel. The west end is dominated by a handsome six-light Jesse window in which each figure carries a scroll with a fragment of text adding up to the Creed in Latin. Below this window stands the elegant Wren font and cover obtained by Nicholson from the crypt of St Mary-le-Bow, Cheapside. The chancel, entered through a fine, intricately carved rood screen, culminates in a magnificent reredos erected in memory of those who fell in the First World War. Filling the whole east wall and lit by side windows it consists of two tiers of figures in canopied niches, with the Holy Family in the centre flanked by the four patron saints of the British Isles. Behind the high altar and forming part of the dark panelling is a painting of the Annunciation. Altogether it makes a strong impact. Around the church are stations of the cross.

WETHERSFIELD (C2) *St Mary Virgin and St Mary Magdalene*

The church, on a hump in the middle of this exceptionally picturesque village, has a massive, unbuttressed early thirteenth-century tower, topped by a short, shingled spire in two stages. Small lancet windows light the way up to the bells. The partly thirteenth-century nave is of flint but a brick clerestory was added in the fifteenth century. There are north and south porches – the former rebuilt in brick in 1750. The lightness of the nave is in contrast to the gloom of the chancel, due to remarkable nineteenth-century stained glass windows. In the chancel is a fine alabaster tomb chest with effigies, possibly fifteenth-century Wentworths. *See also plate 6.*

WICKHAM ST PAUL (C1) *All Saints*

This small church (illustrated above) 'composes' well, adjoining Wickham Hall but away from the village centre. Its stocky Tudor diapered red brick tower, for building which £20 was given in a will of 1505, contrasts nicely with the whitewashed walls of the fourteenth(?)-century nave and chancel, both under one continuous tiled roof. Proximity to Gestingthorp, where the more ambitious tower was built a few years earlier (q.v.), suggests that emulation was the motive of the testator and that the bricks and the skilled and experienced bricklayers came from the brickyard there (likewise probably Castle Hedingham). After this promising exterior, the interior is, frankly, disappointing.

WIDFORD (B3) *St Mary*

In 1862, Arthur Pryor, prosperous brewer and squire of nearby Hylands, was prevailed upon by his pious wife Elizabeth to replace at his sole expense their existing parish church with a new one on the same site at what is now a major traffic roundabout where expanding Chelmsford meets open country. As architect he commissioned Piers St Aubyn, better known in the west country where he 'restored' and rebuilt many churches.

St Mary's is quintessentially High Victorian Gothic in the prevailing Decorated style. Built of Kentish rag it has a graceful freestone tower and tall slender spire rising to 145 feet, and therefore a landmark. There is a north aisle divided from the nave by a four-bay arcade, and a dignified and restrained chancel with a richly coloured three-light east window.

Eleven years later Pryor commissioned St Aubyn to design a larger, more ambitious church for Galleywood (q.v.). In Widford churchyard, north of the church is a large squat stone pyramid commemorating a Viscountess Falkland who died in 1776.

WIGBOROUGH, LITTLE (D3) *St Nicholas*

This lonely little church has only Copt Hall for neighbour but there are wonderful views and walks on National Trust land in the surrounding saltings and marshland of the Blackwater Estuary looking towards Mersea Island. Like others in the neighbourhood it suffered badly in the 1884 earthquake. It was well repaired and re-equipped by the London architect, Joseph Clarke (who also worked at Inworth). The squat tower is only fractionally higher than the fifteenth-century nave and chancel, which display good Victorian wood and ironwork in the screen and other furnishings.

WILLINGALE DOE (B3) *St Christopher*

Willingale is a small village now, but has two churches in the same churchyard, which is very pleasant and well kept. Willingale Doe takes its name from the D'eau family. The nave and chancel of St Christopher's church, which is the one still in use, were built of clunch and flint *c.*1320. The tower and south porch were added in the fifteenth century, but the tower was substantially rebuilt in 1853, when the north aisle was added.

The church has a number of interesting brasses, monuments and ledger slabs. The impressive alabaster and marble monument to Sir Robert Wiseman, 1641, takes the form of an architectural composition with his semi-reclining effigy and his parents kneeling above.

WILLINGALE SPAIN (B3) *St Andrew and All Saints*

This church is still used occasionally and is now looked after by the Churches Conservation Trust, after being restored in the 1950s. The church was given to Blackmore Priory in 1120 by William de Hispania. The twelfth-century nave is constructed of flint, rubble and puddingstone, with Roman brick used for quoins and the arch of the south door; there are two surviving windows in the north wall. The chancel and chancel arch were rebuilt in the fifteenth century, when the belfry, resting on a tie beam with four arched braces and now weather-boarded, was added. The inner side of the modern north door has twelfth-century ironwork. There is a late fourteenth-century octagonal font and the original stone altar is still in use. Graffiti on the west jamb of the sedilia include an archbishop.

WIMBISH (B1) *All Saints*

Not easy to locate, this towerless church lies between Wimbish Hall and the old rectory, approached via a lane between fields, well away from its scattered village. And when you do get there, at first glance it looks disappointingly all renewed in the nineteenth century. Looking more closely, there are signs of a Norman window and mysterious triple arcading, largely hidden by the big two-storey fifteenth-century porch. There are surprises in store. First, the handsome Transitional Norman south doorway; with its pointed arch but two orders, one plain, the other spirally carved with volute capitals; it must date from *c.*1200. The nave, then, is Norman/ Transitional. A north aisle was added *c.*1290, to judge from the three-bay arcade with its quatrefoil piers. The north aisle roof is actually dated in one of its spandrels, 1534. There is a fifteenth-century screen to the north chapel. In the floor in front of it is the church's chief treasure, the exquisite little de Wantone brass of 1347. Some of it is missing, notably its octofoil surround, but it can be reconstructed from the indent. Pevsner, who illustrates it reconstructed (*Essex* 2nd edn p. 427), compares it to the superb Hastings brass at Elsing, Norfolk, one of the finest in England.

The chancel was rebuilt 1868 and the tower demolished as unsafe 1883 and the tower arch bricked up.

WITHAM (C3) *St Nicholas*

This rapidly expanding town's medieval parish church is far from the busy main thoroughfare (Newland Street) in the quiet unspoilt conservation area of Chipping Hill, the site of the old market. It is a large, relatively uncomplicated building. The embattled west tower, nave with north and south aisles and four bay arcades and the chancel are all of the early fourteenth-century (Decorated) period but a good Norman south doorway with zigzag mouldings from an earlier church forms the main entrance. North and south chancel chapels were added in the fifteenth century (Perpendicular). There is a good chancel screen, much restored. The Arms of William III (1694-1702) are in the south chapel. Several notable monuments include a recumbent effigy of Elizabethan judge John Southcotte, at the west end of the north aisle and, in the chancel, Francis Harvey and wife 1592 facing each other and a fine bust of William East of the Middle Temple 1726 on a large mural monument signed by Horsnaile.

WIVENHOE (D2) *St Mary the Virgin*

The church with its late medieval tower topped by a picturesque wooden cupola stands in the old village near the quay and composes well as seen from Rowhedge across the Colne. The church itself is a rebuilding by Hakewill in 1860 'of no interest' (Pevsner), apart from its typically Perpendicular font, and the two fine brasses of William, viscount Beaumont (d.1507) and his wife Elizabeth, d.1537, and that of Thomas Westeley (d.1535) her chaplain.

WOODFORD (London E18) (A4) *St Mary the Virgin*

In 1973 the *Victoria County History* (Vol VI) described Woodford as a 'dormitory suburb for middle class city workers, with only a few working class enclaves'. Its proximity to Epping Forest had long made it, in house agents' jargon, a 'sought after' residential neighbourhood for the well-to-do.

Its original parish church in what is now South Woodford had been enlarged, reordered and rebuilt time and again, notably in 1816 and, as regards the chancel, in 1889. It was this church, apart from its handsome, if stocky, Queen Anne red brick tower (of 1708), which was completely gutted by a fire started by arsonists on a Sunday in February 1969. Its rebuilding within the old walls with John Phillips as architect was completed in 1972. The opportunity was then taken to turn the church completely round, making the new entrance under the old east window and creating a worship area almost completely square and seating 500, with a central west facing altar. 'The effect is of more space and greater participation in the worship of all present' writes Winifred Paramour in her attractive church guide, adding 'The clear glass in the windows gives more light while the loop sound system has vastly improved the acoustics.' Yet another case of good coming out of evil.

WOODHAM FERRERS (C4) *St Mary the Virgin*

Halfway up a steepish hill in the village, this sizeable church is on three sides so closely surrounded by trees it is difficult to see it as a whole.

Consisting of a wide nave with north and south aisles, a chancel and south porch with a rather inadequate wooden belfry and spire perched on the apex of the nave roof, it appears to have been built, probably by the Ferrers family, between *c.*1250 and *c.*1340. The timber porch is fifteenth century and the belfry (which rests, not on the usual posts, but on a stout tie beam) took the place of a collapsed tower of which vestiges remain. The piers of the three-bay arcades are alternately cylindrical and octagonal and two have niches. The windows are mostly glazed with Victorian green tinted 'Cathedral' glass, making one feel like a fish in an aquarium. There is a fine set of Royal Arms of 1788 with the shield and supporters carved in the round against the mantling on canvas or boards but unfortunately it is hidden away behind the organ. Evidently it was removed from its central position over the chancel arch, since the tell-tale legend FEAR GOD. HONOUR THE KING is still up there beneath a very faint and faded medieval Doom painting, no doubt revealed when the Royal Arms were taken down.

There is a notable monument on the north wall of the chancel by the altar. It commemorates Cecilie Sandys d.1610, the 'true widow' of Edwin Sandys, archbishop of York. (Her home was Edwin's Hall, an Elizabethan house a mile from the church.) Mrs Sandys is seen kneeling in prayer under a canopy in an arbour of roses. Father Time stands guard outside (cf. Little Warley).

WOODHAM FERRERS, SOUTH (C4) *Holy Trinity*

Essex's newest New Town, South Woodham Ferrers, was planned in the 1980s and provided in 1982 with an ecumenical church, shared by Anglicans, Roman Catholics and Methodists. The worship area, pleasingly furnished, is surprisingly intimate and its users complain that it is too small for their congregations! Situated in the town centre and plainly built of red brick, it forms part of a complex with the church junior school, and its only distinctive feature externally is a plain wooden cross. The architect was John Breavington.

WOODHAM WALTER (C3) *St Michael the Archangel*

The most remarkable thing about this attractively mellow red brick church (illustrated overleaf), with its characteristic crow-stepped gables and straight-headed windows, is its date, 1563, five years after the accession of Elizabeth I. As such it is a great rarity, one of only six Elizabethan churches in England, and the only one in Essex, albeit its roofs, the stonework of its piers and its font came from its predecessor on (apparently) a different site – an early case of recycling! A royal licence to build it was obtained by the powerful lord of the manor, the courtier Thomas Radcliffe, third earl of Sussex and Viscount Fitzwalter, a supporter of the new queen's Reformation church settlement, and her Lord Deputy of Ireland. The roofs of the nave and chancel can be reliably dated fourteenth century and the stonework of the arcade separating the nave from the north aisle is not only, with its depressed four centred arches, typically late Perpendicular but actually bears graffiti positively dated between 1450 and 1500. The north aisle roof is fifteenth century, as is the font. The belfry, containing three bells, is Victorian, as are most of the furnishings.

WORMINGFORD (D2) *St Andrew*

On high ground, before it begins to fall away to the north into the Stour valley, stands this much loved old church with its rugged stump of a Norman tower built of flint rubble and plenty of thick Roman tiles taken no doubt from some local ruin to form quoins. The texture of the external walls, as always, repays careful observation before going in. A blocked Norman lancet window can be seen, evidence that when the church was rebuilt in the fourteenth century, all traces of its predecessor were not obliterated. The north arcade of four bays dates from this time. There was

Woodham Walter.

a too thorough Victorian 'restoration' and as a result all the furnishings and nearly all the stained glass are Victorian or later. The strong colours of the east window blend well with the alabaster reredos. The single-light window in the north west wall of the nave cleverly incorporates continental renaissance glass in a heraldic design and the Dragon window facing it at the east end of the north aisle has some frightening heraldic beasts. Both commemorate Boggis-Rolfes. In the tower are some small brasses lacking inscriptions.

The churchyard south of the church was transformed into a garden nearly a century ago.

WRABNESS (E2) *All Saints*
A very small church, nave and chancel only, with superb views across the Stour estuary to the Royal Hospital School, Holbrook. Also in the churchyard quite apart from the church is the bell cage, originally constructed of timber in the seventeenth or eighteenth century, but repaired in recent years. It houses one solitary bell. There is a similar one at Wix nearby, both no doubt inspired by the well-known earlier one at East Bergholt in Suffolk, beyond Manningtree. The church itself has a good south doorway and a simple hammerbeam roof.

WRITTLE (B3) *All Saints*

Situated just off one of the most notable village greens in Essex, the church, built of Kentish ragstone, is basically thirteenth century except for the brick south chantry chapel (1526) and the west tower which fell down and was rebuilt in 1802. Writtle, a royal manor on the old main road to London, was far more important than Chelmsford in 1086, when it is known to have had a church, parts of which may have been incorporated in the present building. Approached from the green through the north porch, the interior is spacious with north and south aisles and a clerestory to the nave, which has fifteenth-century roof bosses and corbels. There is a rood stair. One of Writtle's chief delights is its monuments, which range from brasses and armorial ledgers to the work of Nicholas Stone (Sir Edward Pinchon, 1629, costing £66 13*s.* 4*d.*) and Cheere (Sir John Comyns, Chief Baron of the Exchequer, d.1740; erected 1759). The chancel was restored after fires in 1974 and 1991.

YELDHAM, GREAT (C1) *St Andrew*

The church (illustrated overleaf) forms an attractive group with the Hall and the old rectory, overlooking the busy A.604 and the spreading village. Its most impressive feature is its handsome late fifteenth-century west tower. Built in a pleasing mixture of rubble, brick and puddingstone with freestone dressings, it has three-light transomed bell openings, a projecting staircase, and a stone parapet with stepped battlements, pinnacles and intermediate figures of angels, and houses six bells. This ambitious structure, seen to best advantage from due south, dominates the unpretentious church beneath it. It had evidently been the earlier intention, perhaps due to the awkward lie of the land, to build an equally large tower to serve also as an entrance porch, on the south side of the nave, after the fashion of several Suffolk churches around Ipswich. When this was abandoned in favour of a west tower, the unfinished south tower became the porch with a room above it, now the choir vestry, and was completed with a Tudor brick stepped gable. The church itself is briefly described. Besides nave, chancel and north aisle, it has a small south transept/chapel adjoining the porch, with some good monuments and a 1627 brass (Symonds). Fittings include a cleverly restored screen with three painted panels surviving, thought to represent (left to right) St Ursula, St Eligius, patron saint of blacksmiths, and St Edmund, king and martyr, seventeenth-century pulpit, good twentieth-century panelling in the sanctuary, and the Royal Arms of George III. The east window *c.*1860 is by Hardman and there is one of St Andrew by Leonard Walker, also in the chancel.

Great Yeldham.

YELDHAM, LITTLE (C1) *St John the Baptist*

This much restored and rebuilt little church sits prettily at the T junction in the middle of the village, its tiled roof and rubble walls and its unpretentious timber belfry giving it a warm, homely look. It is known that there was a church here in 1090, when it was conveyed by Gilbert, lord of Clare, to the Benedictine priory there, but no identifiable Norman features

206

have survived. The south porch and north vestry, together with a stone pulpit and screen, were added in 1891; the architect was J. P. Seddon and the well-to-do rector paid the bill himself. The west wall with its triple lancet window is also Victorian. But there is a nice fifteenth-century font, with the de Vere mullet (five pointed star) on one of its eight sides, the wooden supports and framework of the belfry are impressive and there is a good set of Royal Arms of George I.

On the way to the gate notice the fine stone coffin lid with carved cross by the porch.

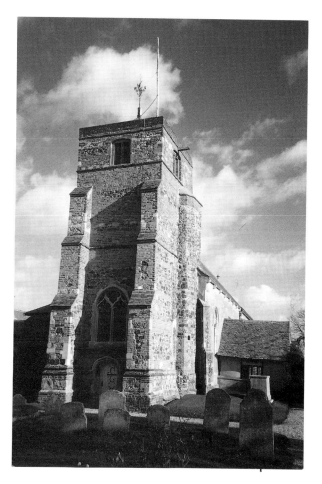

The tower at Lawford, St Mary's (see pp. 122-4).

LISTS OF SPECIAL FEATURES

The following lists make no claim to be exhaustive.

Fonts. (a) *Medieval:* Althorne; Bradfield; Bradwell juxta Mare St Thomas; Bulmer; Chickney; Chignal Smealey; East Mersea; High Easter; Marks Tey; Peldon; Springfield All Saints; Stanford Rivers; Little Totham. (b) *Post-Medieval:* Barking St Margaret; Birdbrook; Little Braxted; Brentwood Roman Catholic Cathedral; Brentwood St George; Debden; Lawford; South Weald; Theydon Mount; Tollesbury; Westcliff St Alban.

Font Covers. (a) *Medieval:* Fingringhoe; Pentlow; Takeley; Thaxted. (b) *Post-Medieval:* Alphamstone; Bradwell juxta Coggeshall; Brentwood St George; Wendens Ambo.

Monuments. (a) *Brasses:* Berden; Bowers Gifford; Brightlingsea All Saints; Great Bromley; Chigwell; Chrishall; Dagenham St Peter and St Paul; Little Easton; Elmstead; Epping Upland; Finchingfield; Fryerning; Gosfield; Ingrave; Little Ilford St Mary; Halstead St Andrew; Harlow; Little Horkesley; Latton; Orsett; Pebmarsh; Saffron Walden; Tilty; Tolleshunt D'Arcy; Walthamstow St Mary; Wivenhoe; South Ockenden; Wimbish. (b) *Wooden Effigies:* Danbury; Elmstead; Little Baddow; Little Horkesley; Little Leighs. (c) *Stone, Alabaster, Marble:* (i) *Medieval:* Layer Marney; Little Dunmow; Halstead St Andrew; Hatfield Broad Oak; East Horndon; Middleton; Wethersfield. (ii) *Renaissance to Early Sixteenth Century:* Castle Hedingham; Dedham; Layer Marney; Saffron Walden. (iii) *1560-1820:* Abbess Roding; Arkesden; Barking St Margaret; Boreham; Borley; Brightlingsea; Chelmsford Cathedral; Clavering; Colchester St James; Debden; East Ham; Little Easton; Faulkbourne; Felstead; Gosfield; Great Waltham; Great Maplestead; Hempstead; Ingatestone; Leigh on Sea St Clement; Leyton St Mary; Little Warley; Little Ilford; Orsett; North Ockendon; South Ockendon; Pentlow; Pleshey; Rettendon; Rivenhall; St Osyth; Stanstead Mountfitchet St Mary; Steeple Bumpstead; Theydon Mount; Waltham Abbey; Walthamstow St Mary; Wanstead St Mary; West Ham; Woodham Ferrers; Writtle.

Organs and Organ Cases: Basildon St Martin; Berden; Black Chapel; Chelmsford Cathedral; Epping St John; Faulkbourne; Harlow St Paul; Harwich; Great Bardfield; Little Bardfield; Quendon; Radwinter; Saffron Walden; Thaxted; West Thurrock; Wanstead St Mary; Wendens Ambo.

LIST OF SPECIAL FEATURES

Pulpits. (a) *Late Medieval:* Henham; Leaden Roding; Rickling; Sandon; Wendens Ambo. (b) *Elizabethan, Jacobean, Caroline:* Bardfield Saling; Berden; Broxted; Great Baddow; Layer Marney; Stondon Massey; Matching; Waltham Abbey. (c) *Late Stuart And Georgian:* Abbess Roding; Bradfield; Canewdon; Colchester St Peter; Gosfield; Greensted by Ongar; Salcott; Thaxted; Theydon Garnon; Wanstead St Mary. (d) *Victorian:* Belchamp Walter; Foxearth. (e) *Twentieth Century:* Chelmsford Cathedral; Hornchurch St Andrew; Tilty.

Roofs, Medieval. (a) *Hammerbeam:* Castle Hedingham; Gestingthorpe; Great Bromley; Little Bentley; Peldon; St Osyth; Sturmer; Wrabness. (b) *Low Pitched:* Bocking; Clavering; Dedham; High Easter; Thaxted; Saffron Walden.

Screens (a) *Medieval, Wooden:* Bardfield Saling; Bradwell juxta Coggeshall; Bulphan; Castle Hedingham; Clavering; Finchingfield; Great Yeldham; Henham; Layer Marney; Newport; Rickling; Stambourne; Witham. (b) *Medieval, Stone:* Great Bardfield; Stebbing. (c) *Nineteenth Century, Iron:* Mistley; Radwinter. (d) *Twentieth Century, Wooden:* Bocking (Comper); Epping; Quendon (Dykes Bower); Saffron Walden; Westcliff St Alban (Nicholson). (e) *Brass:* Great Warley (Reynolds-Stephens).

Stained Glass. (a) *Medieval:* Clavering; Old Harlow; Margaretting; Newport; North Ockendon; Rivenhall; Thaxted; White Notley. (b) *Renaissance, Early Sixteenth Century:* Prittlewell; Stisted. (c) *Seventeenth And Eighteenth Century:* Little Easton; Leigh on Sea St Clement; Old Harlow; Messing; Theydon Mount; Upminster. (d) *Nineteenth Century:* Layer Marney; Ilford Hospital; Thaxted; Waltham Abbey. (e) *Twentieth Century:* Basildon St Martin; Broomfield; Broxted; Clacton on Sea St Paul; Great Coggeshall; Fryerning; Harlow Our Lady of Fatima; High Easter; Hornchurch St Andrew; Little Easton; Maldon St Mary; Ongar; Sheering; Stifford; Stock; Theydon Mount; Grays Thurrock; Tollesbury; Westcliff St Alban.

Wall Paintings. (a) *Medieval:* Belchamp Walter; Bradwell juxta Coggeshall; Copford; Fairstead; Great Burstead; Great Canfield; Hadleigh; Inworth; Lambourne; Layer Marney; Little Baddow; Little Easton; Little Tey; Waltham Abbey; Woodham Ferrers. (b) *Victorian:* Ardleigh; Foxearth; Halstead St Andrew; Little Braxted; Littlebury. (c) *Twentieth Century:* Broomfield (tower); Harlow St Paul (Piper mosaic).

GLOSSARY

AISLE The side part of a church.

APSE A semi-circular or polygonal end.

ARCADE A range of arches supported on PIERS or columns. A blind-arcade, the same attached to a wall.

AUMBRY A recessed cupboard holding the sacred vessels for Mass or Communion, usually on N wall of CHANCEL. Also used in some churches for the purpose of housing the reserved Sacrament.

BALLFLOWER Globular flower of three petals enclosing a small ball, a form of decoration used in the first quarter of the 14th century (DECORATED period).

BATTLEMENT A parapet with gaps at regular intervals.

BOSS An ornamental projection, generally carved with foliage or figures, used to conceal the crossing of the ribs in a vaulted roof.

BROACH SPIRE see SPIRE.

CAPITAL The top or head of a column.

CHANCEL The eastern compartment of the church beyond the nave, and housing the altar or communion table.

CHANTRY CHAPEL A chapel attached to, or inside a church, endowed for the saying of private Masses for the soul of the founder or another individual.

CHAPEL OF EASE A small building for worship which is not a parish church.

CHARNEL HOUSE A room, often below ground level, where the bones of the dead are deposited.

CHEVRON A zigzag ornamentation typical of the NORMAN period.

CLERESTORY The upper part of the NAVE and CHANCEL walls, containing a series of windows.

CLUNCH A soft, chalky stone quarried in the SE of Cambridgeshire.

CORBEL Block of stone projecting just below the roof eaves externally or internally, often adorned with carving.

CROCKETS Decorative projections placed on sloping sides of SPIRES, pinnacles or gables.

DECORATED Stylistic division of English GOTHIC architecture from *c.*1290 to *c.*1350.

DOG-TOOTH Typical EARLY ENGLISH ornament, consisting of a series of raised four-cornered stars.

DRIP MOULDING See HOOD-MOULD.

EARLY ENGLISH Stylistic division of English GOTHIC architecture roughly covering the 13th century.

EASTER SEPULCHRE A recess to hold the consecrated Host prior to the Easter celebration, usually in the N CHANCEL wall.

FLUSHWORK Decorative use of flint to form patterns, monograms, inscriptions, etc.

GOTHIC English architectural term covering the period 1200 to 1539, and including EARLY ENGLISH, DECORATED and PERPEND-ICULAR styles.

GREEN MAN A foliate face, often with leaves coming from its mouth, seen on fonts, CORBELS, etc.

HAMMER-BEAMS Beams projecting at right angles, to provide support for vertical members or braces of a wooden roof.

HOOD-MOULD Projecting moulding above an arch or LINTEL to throw off water.

INDENT Matrix for brass, often visible after a brass has been removed.

JAMB Sidepiece or post of a door.

JESSE TREE or WINDOW Visual genealogy of Christ's descent from Jesse. Jesse is portrayed at the base of a tree trunk with Christ's other forebears depicted in loops of braches.

LANCET Narrow windows which terminate in a sharp point; characteristic of the EARLY ENGLISH period.

LECTERN Free standing reading desk.

LEDGER A flat stone covering a grave, often forming part of a church floor.

LINTEL Load-bearing support over door or window.

LONG AND SHORT WORK Alternate vertical and horizontal stonework, used as corner quoins in SAXON churches.

LOW-SIDE WINDOW A small window low down in the CHANCEL wall, just E of the arch. They were not originally glazed. It is generally thought that a handbell would be rung through the opening at the elevation of the Host during Mass, so that those who heard it could thus share in the Celebration. Their exact purpose is not known for certain.

LYCH-GATE Roofed gate at the entrance to a churchyard, where coffins were traditionally rested before a funeral.

MASS DIAL A sun dial showing the times of Mass, usually close by the porch or entrance, also referred to as a Scratch Dial.

MISERICORD Bracket, often richly carved, on the underside of a hinged choir stall seat which when turned up provided the occupant of the seat with a support during a long period of standing.

NAIL-HEAD EARLY ENGLISH ornamentation, consisting of small nail-like pyramids, regularly repeated.

NAVE The main body of a church.

NORMAN Style of architecture, typified by rounded arches and massive piers, from 1066 to *c*.1200. See also ROMANESQUE.

OGEE A double curved arch, very characteristic of the DECORATED period.

PARCLOSE A screen separating a chapel or aisle from the body of the church.

PERPENDICULAR Stylistic division of English GOTHIC architecture *c*.1335-50 to *c*.1530.

PIER A strong solid support, pillar or column.

PISCINA A stone basin, with a drain, for washing the sacred vessels, usually to the south of an altar.

POPPY-HEAD The carved ornament on top of bench-ends or pew-ends.

QUATREFOIL Four-lobed decorative opening or window.

QUOINS Stones at the angles or corners of a building.

REREDOS Painted or carved screen behind altar.

RETABLE Painted or carved panels behind altar.

ROMANESQUE Architectural style, based on Roman models, used from 7th to 12th centuries. In England early Romanesque is known as SAXON and later as NORMAN.

ROOD A cross or crucifix.

ROOD LOFT Gallery on top of ROOD SCREEN, to contain the ROOD and also for use by singers and musicians.

ROOD SCREEN A screen at the entry of the CHANCEL, occasionally in stone, usually in wood; on which was erected the ROOD LOFT or rood beam.

GLOSSARY

SAXON Style of architecture linked with period before Norman Conquest.

SEDILIA Seats for clergy, usually on south side of CHANCEL.

SPIRE A tall, slender structure tapering to a point.

SQUINT A hole cut in a wall or through a PIER to allow a view of the main altar of a church.

STEEPLE Tower together with SPIRE, cupola etc.

STIFF LEAF EARLY ENGLISH A type of foliage design common in the 13th century.

STOUP Vessel for the holy water, usually placed by a door.

STRING-COURSE A projecting horizontal band set in the surface of a wall. It acts as a division (see drawing for QUOINS).

TRANSEPT An arm of a cross-shaped church.

TYMPANUM Area between lintel and arch of a doorway, often filled with a relief sculpture.

VESTRY A room in which robing takes place.

The bellringers' hats in the tower at Great Bromley.

BIBLIOGRAPHY

The one indispensable book, still in print, is N. Pevsner *The Buildings Of England: Essex*, 2nd edn, revised by E. Radcliffe (Harmondsworth: Penguin, 1965). The Introduction is especially valuable.

Other, smaller books directly on the subject and strongly recommended, but all currently out of print, are:

N. Scarfe *Shell Guide To Essex* (London: Faber & Faber, 1968), a masterpiece by a professional historian, and full of brilliantly perceptive comments.

Essex Churches 600-1800 (Essex Record Office, 1960), an admirable little book with an illustrated introduction.

C. Starr (ed.), *A Guide To Essex Churches* (Essex Churches Support Trust, 1980), a first rate collection of essays by experts on various aspects of the subject.

John Hough *Essex Churches* (Woodbridge: Boydell and Brewer, 1983), is particularly useful for its ground plans and illustrations, but has several unexplained omissions.

Two printed sources for the specialist are, for most readers, only accessible in public libraries:

Royal Commission on Historical Monuments, *Essex*, 4 vols (London: RCHM, 1916-23). When it was compiled the official cut-off date, since revised, was 1714; everything later was 'modern' and ignored.

Victoria County History Of Essex, 8 vols (London, 1903–) (still unfinished). So far only 70 parishes in south west Essex and London, now over the border, are covered in detail. When complete it will be a definitive survey of the county.

The following are useful for historical context or particular studies:

Historical Context: A. C. Edwards, *History of Essex*, 4th edn (Chichester: Phillimore, 1978).

Building Materials, general: A. Clifton-Taylor, *The Patterns of English Building* (place and publisher?, 1962).

Archaeology of Churches: W. J. and K. Rodwell, *Historic Churches, A Wasting Asset* (London: Council for British Archaeology, 1977). This is entirely on Essex and includes important studies of Colchester, Rivenhall and Hadstock.

Timber Work, by the acknowledged expert:

C. A. Hewitt, *Church Carpentry: a Study Based on Essex Examples* (Chichester: Phillimore, 1974).

On Churchyards:

F. Greenoak and C. Roberts, *God's Acre* (London: Orbis, 1985).

The above list is by no means exhaustive. Specialist studies of stained glass, wall paintings, monuments (including brasses) abound, some still in print.

Finally, guides: most churches these days offer for sale leaflets or booklets as guides. Many of these are first rate.

ABOUT THE EDITOR

JOHN FITCH is an Essex man, born in 1922 at Mistley, near the border with Suffolk (where he also has deep roots). After reading history and theology at Cambridge, he was ordained and served in parochial ministry in Suffolk for forty years, returning to Essex when he retired in 1987. He is a Canon Emeritus of St Edmundsbury Cathedral. In 1973-4 he helped to found the Suffolk Historic Churches Trust, of which he is a Vice President. He is a widower with three children and seven grandchildren and lives at Great Yeldham.

As this book goes to press, he has been elected a Fellow of the Society of Antiquaries.

Earls Colne Friends' Meeting House, built in 1674.

TO THE READER

If you are not already a member of The Friends of Essex
Churches and, having read our book, would like to join us,
our membership secretary would be delighted to hear from
you and to send you particulars. He is:

Sir Alistair Stewart, Bt.,
Walters Cottage,
Little Baddow,
Chelmsford,
Essex, CM3 4TQ.